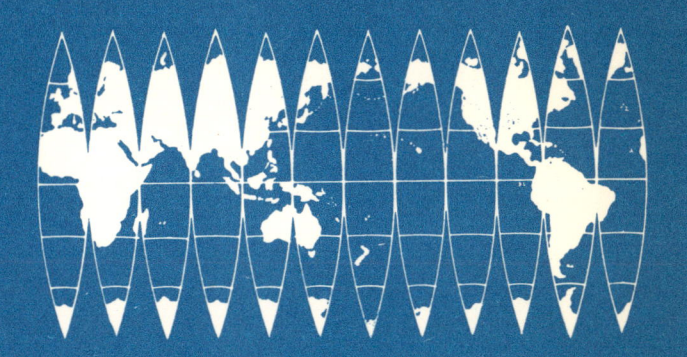

Editor in Chief • PHILLIP BACON
Professor of Geography
Teachers College, Columbia University

Managing Editor • JOANNA ALDENDORFF

Picture Researcher • PETER J. GALLAGHER

Associate Editor • PETER R. LIMBURG

Cartographer • VINCENT KOTSCHAR

Picture Editor • ROBERT J. GARLOCK

Designer • FRANCES GIANNONI

Staff • JUDY KORMAN, BARBARA VINSON, KATHLEEN SEAGRAVES, JOHANNA GREENWALD

Special Section of Statistical Maps • RICHARD EDES HARRISON

Covers • RAY PIOCH

Maps on pages 3, 99, 194-5, 292-3, 294-5, 387, 484-5, 532, 533 are copyrighted by Georg Westermann Verlag. They are produced from the *Westermann Bildkarten Lexicon* by arrangement with Georg Westermann Verlag.

Complete List of Books

These books tell the exciting story of how people live in all parts of the world. You will see how men use the land for farming and industry. You will learn about mountains and deserts, oceans and rivers, cities and towns—and you will discover how the daily life of people in other countries compares with your own.

BOOK 1 • NORTH AMERICA

BOOK 2 • SOUTH AMERICA

BOOK 3 • EUROPE

BOOK 4 • ASIA

BOOK 5 • AFRICA

BOOK 6 • AUSTRALIA, OCEANIA
AND THE POLAR LANDS
WITH A SPECIAL SECTION OF
STATISTICAL MAPS AND INDEX

BOOK 6

AUSTRALIA
OCEANIA
AND THE POLAR LANDS

WITH A SPECIAL SECTION OF STATISTICAL MAPS AND INDEX

BY PHILLIP BACON

*Professor of Geography,
Teachers College, Columbia University*

STATISTICAL MAPS BY RICHARD EDES HARRISON

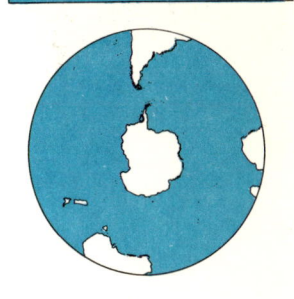

THE GOLDEN BOOK
PICTURE ATLAS
OF THE WORLD
IN SIX VOLUMES

Illustrated with More than 1,000 Color Photographs and Maps

GOLDEN PRESS · NEW YORK

© COPYRIGHT 1960 BY GOLDEN PRESS, INC. DESIGNED AND PRODUCED BY ARTISTS AND WRITERS PRESS, INC. PRINTED IN THE U.S.A. BY WESTERN PRINTING AND LITHOGRAPHING COMPANY. PUBLISHED BY GOLDEN PRESS, INC., ROCKEFELLER CENTER, NEW YORK 20, N. Y.

Plentiful rain supports lush tropical vegetation on the high, volcanic Pacific island of Tahiti.

THIS IS OCEANIA

The Pacific Ocean is the biggest of all the world's oceans. It covers about one third of the earth's surface. Here is an ocean larger than all of the continents put together.

At its widest point, from Panama to the Malay Peninsula, the distance across the Pacific Ocean is about 12,500 miles. This is half the distance around the earth.

The land area in this vast watery region is relatively small. Even the Pacific's island continent, Australia, is smaller than the United States.

A chain of underwater mountains stretches southeast across the Pacific from Asia. The tops of some of them form the islands of Indonesia, New Guinea, the Bismarck Archipelago, and the Solomons. Other islands in this same mountain chain are the New Hebrides and New Caledonia. These mountains again appear above the ocean as New Zealand.

Farther seaward, to the north and east, are other mountains. Most of them are submerged beneath the surface of the Pacific. But here and there a few peaks rise above the open ocean. These peaks form tiny and widely scattered islands.

In so vast a region as the Pacific Ocean you can be sure that there is a great variety of landscapes. Australia alone has broad deserts, tropical forests, and mountain highlands.

There is such a variety of landscapes in the Pacific that geographers have listed seven distinct types of islands. Each type has its own landforms, soils, climates, and plants.

Treeless atolls are low coral islands. They have poor soil and little drinking water. There are plenty of sea birds and fish around the treeless atolls. Yet the Pacific natives do not like these islands. They prefer islands with trees. But the treeless atolls make good landing strips for airplanes. Some of them are used as military airbases. Canton, Howard, and Johnson Islands are all treeless atolls.

Dry-forest atolls are also low coral islands. Because of their salty air and brackish ground water, few plants can grow on them. The plants that do live on these islands are especially suited to the salty conditions. These plants usually form a dry, brushy scrub forest.

Not many people live on the dry-forest atolls. As on the treeless atolls, there is often a shortage of drinking water, and it is hard to grow crops in the salty soil. Most of the Marshall and Ellice Islands, and many of the Tuamotus and northern Cooks, are dry-forest atolls.

Moist atolls are the beautiful coral islands that you sometimes see in movies. They receive plenty of rain. Trees grow closely together. Coconut palms and breadfruit trees are everywhere. Man can grow fine food crops on these islands. The Gilbert and Tokelau islands are typical moist atolls.

Raised coral islands are composed of layer upon layer of old coral. Some have been raised as high as 200 feet or more above sea level. The coral of which they are composed forms limestone rock. Limestone dissolves easily; so the islands have many caves and sinkholes. Because limestone soaks up water rapidly, these islands are often quite dry. Some, like Nauru and Ocean Island, have rich deposits of phos-

Scrub vegetation and barren, eroded hills are characteristic of the drier regions of Australia.

Scott Polkinghorne—Photo Researchers

Luzon
PHILIPPINE ISLANDS
Quezon City
MANILA
Mindoro
South China Sea
Palawan
Sulu Sea
Mindanao
Davao
Mt. Apo
Mt. Mayon
Saipan
Marianas Is. (U.N. - U.S.)
Guam (U.S.)
Micro
Yap
Palau Is. (U.N.-U.S.)
Caroline Is. (U.N. - U.S.)
Truk Is.
Ponape
Sulu Arch.
Borneo
North Borneo
Kinabalu
Celebes Sea
Celebes
Macassar Str.
Molucca Sea
Halmahera
Mapia Is. (Neth.)
Melanesia
Moluccas
Ceram
Ceram Sea
Buru
Amboina
Banda Is.
Sorong
Schouten Is.
Admiralty Is.
Hollandia
New Ireland
Bismarck Archipelago (U.N.-Austr.)
Madang
Rabaul
New Britain (U.N.-Austr.)
Buka (U.N.-Austr.)
Bougainville
Choiseul
Solomon Is. (Br.)
New Guinea
Netherlands New Guinea
Papua
Gulf of Papua
Port Moresby
Huon Gulf
Astrolabe Bay
Aru Is.
Banjermasin
Macassar
INDONESIA
Flores Sea
Banda Sea
Lesser Sunda Islands
Flores
Sumbawa
Lombok
Bali
Sumba
Timor
Timor (Port.)
Savu Sea
Tanimbar Is.
Arafura Sea
Merauke
Torres Strait
C. York
Louisiade Arch. (U.N.-Austr.)
Guadalcanal
Melville I.
Coburg Pen.
Darwin
Timor Sea
Joseph Bonaparte Gulf
Arnhem Land
Gulf of Carpentaria
York Peninsula
Cooktown
Great Barrier Reef
Coral Sea
Cairns
Townsville
Point Denison
Chesterfield Is. (Fr.)
Birdum
Daly Waters
Normanton
Northern Territory
Derby
C. Leveque
King Sound
Broome
Dobbyn
Forsayth
Charters Towers
Cloncurry
Mt. Isa
Hughenden
Mackay
Great Dividing Range
Dajarra
Winton
Queensland
Port Hedland
Great Sandy Desert
Lake Mackay
Macdonnell Ranges
Alice Springs
Longreach
Rockhampton
Curtis I.
Sandy Cape
Onslow
North West Cape
Lake Macdonald
Mt. Bruce
Gibson Desert
L. Amadeus
Bundaberg
Maryborough
Western Australia
AUSTRALIA
Horseshoe
Charleville
Quilpie
Mitchell
Moreton Bay
Brisbane
Carnarvon
Shark Bay
Oodnadatta
Cunnamulla
C. Byron
Lismore
Steep Point
Wiluna
Sandstone
Laverton
Great Victoria Desert
Lake Eyre
South Australia
Woomera
Broken Hill
Bourke
New South Wales
Lord Howe (Austr.)
Geraldton
Nullarbor Plain
Kalgoorlie
Coolgardie
Port Pirie
Newcastle
SYDNEY
Bathurst
Goulburn
Perth
Fremantle
Esperance
Great Australian Bight
Wallaroo
Kapunda
Adelaide
Wagga Wagga
Port Kembla
Canberra
Bunbury
Collie
Albany
Hopetoun
Kangaroo I.
Echuca
Bendigo
Albury
Mt. Kosciusko
Australian Alps
C. Leeuwin
King George Sound
Victoria
Ballarat
MELBOURNE
Cape Howe
Portland
Geelong
Cape Otway
Yallourn
Bass Strait
King I.
Flinders I.
Devonport
Launceston
Tasmania
Strahan
Hobart
South Cape
INDIAN OCEAN
Tasman
Cape Prov

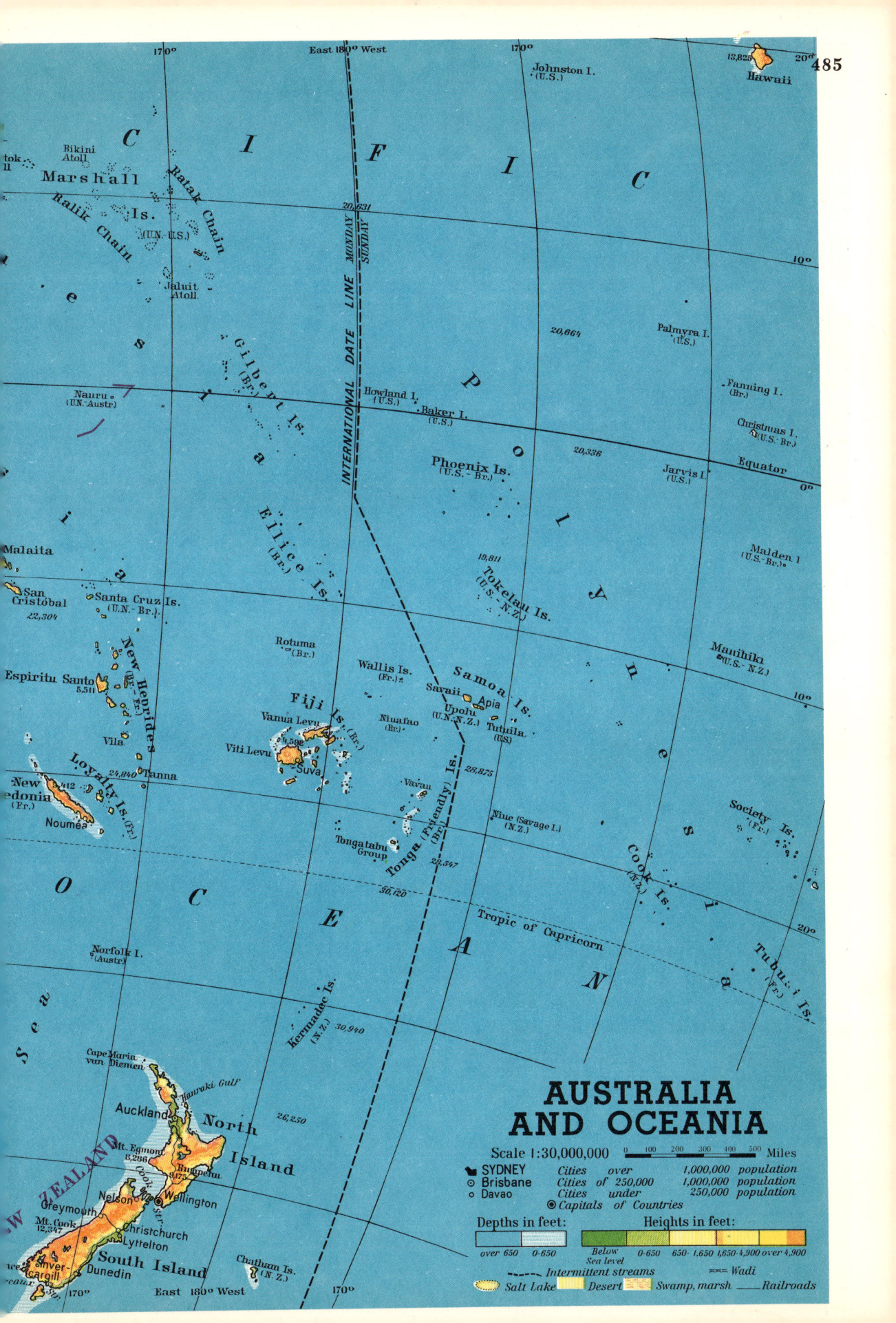

AUSTRALIA AND OCEANIA

Scale 1:30,000,000 — 0 100 200 300 400 500 Miles

- ■ **SYDNEY** — Cities over 1,000,000 population
- ⊚ Brisbane — Cities of 250,000 1,000,000 population
- ○ Davao — Cities under 250,000 population
- ⊙ Capitals of Countries

Depths in feet: over 650 | 0–650

Heights in feet: Below Sea level | 0–650 | 650–1,650 | 1,650–4,900 | over 4,900

--- Intermittent streams   ≈≈≈ Wadi

Salt Lake   Desert   Swamp, marsh   ___ Railroads

Streams of bubbling lava flow into the ocean as Hawaii's great volcano, Mauna Loa, erupts. The Pacific Ocean has long been a center of volcanic activity, and many of the islands are of volcanic origin.

This coral island is part of Australia's Great Barrier Reef. Stretching for 1,250 miles along Australia's northeastern coast, the Great Barrier Reef is the world's longest single coral deposit.

Coral atolls of the Pacific usually have a ring of land surrounding a shallow central lagoon.

phate. Phosphate mining is important on these islands.

Unweathered volcanic islands have little soil and vegetation. When rock is "weathered" it gradually breaks down to form soil. Because these islands are not "weathered" they have little soil. Natives grow their coconut palms and other crops in valley bottoms where a little soil accumulates. The northern Marianas are unweathered volcanic islands.

Weathered volcanic islands often rise hundreds of feet above sea level. These islands have a great variety of plants, soils, and climates. Nearly everything the native needs for life can be found. Only minerals are missing. The Hawaiian, Society, and Samoan Islands are good examples of weathered volcanic islands.

"Continental" islands contain rocks that were formed under conditions of great heat and pressure which occur only on the continents or along their borders. These rocks are often very old. Because the "continental" islands are old, they have an even greater variety of plants and soils than the weathered volcanic islands.

These "continental" islands have a great variety of landscapes, too. They have high mountains, dense forests, and broad swampy areas. On such islands people developed many different ways of life. The "continental" islands also have mineral resources. Some of the Pacific's important "continental" islands are New Zealand, New Guinea, New Caledonia, Guadalcanal, New Britain, and New Ireland.

The spectacular fiords of New Zealand's South Island were formed by the action of glaciers.

The koala is a marsupial, native to Australia. It lives on eucalyptus leaves.

The echidna and the duck-billed platypus are two of Australia's unusual mammals. Both lay eggs.

PACIFIC ANIMALS

Long ago there were land links between Asia, Indonesia, Australia, and other nearby islands. But these land links have been covered by ocean waters for hundreds of thousands of years. During this time, a great variety of plants and animals developed in the Pacific. No matter how small the island, nearly every speck of land is the home of some plants and animals.

Many islands have native plants that are found in no other place in the world. Plants which are found in one place only are called *endemic plants*.

In New Zealand, nearly seven tenths of the flowering plants are endemic. In New Caledonia, four fifths of the island's 2,500 species of flowering plants are endemic.

Winds and ocean currents are the chief means by which living things reach islands. Islands that are far from other land usually have only a few species of plants and

The bearlike Australian wombat is a marsupial, like the kangaroo. From two to three feet long, it lives in a burrow and feeds on plants and roots.

animals. But those islands close to continents have many species.

Oceanic islands have no native mammals at all other than bats. And bats, of course, can travel great distances by flying. Cattle, deer, goats, pigs, rabbits, and rats have all been brought in by man.

Australia has long been separated from other lands, and so many of its animals are endemic. These animals have no close relatives in other continents.

Two thirds of Australia's native mammals are marsupials. Marsupials carry their young in pouches. Kangaroos and opossums are both marsupials. Australia's famous "teddy bear," the koala, is a marsupial too.

The only egg-laying mammals in the world come from Australia and its neighboring islands. One of these odd animals is the platypus, which is found in Australia and Tasmania. The other is the echidna, or spiny anteater, which lives in Australia, Tasmania, and New Guinea.

An emu inspects its eggs. This large flightless bird of Australia is related to the ostrich.

Sharp teeth and a vicious temper gave the Tasmanian Devil its name. About the size of a badger, it sometimes kills sheep.

A baby wallaby peeks out of its mother's pouch, where it nurses. The wallaby is a smaller relative of Australia's famous kangaroo.

PEOPLE OF THE PACIFIC

When white men first sailed the Pacific Ocean, they found dark-skinned people living on nearly every island. These first white explorers of the Pacific mistakenly called the natives "Indians."

The term "Indian" did not last long. As explorers traveled over more of the Pacific they found a great variety of native people. Some had copper-colored skin and straight black hair. These people lived in the western islands and were expert boatsmen. In the islands farther to the east, explorers found brown or black-skinned natives with curly or frizzly hair.

Who were these islanders? Where had they come from? And how did they manage to spread themselves over the thousands of miles of open Pacific Ocean?

From ancient times the large islands close to Southeast Asia have attracted people. Once on the islands, these people became seafarers. As their sailing skills increased, they pushed farther and farther eastward across the Pacific seeking new island homes. The farther east they pushed, the smaller and more widely scattered the islands became. Even so, all of the islands can be thought of as stepping stones from Asia.

The islands of Indonesia, close to Asia, have been occupied by man from the earliest time. The Polynesian islands, in the mid-Pacific Ocean, were the last of this island world to be occupied by man.

People moved eastward, from island to island, over thousands of years. The various people who sailed eastward during these thousands of years differed greatly in appearance, languages, and customs. As a result, many different groups of people came to occupy the Pacific islands.

Scientists have studied the ways of life of the Pacific natives. They have divided the native people into four main groups.

Australian aborigines cook a simple meal of boiled fish. A boomerang lies on the ground nearby.

Richard Harrington—Annan Photo Features

A stone ax is still the main tool of these New Guinea tribesmen, dressed for a ceremonial dance.

Bips—Photo Researchers

Swimming is a popular sport in Australia, since most of the people live on or near the coasts. Here, Sunday bathers enjoy the surf at Bondi Beach in Sydney.

These groups live in four different parts of the Pacific island world.

Australian aborigines occupied Australia long before white men came to this island continent. ("Aborigines" means "first inhabitants.") These aborigines are primitive people. They live in small groups. They hunt kangaroos and the ostrich-like emu. Their favorite weapon is the boomerang.

Aborigines move constantly. They have to move often to find food. They can move quickly because they have no homes, gardens, or even clothing.

The Bismarck Archipelago, the Solomons, New Hebrides, Fiji, New Caledonia, and many nearby smaller islands are all

Indian women on Fiji wear their traditional saris. Indians have become farmers and merchants there.

In sailing canoes like this one, the ancestors of today's islanders voyaged all over the southern Pacific. The outrigger keeps the canoe from capsizing in heavy seas.

called Melanesia. Melanesia means "black islands." The people of Melanesia have dark skins and frizzly hair.

Fishing and trading by canoe are important in the way of life of the Melanesians. Melanesians believe in magic, and magicians are often the richest and most important men in these islands.

The third of the Pacific island groups is called Micronesia. Micronesia means "small islands." Most of the islands of Micronesia are the tiny islets of the Caroline, Mariana, and Marshall groups.

The people of Micronesia are skilled sailors. They use ocean-going canoes. The sails on their canoes are shaped like a triangle. The sail can be quickly shifted from one end of the canoe to the other. An outrigger keeps the canoe from capsiz-

A Fijian, with typical Melanesian features, builds a hut with a wooden frame and reed-matting walls.

New Zealand Maori children, descendants of fierce Polynesian warriors, enjoy their ice-cream cones.

ing in heavy seas. Micronesian sailing canoes are the fastest in all Oceania.

Polynesia is the last of the island groups. Polynesia means "many islands." Polynesia covers a huge area, from Hawaii in the north to New Zealand in the south and Easter Island far to the east.

Of all the native people in the Pacific, the first explorers liked the Polynesians best. They are a handsome, friendly people. Nearly all of the Polynesians are farmers and fishermen. But they do not have to work hard in their beautiful islands. Food is plentiful. There is always time for singing, dancing, and games.

In more recent times many newcomers have arrived in the Pacific. Fiji, for example, has more Indians than native Fijians. Chinese traders have settled on many islands. And white people have come from nearly every country of Europe.

Most of the Pacific's white people live in Australia and New Zealand. The majority are of British origin, but thinly-populated Australia is now encouraging immigration from other European countries.

A Polynesian family on United States-administered Samoa watches dancers at a celebration. Polynesians are fond of singing and dancing, which they have developed to a fine art.

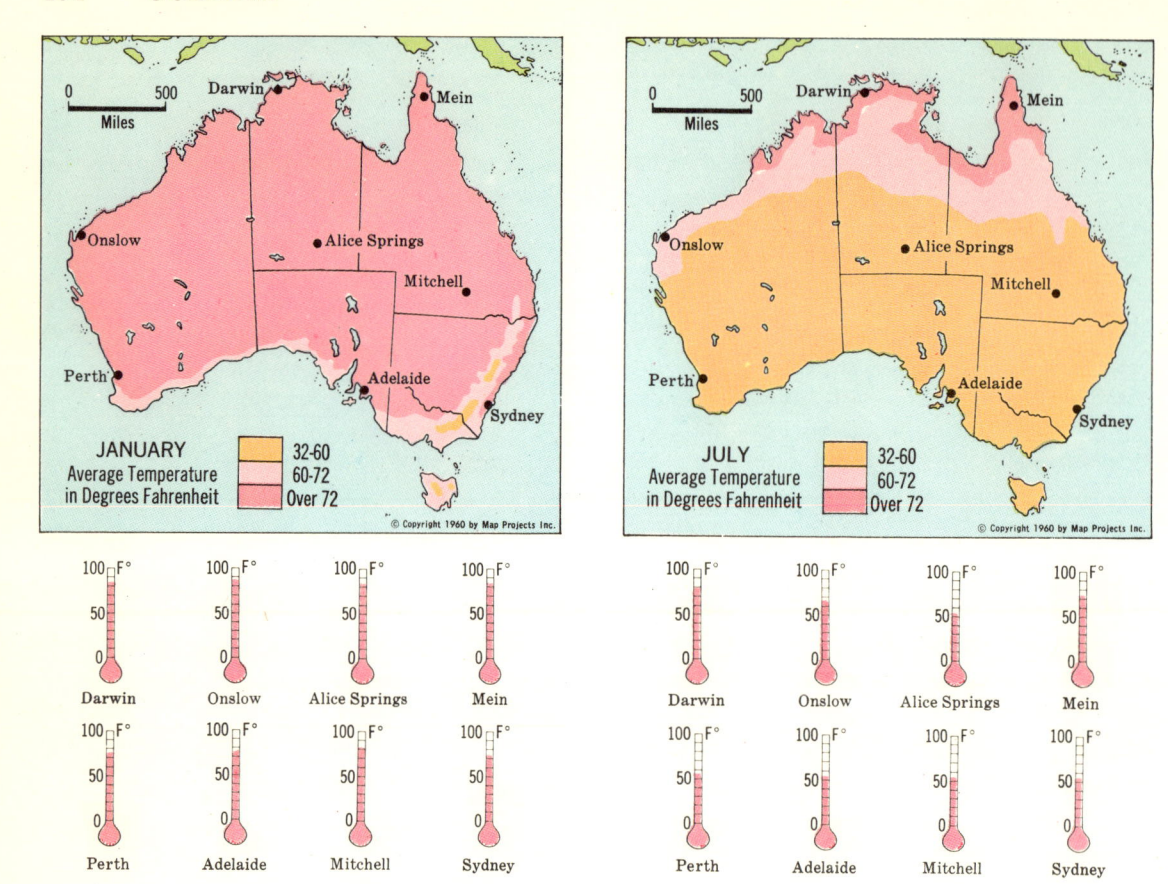

CLIMATE

There are many climates in the Pacific. Variety must be expected in an area that covers one third of the earth's surface. It is mainly latitude, the distance north or south of the equator, that determines the climate of places in the Pacific. But elevation above sea level and ocean currents also affect climate.

Places on or near the equator have an everlasting sameness of weather. Even temperatures—little variation between the warmest and coldest months of the year—are a characteristic of equatorial islands. Heavy and frequent rain is another characteristic of this region.

High islands get the most rainfall. Air is forced to rise to pass over the mountains. It cools as it rises. Cool air cannot hold as much moisture as warm air. So as the air cools, rain begins to fall. Thus, high islands are often quite wet. Low-lying islands, on the other hand, receive less rainfall.

Typhoons (great tropical storms) sometimes develop in the Pacific. The strength of the winds in such storms often causes tremendous damage. Fruit is shaken from the trees. Branches of coconut palms and other trees are broken. Tin roofs from buildings swirl through the air. Everyone has to stay under cover for protection.

When typhoon winds are especially strong (some have velocities of over 150 miles an hour), huge waves are whipped up on the ocean. Even the largest ships have trouble riding out these waves. And sometimes the gigantic waves wash completely over low-lying islands. When this happens, people are forced to tie themselves to the tops of trees to keep from drowning.

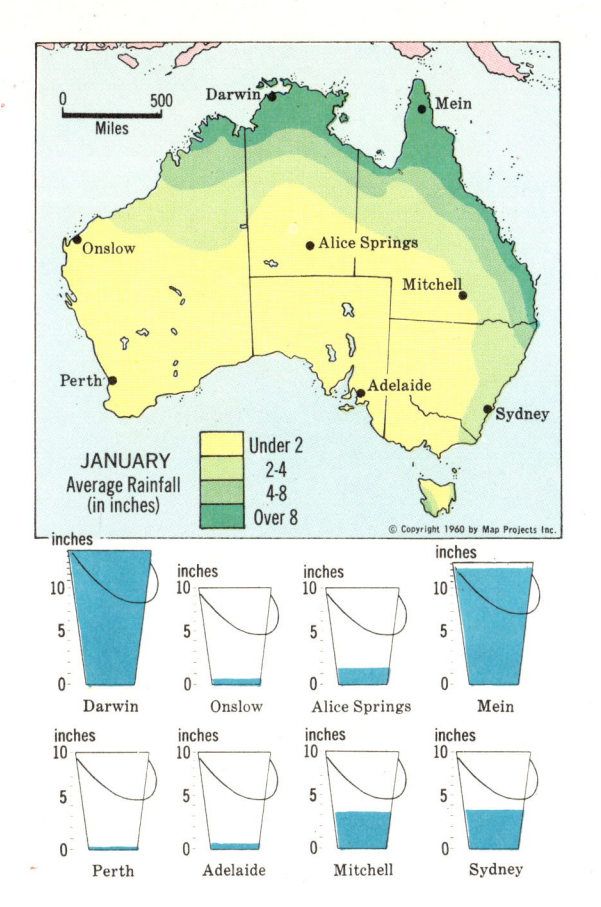

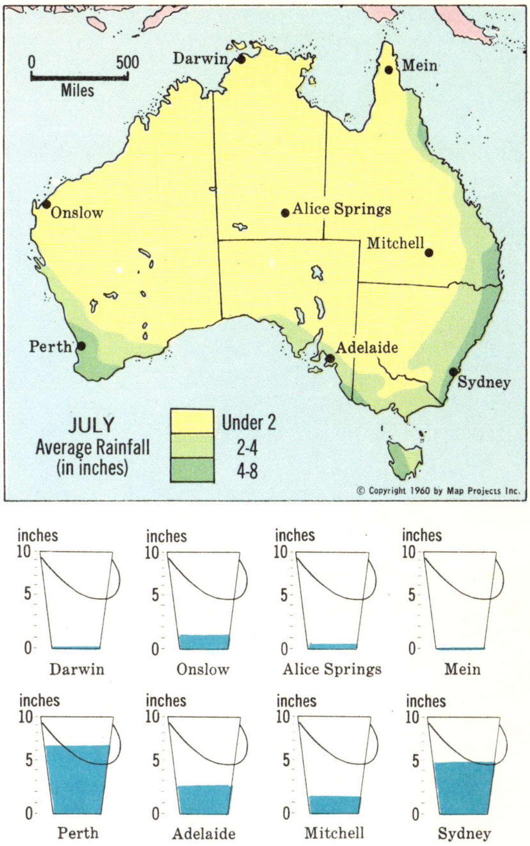

The maps on these pages show the climate of the Pacific's largest landmass—Australia. Australia's climate is affected by its location. It is south of the equator; so seasons are reversed from those of the Northern Hemisphere. In December, January, and February, when boys and girls are sledding and ice-skating in North America and Europe, Australian children are playing at the beach. The winter season is from June to August in Australia.

Australia's climate is also related to its location between 10 and 40 degrees south latitude. The tropical portions of Australia are warm all year round, and the areas which are beyond the tropics become nearly as warm as the tropics in the summer. Winters are generally mild throughout Australia, except in the high plateau and mountain regions.

Tropical northern Australia gets its rain from the summer monsoon winds. Rainfall is heavy near the coast but dwindles rapidly inland. The six-month cool season from May to October is very dry.

The interior and much of western Australia are very dry. Most of these areas is desert country. In fact, the Great Sandy and Victoria deserts rank among the largest deserts of the world.

Southwestern Australia and the coast of South Australia have mild, rainy winters. The summers are hot and dry.

Southeastern Australia receives some rain throughout the year. This more abundant rainfall has helped make this portion of the continent more densely settled than other parts of Australia. Southeastern Australia has cool to mild winters. The summers are more comfortable than in the regions closer to the equator.

Tasmania, off the southeastern coast of Australia, has a climate somewhat like that of New Zealand. Tasmania is far enough south of the equator to provide relief from both heat and drought.

Sydney, Australia's largest city and leading port, has one of the world's finest natural harbors.

COUNTRIES AND CITIES OF THE PACIFIC

Over the years many countries have controlled islands in the Pacific. Today the United States, Great Britain, and France control most of them. Australia and New Zealand also have some islands.

Australia and New Zealand claim large portions of the Antarctic continent in addition to islands in the Pacific. Together they claim nearly half of Antarctica.

Australia and New Zealand are both members of the Commonwealth of Nations. The capital of the Commonwealth of Nations is London, England. But the people of Australia and New Zealand are not governed by England. They elect their own officials, make their own laws, and conduct their own affairs independently.

Until the twentieth century the Australian continent was divided into five British colonies. The island of Tasmania was the sixth colony. On January 1, 1901, these six colonies became states in a new country, the "Commonwealth of Australia."

Australia's people are city dwellers. Less than one third of the population lives outside Australia's cities and towns. These cities and towns are continuing to grow. More and more of Australia's people are moving away from the rural areas into the towns and cities.

Mechanical farm equipment makes it possible for fewer farmers to grow Australia's crops. And manufacturing is becoming ever more important in Australia.

Melbourne is Australia's second largest city and an industrial center. It serves a rich farming area.

Canberra, Australia's capital since 1927, is a modern, well-planned city with fine homes and gardens.

Manufacturers like to locate their factories in cities. Industries have to be near markets. They also have to be near a good supply of labor. These conditions can only be found in the larger cities.

Half of Australia's people live in the capital cities of the six states. Indeed, the two largest of these capital cities, Sydney and Melbourne, contain one third of all of the people on the Australian continent.

Sydney and Melbourne are the fourth and fifth largest cities in the Southern Hemisphere. Only the South American cities of Buenos Aires, São Paulo, and Rio de Janeiro are larger. Sydney and Melbourne each have more than one million residents.

Both Sydney and Melbourne are modern seaports. Sydney has one of the world's finest natural harbors. Both Sydney and Melbourne have many industries producing goods for local consumption. Their principal exports are the wool, meat, hides, and wheat of the interior.

Canberra is not one of Australia's largest cities, but it is certainly one of the most important. Canberra is the capital of Australia. The government of Australia moved from Melbourne, the old capital, to Canberra in 1927.

New Zealand, with a total population of two and a quarter million, has few large cities. Nevertheless, the four largest cities —Wellington, Auckland, Christchurch, and Dunedin—contain more than half of New Zealand's people.

Auckland is the largest city in New Zealand. It is the country's leading seaport. New Zealand's first European settlers founded Auckland in 1841. Wellington, the capital, is the country's second largest city and an important seaport.

The islands beyond Australia and New Zealand have few real cities. Most of the

Suva, the capital of Fiji, is a chief port of call for regular shipping lines and inter-island traders.

Sheep graze on this wooded hillside overlooking Auckland, New Zealand's chief city and port.

In Wellington, where British traditions are strong, traffic moves on the left as it does in London.

people of Oceania live in tiny villages. But there are two cities that you should know. One is Suva, capital of Fiji. The other is Papeete, on the French island of Tahiti.

Suva has a fine sheltered harbor. It is on Viti Levu, largest of the Fiji Islands. Most ships crossing the Pacific stop at Suva. Cargo ships take on sugar and copra here. Passenger liners also call at this largest of the South Pacific island cities. A medical school here trains native doctors.

Papeete is the largest and only real city in all of eastern Polynesia. Even so, its population is only 18,000. Most of the larger business houses in Papeete are operated by Europeans, but Chinese own many of the small shops. Nearly one fifth of Papeete's population is Chinese.

Tahiti's lush green mountains rise behind the harbor of Papeete, the capital of France's Pacific territories. This port city ships copra, vanilla, phosphates, and mother-of-pearl.

Ewing Krainin—Photo Researchers

A desolate, dry plateau—about 1,500,000 square miles—covers the western half of Australia.

Cattle and sheep graze on the well-watered uplands between New South Wales and Victoria.

Tasmania, Australia's island state, is separated from the mainland by 150-mile-wide Bass Strait.

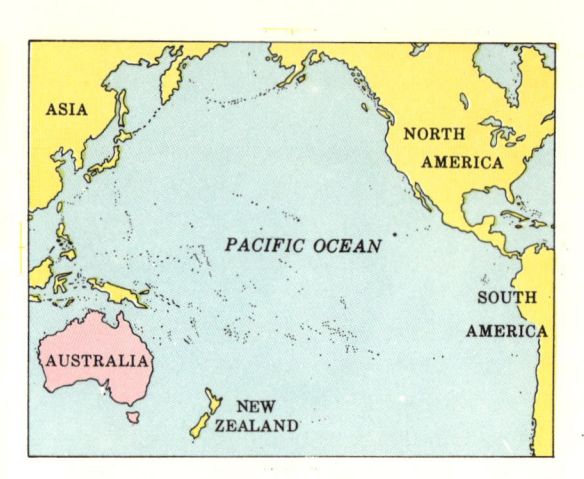

AUSTRALIA, THE ISLAND CONTINENT

Australia has long been little known to most of the people of the world. But this is not hard to understand. Australia is the newest of the inhabited continents. It was just a little more than 350 years ago that the Australian continent was discovered by white men. And the first European settlement in Australia was not made until 1788.

Yet in some ways Australia is a very old continent. Rocks discovered in northwestern Australia tell us that Australia may be the very oldest of all the continents. These rocks have been above water for 1,600 million years.

Australia is old in another way too. The aborigines, who inhabited Australia before the coming of Europeans, were Stone Age people. Some of them may have been living in Tasmania as long as 30,000 years ago.

Australia may be little known to many of the people of the world because it is so far away from the places where most of the world's people live. Even by air, Sydney, Australia's largest city, is almost 10,000 miles from New York City. Sydney is 10,500 miles from London and 9,000 from Moscow. Sydney is even 8,400 air miles from Rio de Janeiro, which, like Sydney, is in the Southern Hemisphere.

AUSTRALIA

Heron Island, part of the Great Barrier Reef, is a popular Australian tourist resort.

Australia and Antarctica are the only continents that lie wholly south of the equator. Antarctica has the highest average elevation of all the continents. Australia has the lowest.

Australia's average elevation is less than 1,000 feet. Only one seventeenth of the entire Australian continent has an elevation of over 2,000 feet. Australia's highest peak, Mt. Kosciusko, is but 7,305 feet above sea level. The main highland areas are the vast plateau of Western Australia and the Great Dividing Range in the east.

Keith Gillett—Shostal

AUSTRALIA

MELBOURNE	Over 1,000,000 population
Perth	250,000–1,000,000 population
Newcastle	100,000–250,000 population
Geelong	50,000–100,000 population
Alice Springs	Under 50,000 population

© Copyright 1960 by Map Projects Inc.

The barren Nullarbor Plain of South Australia is a 300-mile stretch of sand, rock, and sparse vegetation.

The first European settlements were made on the eastern coast. A few miles inland, the Great Dividing Range raises its mountain barrier. The Great Dividing Range is not high, but it is quite rugged. It was 1813 before European settlers crossed the Great Dividing Range.

On the western slopes of the mountains farmers found good country for growing wheat. The soil was fertile, and the rainfall, while not heavy, was sufficient for growing wheat and for mixed farming. Farther west, the grassy plains of New South Wales seemed ideal for sheep grazing. And to the north, in tropical Queensland, the grasslands proved suitable for cattle, despite the long winter droughts.

As settlers pushed on to the west the country became much drier. Beyond the Darling River the tufts of grass grew farther and farther apart. How disappointed the early settlers must have been

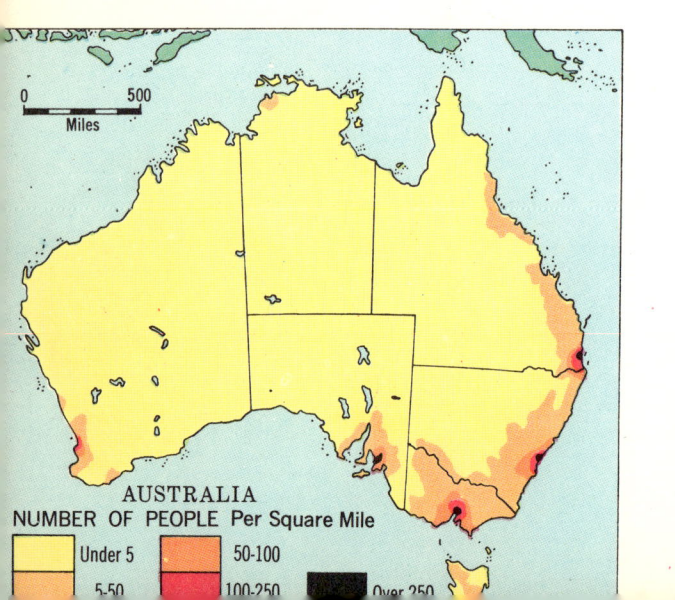

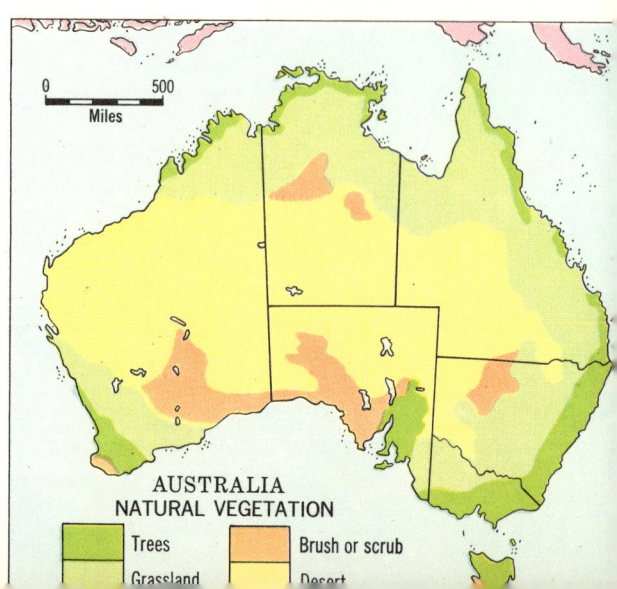

AUSTRALIA
NUMBER OF PEOPLE Per Square Mile
Under 5
5-50
50-100
100-250
Over 250

AUSTRALIA
NATURAL VEGETATION
Trees
Grassland
Brush or scrub
Desert

to discover that the interior of Australia was a vast, dry desert!

The population map on page 502 helps tell you what dryness means to Australia. Most of Australia's people live on the southeastern and southwestern coasts. The interior is Australia's vast "empty land." The coastal areas have water—far more water than the dry interior.

People and industries are concentrated in the southeast and southwest. The interior is empty. This population pattern affects the location and construction of highways and railroads. Only one railroad, far to the south, crosses Australia from east to west. And there is only one well-traveled route crossing the continent from north to south. A narrow-gauge railroad runs to Alice Springs, in the interior. A highway joins this railroad at Alice Springs. From there the highway runs north to Port Darwin on the coast.

Highways, as you might guess, are concentrated around the larger cities. But most of Australia's chief cities are seaports. Much of the freight carried between these cities travels by ship rather than by truck or railroad.

In few countries of the world is the airplane more important than in Australia. Australia is thinly populated. Towns are far apart. The airplane helps bring the people and places of Australia closer together by reducing the travel time between them. In Australia, doctors and nurses even call on their patients on remote ranches by airplane.

The natural vegetation of Australia is strongly influenced by temperature and rainfall conditions. The most common tree is the evergreen eucalyptus. There are over 400 species of eucalyptus, ranging in size from the 200-foot giants of the rainy southeastern uplands to the dwarfed, bushlike forms of the dry interior. Another very common tree is the acacia. In the deserts there are also sagebrush-like bushes and tough, spiny bunch grasses.

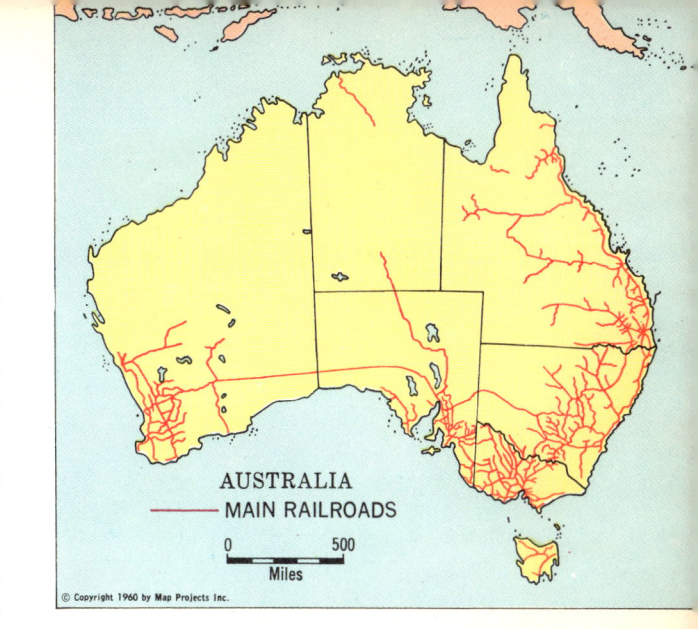

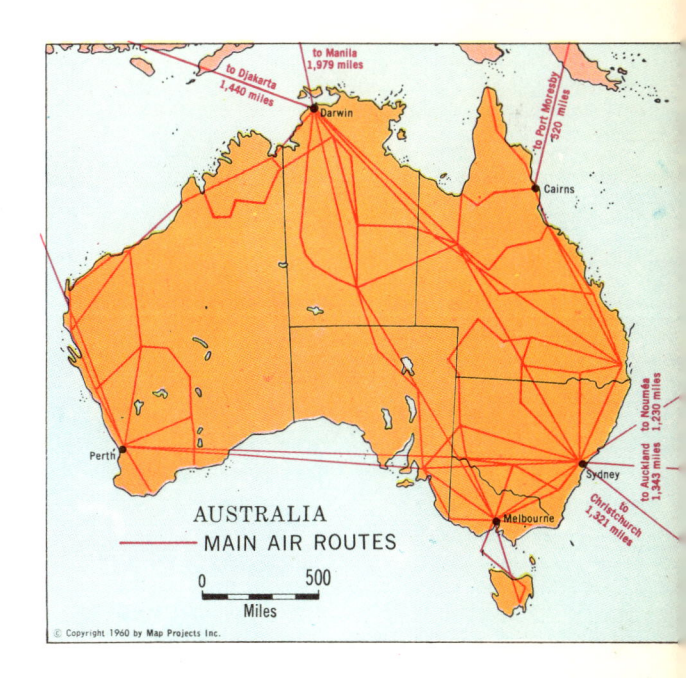

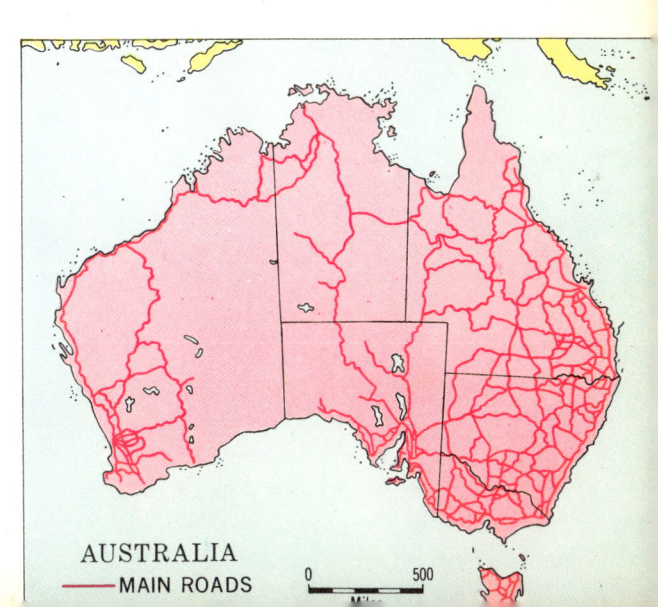

Ninety-five per cent of Australia's sugar cane is grown on the tropical coastal plain of Queensland.

Australian Farms and Ranches

Australia is one of the world's great food-producing countries. Its people are well fed. But far more food is produced than Australians could possibly eat. Plenty is left over to be shipped to markets overseas.

Great fields of wheat ripen on Australia's rolling plains. Two thirds of all of Australia's cropland is used for growing wheat, which can tolerate hot, dry conditions.

Wheat is grown in areas that receive at least 12 inches of rain each year. The more rain, the higher the yield of wheat. In dry areas the yield is often only 5 or 6 bushels per acre. Where 20 or more inches of rain fall, 30 or more bushels of wheat per acre may be harvested. The average yield for the entire country is about 12 bushels per acre.

This is slightly lower than the nationwide averages for the United States, Canada, and Argentina, three of the world's other leading wheat producers.

Australia's dry summers help the wheat farmers. The grain can be allowed to ripen on the stalk. Then the wheat can be harvested and threshed in one operation. In a recent year, Australian farmers harvested and threshed nearly 135 million bushels of wheat.

Some of the wheat farms are huge. Heavy machinery is used in growing Australian wheat. With good machinery one or two men can manage hundreds of acres. Only about one third of Australia's wheat is eaten by Australians, and the rest is sold to other countries. Much of the rest travels half way around the world to markets in Great Britain.

One of Australia's six states, Queensland, is in the tropics. Tropical crops can be raised here. Sugar production began in Queensland nearly 100 years ago. At first workers came from Pacific islands. Later, the government decided to stop bringing in islanders. Today all of the heavy work of growing and harvesting sugar cane is done by Australians.

Queensland grows more sugar cane than Australians can use. Most of the excess sugar is shipped to Australia's "neighbor," New Zealand.

Australians are proud of their fine orchards and vineyards. Millions of bushels of apples are grown in Tasmania, Victoria, and Western Australia. Some of these apples are shipped to Europe. They reach European markets from March to June, when there are no European apples in the stores. The reversed seasons of the Southern Hemisphere help Australian fruit growers get good prices for their products in Europe.

In some years Australian farmers grow nearly half a million tons of grapes. About one fourth of the grapes are used in making wine. Most of the remainder are dried for raisins and currants.

Cultivating Australia's cropland is important work. But only slightly more than one one-hundredth part of Australia's total land area is used to cultivate crops.

To really understand Australia's importance as a food-producing country, you must travel to the "outback"—the ranch country far inland from the eastern coast.

The outback is the home of Australia's great sheep ranches. Australians call their ranches "stations." Some stations on the drier pastures of the outback cover thousands of acres.

The outback is lonely country. Stations are often many miles apart. The people who live on these lonely stations keep in

Courtesy of Australian News and Information Bureau
Australia's wheat farmers depend on machinery for plowing, planting, and harvesting.

Birnback
A Tasmanian apple orchard in bloom. Refrigerated ships enable Australia to export fruit to Europe.

Hot, dry summers make the irrigated Murray River Valley a leading grape-growing district.
Birnback

Australian stockmen inspect their flock of Merinos on a sheep station in New South Wales.

touch with their friends by radio. Children even go to school by radio. Australia has a "School of the Air" for the boys and girls who live on the stations of the outback. The School of the Air broadcasts lessons to these boys and girls every day.

A few sheep arrived at Botany Bay, on Australia's east coast, with the first European settlers. Today, in good years, Australia's sheep population numbers 140 million. This means that there are 14 sheep for every person in Australia.

Three fourths of these sheep are Merinos. Merinos are famous for their fine wool. A Merino sheep is literally covered with a fleecy coat of wool from the tips of his toes to the end of his nose. The other fourth of Australia's sheep are mainly mixed breeds. They are raised for meat—mutton and lamb.

Half of Australia's sheep are raised in New South Wales. Most of the remainder are found on stations in southern Queensland, Victoria, and coastal South Australia and Western Australia.

Shearing time is anxiously awaited by station owners, for that is when the crop of wool is harvested.

Shearing begins in June in Queensland. The shearers are at work in western Australia in November. Shearers are skilled workers. They travel across the country in groups called shearing gangs. The long shearing period gives the shearing gangs time to move from station to station and from state to state.

When the shearers arrive, the sheep are herded into pens. The shearers reach into the pens and grab a "customer." It takes the shearer only a few minutes to remove the sheep's heavy woolen coat. Each sheep yields about 9 pounds of wool. Expert shearers can clip 150 sheep in a day. In all, Australia produces about a billion pounds of wool each year. This is one fourth of the world's total wool production.

Out in the center of Australia is a stone marker. It points out the line that divides the state of South Australia from the Northern Territory. The Northern Territory is nearly as large as Alaska.

In this vast, sparsely populated land are some of the world's largest cattle ranches. One of them covers 12,686 square miles.

Getting cattle to market is a real problem in the Northern Territory. Many ranches, or stations, are hundreds of miles from a railroad. So the cattle must be herded on long drives to the railroad. Some drives take months. The cattle can only travel 10 or 12 miles a day. If they are rushed, they will lose too much weight before they reach market.

The Northern Territory is still pioneer country. The rewards are great for those who have learned to conquer the loneliness and rigors of pioneer life.

Dick Hanley—Photo Researchers

Australian sheep shearers use mechanical clippers to remove the heavy fleece.

Cowboys drive a herd of beef cattle near Alice Springs, an oasis in the dry Northern Territory.

Courtesy of Australian News and Information Bureau

A solitary acacia tree and barren red sands form a typical Australian desert scene.

Artesian "bores" tap underground water supplies Overuse makes many wells run dry each year.

Problems on the Land

Much of Australia is dry. At times the owners of sheep and cattle stations desperately need water. During dry years flocks and herds often have to be reduced by one fourth. Even then millions of sheep and cattle may die of thirst.

Once, long ago, Australia had a drought that lasted for 10 years. The flocks were reduced by half. When the drought finally ended, it took 30 years to rebuild the flocks to their original number.

When you look at a map of Australia (p. 484), you might think that the continent had plenty of water. The map shows many rivers and lakes. But the rivers are often dry, and the large lakes of South Australia, Eyre and Torrens, are really only lake beds. They are covered with water after occasional rainy periods, but most of the time they are dried up and covered with glistening salt. The big lakes of Western Australia —Austin, Macdonald, and Mackay—are dry most of the year.

Fortunately for station owners, some portions of Australia have large stores of underground water, which can be reached by drilling deep wells. These wells are called "bores" in Australia.

Thousands of bores have been drilled. In fact, too many may have been drilled. In some parts of Australia so much underground water has been removed that the supply is not as good as it used to be. The search for water must go on, and better ways of using the existing supplies must be found, if Australia is to continue to supply the world with large quantities of wool and meat.

Like farmers all over the world, Australians are learning that they must take better care of their land. Australian wheat farmers, year after year, plowed the soil west of the Great Dividing Range. Then came a time of drought. The cover of grass that once held the soil in place was gone. The soil began to blow. Great clouds of dust swirled over the countryside. Once gone, this wind-blown soil could not be replaced. Australian farmers today are busy learning new methods of tilling their land to prevent its blowing away again.

Plants and animals cause problems on the land too. One plant pest is the prickly pear. The prickly pear is a kind of cactus. Settlers brought some prickly pears with them when they came to Australia more than one hundred years ago. By 1920, prickly pear cactus had spread over 60 million acres of good grazing land. The growth was so thick that the land was useless for grazing.

Finally, in 1925, an insect called *Cactoblastis* was brought to Australia from Argentina. *Cactoblastis* kills prickly pear plants. Within a few years more than half of the ruined land was again available to station-owners and farmers.

The station-owner's worst enemy is the rabbit. Australia has millions of rabbits. These rabbits devour the grass and brush needed to feed sheep. Like the prickly pear, the rabbit is an introduced pest, brought in by settlers for hunting.

Australians have worked hard to get rid of their rabbits. They have killed as many as 25 million in a single year. They have even built thousands of miles of fences to keep rabbits out of good pastures.

A few years ago a rabbit disease was introduced in Australia to help wipe out the rabbits. The first year four fifths of them died from this disease. But those that survived have built up a resistance to the disease. It looks as though Australians will be having trouble with their rabbit population for many years to come.

Kangaroos are another pest. Like the rabbits, kangaroos feed on grass. Building fences will not keep kangaroos out of the pastures. They can leap 20 feet into the air. Great kangaroo hunts are organized in the outback. But kangaroos are not easily killed. They can travel more than 40 miles an hour.

A windmill pumps water for irrigation in the dry "outback" near Alice Springs.

Where forest cover has been removed, rainstorms leave jagged gullies in the earth.

A heavy dredge brings up huge quantities of gold-bearing mud in New South Wales.

Mineral Resources

In 1849 all the world rushed to the newly discovered California gold fields. Two years later, and half way around the world, another gold rush began. Gold was discovered in Australia.

The first gold was discovered in New South Wales. Shortly afterward, even richer deposits were uncovered in Victoria. In just 10 years Victoria's population increased five times.

Gold is mined in every Australian state and territory. More than a billion and a half dollars' worth has come out of Victoria alone. But today the center of gold mining is at Kalgoorlie, in the deserts of Western Australia.

Australia has other important minerals too. It is a leading producer of lead and zinc. The lead and zinc mines at Broken Hill, in dry western New South Wales, are among the greatest in the world. These mines have operated for nearly 80 years, and there is still plenty of valuable ore left.

Australian mines produce enough copper for the country's use. Small amounts of tin are also mined. But far more important than copper and tin are Australia's coal and iron ore deposits, for it is coal and iron ore that have helped Australia become a manufacturing country.

This zinc refinery in Hobart, Tasmania, provides Australia with a valuable mineral export.

This giant pipeline carries coal from the mine to the steelmaking center of Port Kembla.

For many years Australia had to depend on manufactured goods from overseas. Because Australia is so far from the world's manufacturing countries, the cost of these goods was high. Using its own coal and iron ore has enabled Australia to manufacture its own goods at home.

The most important coal fields are in eastern New South Wales. Four fifths of all the coal mined in Australia comes from this state. The most important mines are near Newcastle.

Limestone is just as necessary as iron ore and coal in iron- and steelmaking. Fortunately for Australia, there are large deposits of limestone in the states of Tasmania and South Australia.

Australia's iron ore mining center is at Iron Knob, a few miles inland from Spencer's Gulf in South Australia. Railroads carry the ore to the docks at Whyalla. There the ore is loaded on freighters and carried to the great blast furnaces at Newcastle and Port Kembla on the eastern coast.

A few years ago Australians began to develop some new iron ore deposits. These deposits are on the northwest coast at Yampi Sound. It is 3,200 miles by sea from Yampi Sound to Whyalla. But these new deposits assure Australia of a good supply of iron ore for many years to come.

Coal is Australia's chief source of power. In this land of limited rainfall, there are few dependable sources of waterpower, and the search for oil has had only limited success. Some wells have been drilled, but so far they have produced only a small quantity of oil. Perhaps some day nuclear power will be used in Australia to supplement the power that comes from coal. Several important fields of uranium have been discovered. Ore from these fields is refined at Port Pirie.

Iron ore is unloaded at Port Kembla's docks. Railroad cars carry the ore to the steel plants.

Birnback

A steel plant at Port Kembla. Australia's steel industry employs about 25,000 men.

This factory produces the Holden, the first automobile made entirely in Australia.

Courtesy of Australian News and Information Bureau

Growth of Australian Industry

Two world wars greatly affected manufacturing in Australia. During World War I, Australia was cut off from overseas supplies of manufactured goods. This is the time when Australia's iron and steel industry began to expand.

The second World War affected Australian manufacturing in a different way. World War II came to the Pacific. For a time many Australians feared that their country might even be invaded. Australian factories quickly began to manufacture guns, ships, and airplanes. The electrical, chemical, and metallurgical industries grew rapidly. When the war ended, Australia was truly a manufacturing country.

Today one third of all the workers in Australia are employed in manufacturing industries. The value of the products manufactured is actually greater than the value of all of Australia's farm, ranch, and mine products put together.

Australia's manufacturing is especially important in the states of New South Wales and Victoria. Manufacturing has concentrated in the port cities. Here railroads deliver raw materials from the outback. And here ships are available to bring in raw materials and to export finished manufactured goods. There are plenty of people to work in the factories. And the largest markets are found in these cities.

What are Australia's chief industries? Meat-packing, food-processing, and flour-milling are all important. So is the manufacture of woolen textiles. Agricultural implements are made from the iron and steel of Australia's blast furnaces. And electrical equipment is produced from Australian copper. But some important goods are manufactured from materials shipped to Australia from overseas. Especially important are the assembly plants of American and British automobile manufacturers.

Australia is a great trading country. Wool is its most important export. Sydney is the world's leading wool-exporting center. More than a million bales of wool are shipped from Sydney each year.

Most of Australia's exports are raw materials from the ranches, farms, and mines. Very few manufactured goods are sold abroad. Most of them are used at home.

Australian truck farms supply food-processing plants like this soup kitchen.

Wool grease is removed from fleece and refined into lanolin, a valuable by-product.

NEW ZEALAND

Travel 1,200 miles southeast of Australia. Or travel 1,600 miles north of Antarctica. Or travel 6,000 miles west of Chile and 4,000 southwest of Hawaii. All of your travels would put you in New Zealand.

The Dominion of New Zealand consists of two large islands and several small islands. All together they have an area of just a little over 100,000 square miles—about the same size as Colorado in the United States. New Zealand's population is more than 2¼ million.

Sometimes people think of Australia and New Zealand together. But in many ways they are quite different. Australia is fairly flat. New Zealand is very mountainous. Australia is mostly dry. New Zealand is very rainy. Much of Australia is covered by deserts, while much of New Zealand was originally covered by forest. And the Maoris, New Zealand's native people, developed a much more advanced culture than the primitive aborigines of Australia.

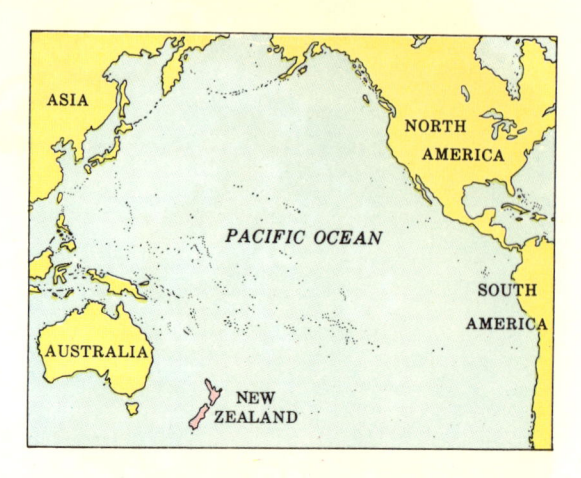

As a whole, New Zealand has a cool oceanic climate. The climate is much like that of the northwest coast of North America—Washington, British Columbia, and southern Alaska. Because New Zealand is in the Southern Hemisphere, it gets colder toward the south. Snow and frost are rare on North Island. But the southern portion of South Island has cold winters.

South Island has a high, rugged mountain chain. The highest of the peaks is Mt. Cook. It is 12,349 feet above sea level. The native Maoris call Mt. Cook "Aorangi,"

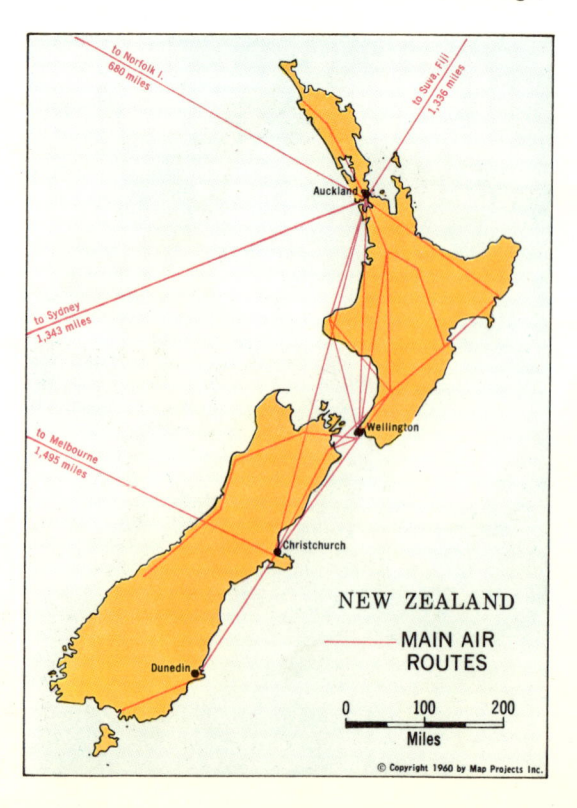

515

Forest-clad mountains look down on Doubtful Sound in Fiordland, on New Zealand's South Island.

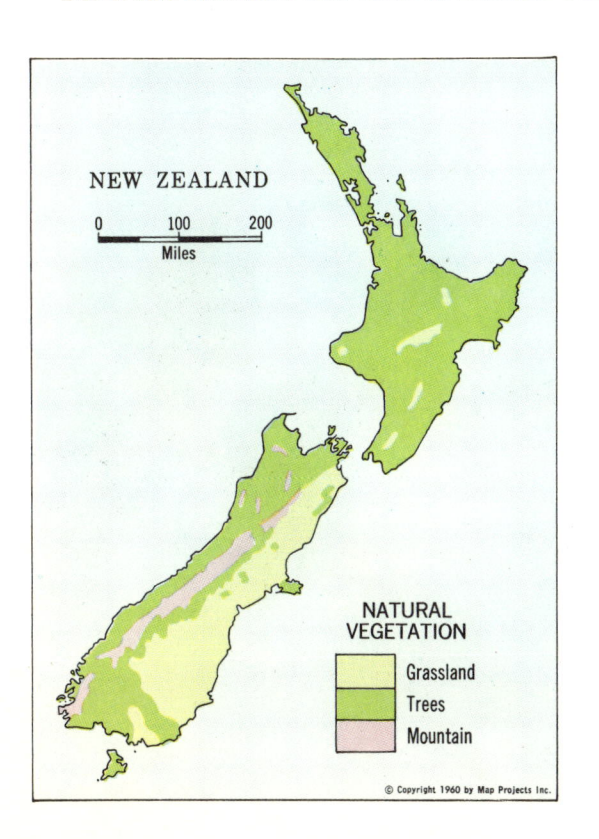

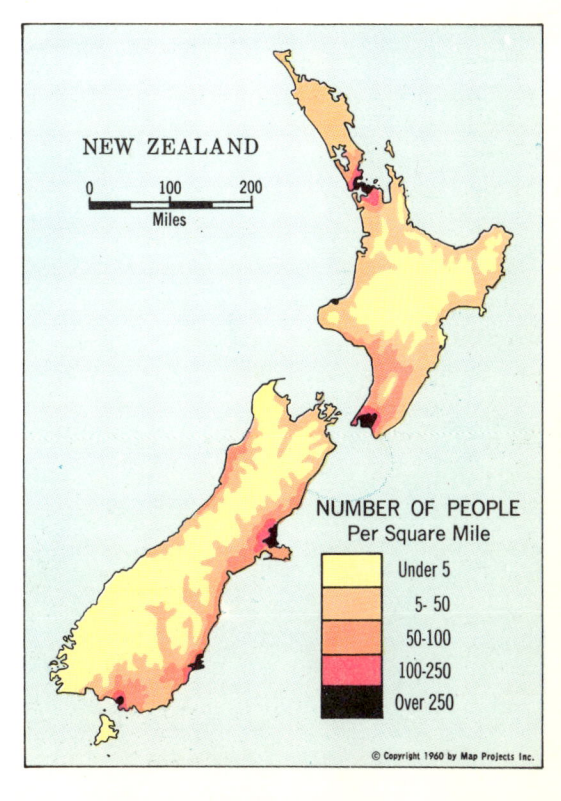

Katherine Tweed Robertson—Monkmeyer

NEW ZEALAND
0 100 200
Miles

NATURAL VEGETATION
- Grassland
- Trees
- Mountain

© Copyright 1960 by Map Projects Inc.

NEW ZEALAND
0 100 200
Miles

NUMBER OF PEOPLE
Per Square Mile
- Under 5
- 5- 50
- 50-100
- 100-250
- Over 250

© Copyright 1960 by Map Projects Inc.

which means "cloud piercer." In all, South Island has 17 peaks over 10,000 feet.

The southwestern coast of South Island is called Fiordland. Here many deep fiords have been scoured out of the rock by glaciers. These lovely fiords, the mountains, lakes, and wonderful snow fields for skiing make South Island popular with tourists.

North Island has its mountains, too, but they are not so high as those of South Island. Even so, North Island has some active volcanoes and many hot springs and geysers.

New Zealand has long been isolated from other lands. As a result, many of its plants and animals are endemic. They are found in no other place in the world. There are giant tree ferns and rimu, totara, and kauri trees, valuable for their fine lumber.

The most fascinating of all New Zealand's animals are the birds. One, the ostrichlike moa, grew to a height of 12 feet. But the moa were all killed hundreds of years ago. Only their skeletons remain to tell scientists of their existence.

The bat was New Zealand's only land mammal. There were no snakes at all. But Europeans brought many animals with them when they came to settle New Zealand. Some of these animals have become pests. Rabbits have caused much trouble in New Zealand, as in Australia. Deer, too, nibble the pastures that were meant to feed sheep.

The first European to sight New Zealand was a Dutch seaman, Abel Tasman. He sailed along the coast in 1642. But it was almost two hundred years later before many Europeans came to settle New Zealand. The majority of these settlers came from Great Britain.

At first the Maoris, New Zealand's native people, welcomed the settlers. But soon they discovered that these white intruders from across the seas were taking Maori land. The Maoris rebelled. Many years of bloody warfare followed. Finally the wars were ended and the Maoris were allowed to keep their land. Today they are respected citizens of New Zealand.

Volcanic peaks, some so high that they are snow-covered, surround Lake Wanaka on South Island.

Rupert Leach—FPG

A Maori mother bathes her little son in one of the volcanic hot springs on North Island.

McKelzie—Shostal

A typical New Zealand farmhouse stands among rolling fields. Most New Zealand farms are family-owned.

Farms, Ranches, and Factories

Plenty of rain and mild temperatures are ideal for growing grass. New Zealand has some of the world's finest grassy pastures. Grass is New Zealand's most important crop. This grass is fed to purebred sheep and dairy cattle, whose wool, meat, and dairy products have made New Zealanders prosperous.

North Island is a grazing land supreme. Nearly all of the crops produced on this island are fed to livestock. Hawkes Bay Province is known as the finest sheep country in the world, and the dairy farms of North Island produce the richest possible milk.

The excellence of New Zealand's grazing land is partly due to the climate, the soil, and the landforms. But the farmers deserve credit too. They have worked hard to constantly improve their pastures. New Zealand farmers have planted the best grasses, they use plenty of fertilizer and lime, and they watch their pastures carefully to keep them from being overgrazed.

South Island has a larger area of cropland than North Island. South Island farmers grow wheat, fruit, and many vegetables. But the raising of livestock is important on South Island too.

Because the climate is mild, neither dairy cattle nor sheep require shelter in New Zealand. They can graze on the green pastures the year around.

The size of the dairy herds is not great. Most dairy farms have about fifty cows. But all together New Zealand's stockmen have nearly six million cattle.

The number of sheep is even greater. New Zealand has more than 40 million sheep. This means that there are 20 sheep for every person in New Zealand. But these sheep are not the Merinos that graze on the dry lands of the Australian outback. New Zealand's rich pastures make it more profitable to fatten lambs and sheep for meat than to concentrate on producing fine wool. Even so, New Zealand produces one fourth of the world's wool.

New Zealand's cool, damp climate and rich grasslands are ideal for raising high-quality sheep.

Shocks of wheat dot the fields of New Zealand's grain farms at harvest time.

Trained dogs are used on New Zealand's cattle and sheep ranches to help herd the animals.

As you might expect from a land of sheep and dairy cattle, many of New Zealand's factories are busy processing food. Meat packers and freezers, and butter and cheese makers, are among New Zealand's most important manufacturers. So are its producers of canned and dried milk.

New Zealand is the world's greatest exporter of lamb and mutton. This island country ranks second only to Denmark as an exporter of butter. No country in all the world exports more cheese than New Zealand.

New Zealand became important as an exporter of food products at the beginning of the 20th century. At that time refrigeration equipment was installed on ships. Refrigeration made it possible to ship food across the equator and halfway around the world to European markets. Great Britain buys most of the food products which New Zealand exports.

Wool is an important export too. Only Australia and Argentina are greater wool exporters. Animal products rank highest among New Zealand's exports. Wool, meat, hides, and dairy products make up more than nine tenths of its exports.

Food products are not the only things produced by New Zealand's factories. But most of the other products are meant for home use rather than for export. Clothing, woolen cloth, flour, and lumber have long been important industries. Some newer industries are motor assembly, chemicals, printing, fertilizer, and paper.

About one fifth of all New Zealand's workers are kept busy in factories. Auckland is the chief manufacturing city and also the center of the rich Waikato dairy region. Here over half of New Zealand's dairy products are processed.

New Zealand's mineral resources are not large, but they are varied. There are deposits of coal and gold on both North and South Island. Iron ore is mined on South Island. Other mineral products include mercury, manganese, tin, platinum, silver, tungsten, and oil. A steel plant on South Island uses local ore and coal. The chief mineral export is gold.

New Zealand does not depend on its coal supplies for power. They are not large enough to fill the needs of industries and homes for more than a few decades. Instead, New Zealand makes use of the many rivers that tumble down the steep mountain slopes. Their water power is converted into electricity by hydroelectric plants. Abundant rainfall ensures a steady water supply. As a result, electricity is plentiful and cheap in New Zealand.

Government reforestation projects control erosion and ensure a future supply of timber.

Katherine Tweed Robertson—Monkmeyer

Water from melting glacier ice supplies power for the Roxbrough hydroelectric plant on South Island.

Katherine Tweed Robertson—Monkmeyer

Map of Pacific Islands

LOYALTY ISLANDS
- Uvea
- Chépénéhé
- Lifu
- Tadinou
- Maré

NEW CALEDONIA (Fr.)
- Art I.
- Paāba I.
- Balabio I.
- Mt. Panié 5412
- Koné
- Bourail
- Thio
- Nouméa
- Isle of Pines

FIJI (U.K.)
- LAU GROUP
- Vanua Mbalavu
- Thithia
- Nayau
- Lakemba
- Kambara
- Lambasa
- Vanua Levu
- Taveuni
- Koro
- Nairai
- Moala
- Matuku
- Koro Sea
- Viti Levu
- Nandi
- Yavuu
- Suva
- Ovalau
- Ngau
- Ono
- Kandavu
- YASAWA GROUP

TUAMOTU ISLANDS (Fr.)
- Pukapuka
- Napuka
- Tepoto
- Takumé
- Raroia
- Taenga
- Makemo
- Marutea
- Puka Ruha
- Reao
- Vahitahi
- Pinaki
- Amanu
- Hao
- Tatakoto
- Aratika
- Raraka
- Katiu
- Fakarava
- Anaa
- Hikueru
- Marokau
- Nengonengo
- Vanavana
- Tematangi
- Mururoa
- Moraně

GAMBIER ISLANDS

SOCIETY ISLANDS (Leeward Group)
- Huahine
- Tahaa
- Uturoa
- Raiatea
- Bora-Bora
- Maupiti
- Motu Iti
- Moorea
- Papeete
- Mt. Orohena 7618
- Mahina
- Faaitira
- TAHITI

ELLICE ISLANDS (U.K.)
- Nanumanga
- Niutao
- Nui
- Vaitupu
- Nukufetau
- Funafuti
- Nukulaelae
- Niulakita
- Vaitupu (US-UK)

GUAM (U.S.)
- Ritidian Pt.
- Pati Point
- Yigo
- Agana
- Orote Pen.
- Piti
- Lamlam 1335
- Merizo
- Cocos I.

WAKE ISLAND (U.S.)
- Toki Pt.
- Peale I.
- Wilkes I.
- Peacock Pt.
- Lagoon
- Matahiva

SOLOMON ISLANDS (U.K.–Aust)
- Ontong Java
- Buka
- Bougainville
- Kieta
- Buin
- Choiseul
- Treasury Islands
- Santa Isabel
- Kia
- New Georgia
- Vangunu
- Rendova
- Malaita
- Auki
- Ulawa
- Honiara
- Guadalcanal
- San Cristobal
- Bellona
- Rennell

KINGSMILL GROUP / GILBERT ISLANDS (U.K.)
- Makin
- Meang
- Marakei
- Abaiang
- Tarawa
- Maiana
- Kuria
- Aranuka
- Abemama
- Nonouti
- Tabiteuea
- Beru
- Nikunau
- Onotoa
- Tamana
- Arorae

SAMOA
- Tutuila (U.S.)
- Pago Pago
- Apia
- Lepa
- Apolima
- Upolu (N.Z.)
- Palauli
- Safotu
- Savaii

MARSHALL ISLANDS (U.S. Trust Territory)
- Bikar
- Utirik
- Ailuk
- Mejit
- Wotje
- Maloelap
- Aur
- Arno
- Majuro
- Mili
- Knox Atoll
- Jaluit
- Ailinglapalap
- Namu
- Kwajalein
- Likiep
- Rongerik
- Rongelap
- Bikini
- Ailinginae
- Wotho
- Ujae
- Ebon
- Namorik
- RATAK CHAIN
- RALIK CHAIN

SANTA CRUZ ISLANDS (U.K.)
- Ndeni
- Utupua
- Vanikoro

BANKS ISLANDS
- Ureparapara
- Vanua Lava
- Gaua
- Mera Lava

TORRES ISLANDS

NEW HEBRIDES (Fr.–Br.)
- Espiritu Santo I.
- Luganville
- Aoba
- Maewo
- Pentecost
- Malo
- Malekula
- Ambrym
- Paama
- Lopevi
- Epi
- Emae
- Efate
- Vila
- Erromanga
- Tanna

OCEANIA

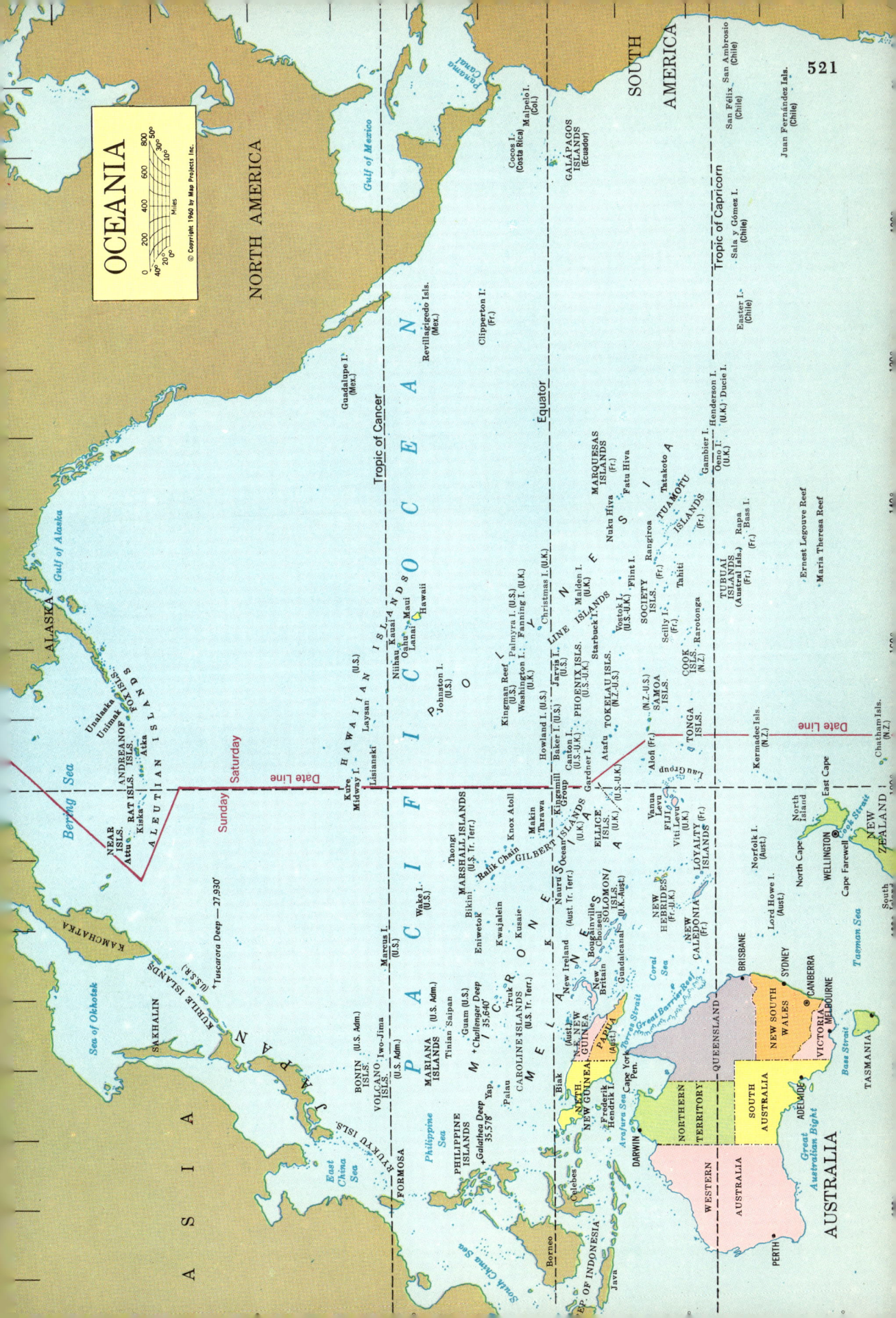

THE PACIFIC ISLAND WORLD

So much water—so little land. This is Oceania. Oceania covers a vast area. In this vast area there is a great variety of landforms, climates, soils, vegetation, animal life, and people.

Most of the islands of Oceania appear in clusters (see the map on pages 520-521). These clusters of islands are usually found in places where the ocean waters are fairly shallow. There the peaks of underwater mountain ranges and volcanoes break the surface of the water.

The floor, or bottom, of the ocean is quite uneven. There are mountains, hills, and valleys on the ocean floor just as on the surface of the land. In places on the ocean floor there are some very deep spots. Such places are called "deeps." The deepest of the deeps is in the Pacific Ocean near the Philippine Islands. There the ocean is

Ewing Krainin—Photo Researchers

Craggy rock formations reveal the volcanic origin of Moorea, one of the Society Islands.

Rugged mountains and palm-clad shores are a frequent sight on volcanic islands like Huahine.

Ralph Luce—Shostal

Coconut palms shade the thatch-roofed huts of Nandi, a typical Fijian village.

six and one half miles deep. You can understand just how deep this is when you realize that Mt. Everest, the world's highest mountain, is five and one half miles high.

Some of the islands rise out of the Pacific Ocean to amazing heights. In western New Guinea there are peaks that tower above 15,000 feet. Here, on a tropical island, just a few miles from the equator, are perpetual ice and snow.

Of course, few islands are high enough to have ice and snow. But many islands are quite rugged. Other islands are very low. They are so low that as you approach them by ship it appears as though the coconut trees are growing right out of the ocean. These low islands are called coral atolls.

Corals are tiny animals which live in warm ocean water. They are simple animals—they have no bones, heads, or legs. Whole colonies of corals grow together. These animals take lime from the ocean water and build walls around themselves. When the animals die, their limestone walls remain.

Coral often builds up around a mountain top that lies submerged beneath the ocean. In time coral columns reach the surface of the water. Waves then break over the coral. The waves break the coral into particles of sand, which slowly build up over the top of the coral. In time plants may wash ashore and take root. In this way thousands of coral atolls have been formed in the tropical waters of Oceania.

This aerial view shows clearly the coral reefs surrounding a typical South Pacific atoll.

524 THE PACIFIC ISLANDS

Sleek, swift canoes like this one are both a necessity and a source of pleasure to Polynesian islanders.

Samoan boys learn how to handle outrigger canoes at a very early age.

This Samoan father is teaching his young son how to spear fish with the traditional wooden spear.

These natives of Maupiti, in the Society Islands, are netting fish in the shallow lagoon.

The stone traps in this lagoon are 200 years old. Fish are driven into the traps and then netted.

Life on the Islands

What are the ways of life of the people who live on the coral atolls? Their ways are simple. Their wants are few.

From the air the atolls look like tiny beads of coral sand strung around a reef-enclosed lagoon. The quiet water of the lagoon provides a safe harbor for the islanders' outrigger canoes. And the lagoon also provides the islanders with a good supply of fish.

At night islanders wade out into the still water of the lagoon. Some carry torches. The light of their torches attracts fish. When the fish appear, a swirl of net is thrown on the water. The men work quickly to close the net. Women and children help drag the net to the beach. Everyone tries to grab the slippery fish. Soon the delicious aroma of baking fish fills the air.

Fish are wrapped in leaves, cooked over white-hot stones, and then eaten with the fingers.

Herbert Knapp

This island boy has shinnied up the trunk of a coconut palm and is now selecting nuts to pick.

The islanders are farmers as well as fishermen. But the soil of the atolls is poor. Only a few plants will grow. The most important of these plants is the coconut palm.

Coconut meat is white and oily. It is an important food on the atolls. In the hollow of the nut is "milk." This milk is delicious. It is also very nourishing. On the drier atolls coconut milk is almost the only source of liquid.

Islanders use the coconut for far more than food and drink. The hollow shell becomes a flask, a cup, or material for carved ornaments. Fibers from the husk become cord. The tough trunk of the tree becomes building material and furniture. And the broad leaves are used to thatch huts or to weave baskets. The coconut is truly the center of the islanders' life.

After the coconuts are picked, they are cracked open. The meat is then pried from the shell and spread out to dry in the sun. Dried coconut meat, called copra, is a valuable export.

Herbert Knapp

Herbert Knapp

THE PACIFIC ISLANDS

Watermelons, raised on the low coral island of Maupiti, find a ready market in nearby Tahiti.

Above: taro grows in fertile, swampy soil. Below: parts of selected stalks are replanted.

The coconut is important to the white man too. The people of nearly every atoll sell some dried coconut meat, which is called copra, to island traders. Oil is squeezed from copra. This oil is used in making margarine, cooking and salad oils, cosmetics, and fine soaps.

Preparing copra for the trading ships that call at the atolls is an important part of the daily chores. The coconuts are chopped open and the meat is scraped from the shells. On the low-lying atolls the meat is spread out to dry in the sunshine. This sun-dried copra is clean and highly valued. It is better than the darker smoke-dried copra of the high, rainy islands.

Scattered among the coconut palms are banana plants and breadfruit trees. Here and there are tiny patches of taro. Taro is a plant with a starchy root. It is an important food for the atoll dweller.

A few pigs and chickens roam in and out of the palm-thatched huts. They are saved for special feasts. Fish from the lagoon, and tuna and bonito caught in the open Pacific, provide most of the islanders' meat.

Ways of life are changing for the atoll dwellers. Airplanes and radios are now part of their world. But most of the atolls are small. They have few people. The lives of these people are still closely tied to their tiny islands and the beautiful waters that surround them.

Pacific Island Resources

In the past the people of Oceania depended upon their islands and the surrounding sea to furnish all they needed. The material for their homes, their tools, their clothing, and the food they ate, all came from their island or the sea.

Then European traders began coming to the Pacific. They showed the islanders shiny knives, beads, cloth, and other European goods. The islanders wanted these fine things of the white man's world. But how could they get them? What did they have that the white man could possibly want?

The islanders were surprised at some of the white man's interests. White men scoured the islands of the Pacific seeking minerals. The natives did not even know how to make metal. They were still living in the Stone Age. They had no use for the minerals that the white man wanted so badly.

Mineral hunters found gold, nickel, bauxite, and chromium. Natives were hired to work in the mines. But more often workers were brought to the islands from China, Java, and Japan. The hard work and rough life of the mining camps did not appeal to the islanders.

The islanders really gained little from the mining operations. In fact mining almost destroyed some islands. These were

Along with copra, bananas are a major Samoan export. They grow well on many Pacific islands.

the "guano islands." Guano is the powder-dry excrement of sea birds. It is a rich fertilizer.

The life of the guano diggers was hard and lonely. The best deposits were found on barren and treeless rocks. There was no protection from the blistering sun. Almost all supplies came in by ship. The food was poor. The workers often became sick and many died. As soon as the deposits were mined out, the islands were abandoned to the sea birds.

This train carries workers to the fields of a large sugar plantation on Viti Levu, Fiji.

Two islands are especially famous for their mines. They are Ocean Island and Nauru. Here are some of the world's richest phosphate rock deposits. Fertilizer made from this phosphate rock is vital to the farmers of Australia, New Zealand, and Japan.

Far more important than mining are the plantations. Coffee, cacao, citrus fruits, bananas, pineapples, and cotton are all grown in Oceania.

The Fiji, Hawaiian, and Mariana Islands have huge sugar plantations. Sugar has changed the lives of the people of these islands. The cultivation and harvesting of sugar cane require many workers. Thousands of Asians came to these islands to work in the cane fields. Even in places where the plantations have been abandoned, many Asians have remained.

More sugar than copra is produced in Oceania, and the total value of the sugar crop in Oceania is greater than that of copra. But sugar is important on only a few islands, while coconuts are important on nearly every island.

Elvajean Hall

Fijian copra is boxed at a company plantation and then shipped overseas from the port of Suva.

In many of the island groups copra is the chief industry. But the ways of growing coconuts vary greatly. In some places, such as the Gilbert and Ellice islands, all of the copra is produced by natives. In other islands, scattered over all of Oceania, copra is produced on small white-owned plantations. And in the Solomons, Fiji, and New Guinea, copra is produced on large company plantations. But, regardless of how it is produced, copra is important to nearly all of the people of Oceania.

An inter-island schooner unloads cattle at Tahiti. These boats carry most of the islands' freight.

Ralph Luce—Shostal

Cheap hydroelectric power from plants like this one is attracting new industries to Tasmania.

THE FUTURE OF THE PACIFIC REALM

What does the future hold for Australia, New Zealand, and the thousands of islands of Oceania? Throughout the Pacific today many places have already taken on new importance. Islands that a few years ago were so isolated that months passed without a visit from an outsider now have become vital landing and refueling bases. In the future, Pacific air lanes will become even more important. More and more airplanes will be linking the continents of North America, Asia, and Australia.

Australia and the "continental" islands contain some very ancient crystalline rocks. And these ancient crystalline rocks contain minerals. In other rocks, called sedimentaries, oil is sometimes discovered.

A new home goes up on Maupiti, in the Society Islands. Concrete is replacing bamboo and thatch.

Sedimentary rocks are also found in this region. Valuable minerals have been mined for years in the Pacific. And some oil is now being produced in New Guinea and Australia.

The future seems certain to see the discovery of a greater amount and variety of minerals in the Pacific. The future of mineral industries looks bright for Australia and the "continental" islands.

The people of the island world have scarcely begun to make use of their fish resources. Radar equipment will help fishermen find large schools. And scientists will improve methods of preparing tropical fish for market. Quick freezing and packing, and floating canneries, will do much to increase the importance of fishing.

Australia and New Zealand have long looked to Europe for markets. Nearby neighbors in the Pacific and Asia are rapidly turning to industry. The incomes of these neighboring countries are rising. Australia and New Zealand will be finding increasing opportunities for trade in the Pacific and Asia in the future.

The scenic wonders of Australia, New Zealand, and Oceania have long been known. Hundreds of books have been written describing them. Artists and photographers have traveled halfway around the world to paint and photograph them. But only a handful of the world's people have ever been able to see these scenic attractions for themselves. Throughout the years they have simply been too far away from the centers of dense population in Europe and North America.

The beauty of Australia's Great Barrier Reef and crashing surf; New Zealand's fiords, snow-capped peaks, hot springs, and lovely mountain lakes; and the palm trees, blue water, and coral beaches of Oceania are all waiting for visitors to see and enjoy. In the future more and more of the world's people will be seeing these scenic wonders. Distance will no longer be measured by miles. Time will be the measuring device of the future.

Fiji youngsters learn to read in an outdoor classroom. Education means progress for the islands.

In a few short years Australia, New Zealand, and Oceania will be only hours away from the world's population centers. More and more people will visit these lands and come to know their people. To really understand others, you must know them. And how better can you get to know the people of the world than to see and talk with them yourself?

New Guinea plywood factory workers travel back to their native village by airplane.

ARCTIC REGIONS

Scale 1:60,000,000

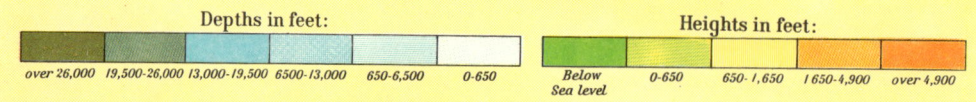

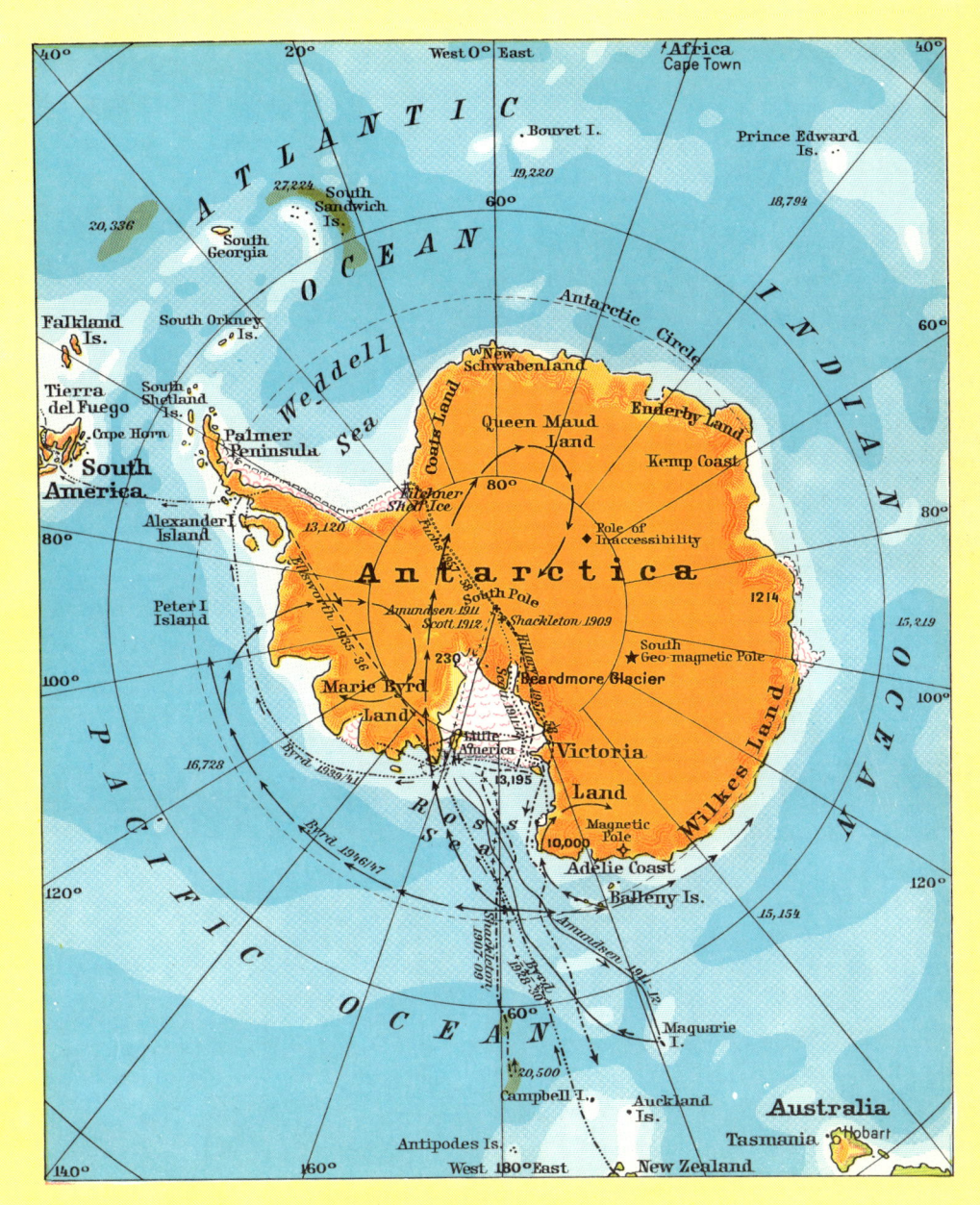

ANTARCTICA

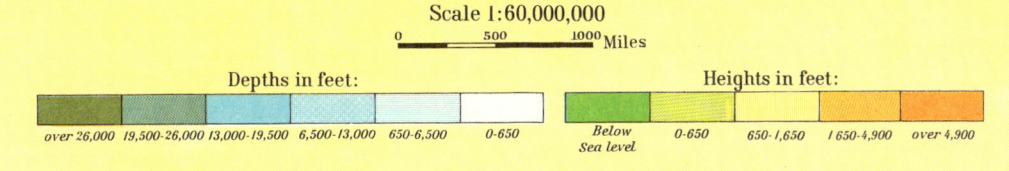

Scale 1:60,000,000

Depths in feet: over 26,000 | 19,500–26,000 | 13,000–19,500 | 6,500–13,000 | 650–6,500 | 0–650

Heights in feet: Below Sea level | 0–650 | 650–1,650 | 1,650–4,900 | over 4,900

The midnight sun lights up the sky over Narvik, Norway, north of the Arctic Circle.

Joe Barnell—Shostal

POLAR LANDS

If you travel far enough to the north or south, you will cross the Arctic Circle or the Antarctic Circle. Beyond these imaginary lines on the earth's surface are the polar lands.

What are the characteristics of the polar lands? The polar lands have cold weather —cold in summer as well as winter. The year-round average temperature is well below freezing. At the South Pole a temperature of 102 degrees below zero has been recorded. Snow and ice can be found even in the summertime.

Many parts of the world have cold weather and ice and snow during some part of the year. But the polar lands are the only regions on earth where the winter months are completely without daylight. The sun does not rise at all for a period ranging from one day at the Arctic and Antarctic Circles to six months at the North and South Poles. The rest of the time it barely appears above the horizon for a few moments. But the summers are as light as the winters are dark. The sun circles the horizon without setting.

But the Arctic and the Antarctic are not completely alike. Indeed, except for their long, dark, cold winters and their short, cool summers, these two polar regions are really quite different.

The Arctic is a "hollow"—a deep ocean basin. This Arctic Ocean basin is surrounded by the northern plains of North America, Europe, and Asia.

The Antarctic is a "hump"—a great land mass. This land mass is the Antarctic continent. The Antarctic continent covers

Vast snow-covered plateaus and towering mountains characterize Antarctica's frozen landscape.

Elmo Jones

This huge iceberg was once part of a glacier. The hole in it was carved by an underground river in the glacier.

more than five million square miles. It is larger than either Europe or Australia. Besides being so large, the Antarctic continent averages more than one mile in elevation. No other continent on earth has such a high average elevation.

The land surrounding the Arctic Ocean has provided a home for man for a thousand years or more. Sturdy Eskimo people have long hunted and fished on the Arctic plains and waters. But man has never lived permanently on the Antarctic continent.

ANIMAL LIFE

The Arctic is rich in animal life. There are great herds of reindeer in northern Europe and Asia. In North America the reindeer's relative, the caribou, roams the Arctic plains. Also important in the North American Arctic is the huge musk ox. His thick coat of shaggy hair makes it possible for the musk ox to live through the coldest Arctic winter.

Wolves and foxes sometimes follow reindeer, caribou, and musk ox. They attack stray animals that have wandered from the herd.

The ice of the Arctic Ocean is the home of another familiar Arctic dweller. He is the polar bear. Polar bears feast on the seals and walruses that live in the freezing water of the Arctic Ocean.

Birds and insects are found in great number in the northern polar lands. Millions of birds fly north each year to nest during the summer months. They have no

Mary Carrick
A polar bear cub prowls over an Arctic ice floe searching for food.

Penguins live in colonies. Their flipperlike wings make them at home in the water of Antarctica.
Jack Couffer

trouble finding plenty of food. Swarms of mosquitoes and flies hatch in the pools of stagnant water that collect on the Arctic plains in the summertime. These mosquitoes and flies provide tasty meals for hungry Arctic bird families.

How different is the Antarctic! A tiny wingless mosquito is the Antarctic's only land animal. And this mosquito is found only in a few protected areas on the Antarctic continent.

The Antarctic has no land mammals at all and the continent itself has no birds. The famous Antarctic penguins live on the pack ice around the edges of the Antarctic continent. These penguins are graceful fishing and diving birds, but they cannot fly and they are quite awkward on land.

The Arctic and the Antarctic differ in plant life too. In the Antarctic only a few mosses and hardy grasses grow on the sunward-facing slopes of ice-free rocks. Most of the Antarctic landscape is buried beneath a deep mantle of snow and ice. In some places this snow and ice is more than 10,000 feet thick.

Summer months in the Arctic are warmer than in the Antarctic. Even so, temperatures are not high enough for trees to grow.

A herd of walruses sun themselves on the rocky Alaskan coast. These warm-blooded animals spend most of their lives in the water. Eskimos hunt them for their meat, blubber, hides, and valuable ivory tusks.

This treeless region of the Arctic is called the tundra. But the tundra is not without vegetation. Indeed, in the summertime the Arctic tundra bursts into bloom.

Travelers are often amazed to find beautiful meadows of rich grasses and flowering plants in this far northern land. The tundra is fine grazing land for reindeer, caribou, and musk ox. Even in winter these animals can paw through the snow to find food on the tundra. Arctic hares and lemmings also inhabit the tundra.

The caribou, wild cousin of the European reindeer, ranges the North American tundra in search of lichens and grass. The caribou is a principal source of food for the Indians and Eskimos of the far north.

When a whale is killed, whole families of Eskimos with their dog teams go to bring the meat home.

LIFE IN THE ARCTIC

Nowhere in the inhabited world is life more difficult than in the northern polar lands. Eskimos are the only people who have lived permanently in this Arctic region. Reindeer-herding tribes in northern Europe and Asia drive their herds onto the Arctic tundra each summer in search of pasture. But when winter darkness approaches, these tribesmen return to the shelter of the vast northern forests.

Eskimos live along the edges of the polar seas from northeastern Siberia, across northern North America, to Greenland. Fifty thousand Eskimos are scattered over this Arctic wilderness.

Gambell, on St. Lawrence Island off the Alaskan coast, is a typical modern Eskimo village.

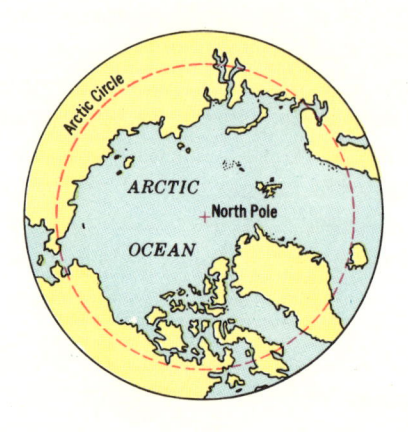

Long ago Eskimos learned the best ways of living in the polar lands. It would have been impossible to grow crops in the frozen tundra soil. So Eskimos became skilled hunters. Seals provided these hunters with almost all of their food, clothing, and bone for tools. They even provided the Eskimo with oil for fuel and light.

At best starvation was never far way in the Arctic. The Eskimo learned that if he killed too many seals in one place, his source of food would be gone.

Eskimo people moved often to remain close to the source of their food. They learned to travel by dog-sled over the frozen surface of the polar seas or the snow-covered tundra. In the summer they traveled and hunted from skin boats called kayaks.

Today only in a few isolated places do Eskimos still live like their ancestors. For most Eskimos the old ways of life are changing rapidly. Contact with Americans and Europeans is causing these changes.

Fur traders started some of the changes in the Eskimos' way of life. To help them kill more seals, fur traders gave the Eskimos rifles. The rifle was a better tool for killing seals than the Eskimos' harpoon.

When they first got rifles, Eskimos easily secured great supplies of seal meat and furs. But they killed too many seals. Soon no seals were to be found in the old, familiar hunting places. And with the seals gone, the Eskimos had nothing to trade to the white men. Nor did they have any food. In some parts of the Arctic, whole villages of Eskimos starved.

Some Eskimos have completely changed their way of life. They have given up all of the ways of their ancestors. Some have become radio operators and pilots. Others have become teachers and skilled mechanics. Eskimo boys and girls go to school. They play records on jukeboxes. They wear the same kind of clothes and play the same kind of games as boys and girls in lands to the south.

Lew Merrim—Monkmeyer
Releasing weather balloons at Thule, Greenland, one of the world's northernmost weather stations

In Greenland many Eskimos have left their igloos and kayaks. They have moved into fishing villages along the coast and live in wooden houses. They fish from motor boats. Probably no people on earth have changed their way of life so rapidly as have these Eskimo people of the northern polar lands. Unfortunately, many of them find the change difficult to make.

Brightly patterned sweaters display the artistry of Greenland's Eskimo craftsmen.

William Fortin

As penguins play in the foreground, a ship passes through a fog bank beneath towering Antarctic ice peaks.

ANTARCTICA, A FROZEN CONTINENT

Imagine a tract of land larger than either Australia or Europe, without a single inhabitant. There is such a place. It is the Antarctic continent. Certainly there is no lonelier place on earth.

And there is no place on earth with a more severe climate than Antarctica. Winter temperatures of 70 and 80 degrees below zero are common. Winds of nearly 100 miles per hour often sweep across the frozen landscape. Even in the brief summer, temperatures are almost constantly below freezing.

This great continent was almost unknown until modern times. Much of it is still little explored.

Antarctica is an isolated continent. The other continents of the Southern Hemisphere—South America, Africa, and Australia—are far away. The seas that surround Antarctica are dangerous. Cold winds pour off Antarctica's icy slopes. These winds whip the seas into huge waves. And the seas are often clogged with drifting ice, ice packs, and giant icebergs.

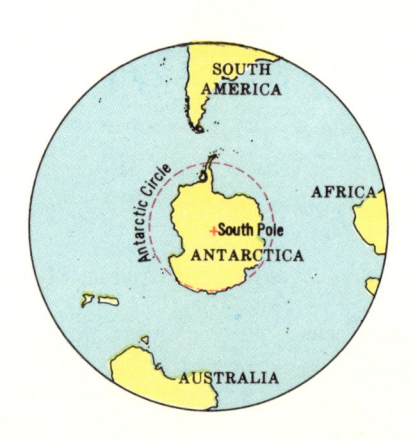

It is no easy task to approach the coasts of Antarctica by ship. The coasts are well protected against intruders. Sometimes great belts of pack ice extend out from the coasts for hundreds of miles. Towering ice cliffs, 50 to 200 feet high, greet explorers who try to come ashore. It is little wonder that most of the exploration of Antarctica had to wait until airplanes made it possible to land men and equipment on the continent.

Beneath the Antarctic ice cap lie some of the world's great mountain ranges. In the Palmer Peninsula, peaks rise above 10,000 feet. In Marie Byrd Land there are peaks that tower 20,000 feet above sea level.

Eastern Antarctica is a high plateau. Geologists (men who study rock formations) say that this Antarctic plateau is much like the African plateau. The African plateau is rich in minerals. Some geologists believe that great mineral wealth may lie beneath the Antarctic ice cap too.

So far little is known about the minerals of Antarctica. It is not easy to study rocks that are buried under thousands of feet of ice. But geologists have studied the rocks in those few places where they rise above the ice. Some coal, copper, nickel, and a few other minerals have been found.

Miners are not rushing to the Antarctic continent. No large or especially valuable mineral deposits have yet been discovered. Besides, the problems of mining on this frozen continent would be great. And it would be too expensive to ship even the most valuable of ores the many thousands of miles to world markets. It is not likely that Antarctica will become a great mining center anytime soon.

Men first came to the Antarctic hunting for a different kind of wealth. They hunted whales. Whaling ships entered the waters around the continent as early as 1820. Giant factory ships still find the rough Antarctic seas the world's best whaling region.

All of the countries interested in Antarctic whaling work together to protect whales. If too many whales were killed there would soon be no whales left. So each country's ships are allowed to take only a limited number of whales each year.

Although whalers sailed Antarctic waters for many years, it was not until the 20th century that explorers set out across the continent for the South Pole. Roald Amundsen of Norway reached the South Pole first. Amundsen raised his country's flag over the Pole on December 14, 1911. Less than three years before, on April 6, 1909, an American, Robert E. Peary, discovered the North Pole.

Crewmen of an Antarctic whaler strip the blubber from a sperm whale before boiling it down for oil.

K. Schubert

This observation tower at "Little America" is part of an Antarctic weather station.

An airplane is unloaded for use in Operation Deepfreeze, an Antarctic exploration project.

In recent years many scientists have gone to the Antarctic. They have built scientific stations on both the continent and the surrounding islands. Important new information about the world's least known continent is being gathered.

Some scientists are eagerly studying Antarctic weather. They believe that the weather of this giant "refrigerator" affects the weather of other parts of the world. Other scientists are measuring the depth of the ice cap. And still others are studying the nature of the Antarctic's rock formations and the direction of flow of offshore ocean currents.

Aerial photographs are also being taken. These photographs will provide the information needed to make new maps of the Antarctic.

Scientists from many countries are working closely together to learn the secrets of the Antarctic. The United States and the Soviet Union both have stations in the Antarctic. So do Argentina, Australia, Chile, France, Great Britain, New Zealand, Norway, and Japan.

This titanium mine on Greenland exploits one of the polar lands' barely touched mineral resources.

FUTURE OF THE POLAR LANDS

What does the future hold for the polar lands? Until the present, man has done little to change the natural landscape of the Arctic and Antarctic. It is hard to believe that he ever will. Permanent settlement of large numbers of people in the polar lands is not likely.

Antarctica will increasingly become the world's only continent-sized scientific laboratory. Some countries now claim parts of Antarctica as their own territory. But in the future these countries may give up their claims. Some international organization, such as the United Nations, may administer Antarctica for scientific purposes.

A different kind of future awaits the northern polar region. Its importance for national defense has already been proven.

With nuclear submarines like the *U.S.S. Skate*, man is better able to explore the ice-clogged Arctic.

Military air bases and a radar warning network now stretch across the North American Arctic. It seems quite likely that similar bases and radar nets have been built in the portion of the Arctic belonging to the Soviet Union. The nuclear submarines *Nautilus* and *Skate* have also shown us that the frozen Arctic Ocean can be navigated in spite of its cover of ice.

The Arctic is an air-age region. The shortest distance from Europe to North America, and to eastern Asia, is across the Arctic. The future will see many more airplanes crossing parts of the northern polar lands.

Valuable minerals, such as uranium, have already been discovered in the Arctic lands. The need for these minerals will increase in the future as more easily mined sources of ore are used up. Sometime in the future many small mining communities will be scattered across the Arctic.

Heat and power would now prove to be serious problems for such communities. But soon nuclear reactors will be available to provide the heat and power needed in the Arctic. These nuclear reactors will help push the Arctic frontier farther northward.

AUSTRALIA AND OCEANIA—FACTS AND FIGURES

PRINCIPAL COUNTRIES AND ISLANDS: AREA AND POPULATION

Country or Island	Area in sq. miles	Population (est. 1960)
Australia	2,974,600	10,272,500
New Guinea	304,200	2,560,400
New Zealand	103,500	2,337,900
Polynesia		
Cook Is.	84	17,400
Ellice Is.	9	5,200
Marquesas Is.	492	4,200
Samoa	1,211	127,400
Society Is.	650	48,900
Tokelau Is.	6	1,700
Tonga Is.	250	60,300
Tuamotu	330	8,100
Micronesia		
Caroline Is.	461	40,800
Gilbert Is.	144	31,600
Mariana Is.	370	34,500
Marshall Is.	70	14,400
Nauru	8	4,500
Melanesia		
Bismarck Archipelago	19,200	162,600
Fiji Is.	7,056	398,000
New Caledonia	8,550	75,800
New Hebrides	5,700	56,400
Solomon Is.	16,000	193,800

LARGE CITIES AND THEIR POPULATION

City and Country (or Island)	Population (est. 1960)
Sydney, Australia	2,017,000
Melbourne, Australia	1,726,100
Brisbane, Australia	555,000
Adelaide, Australia	544,000
Auckland, New Zealand	401,500
Perth, Australia	382,000
Christchurch, New Zealand	205,500
Newcastle, Australia	192,900
Wellington, New Zealand	141,300
Hobart, Australia	105,100
Dunedin, New Zealand	101,600
Hutt, New Zealand	90,600
Geelong, Australia	82,800
Launceston, Australia	56,000
Hamilton, New Zealand	43,700

LARGE CITIES AND THEIR POPULATION

City and Country (or Island)	Population (est. 1960)
Canberra, Australia	39,100
Suva, Fiji Is.	37,400
Nouméa, New Caledonia	22,200
Papeete, Tahiti	18,000

PRINCIPAL MOUNTAINS AND THEIR ELEVATIONS

Mountain and Country (or Island)	Height in feet
Carstenz, New Guinea	16,400
Idenburg, New Guinea	15,750
Wilhelmina, New Guinea	15,584
Wilhelm, New Guinea	14,107
Victoria, New Guinea	13,240
Albert Edward, New Guinea	13,000
Cook, New Zealand	12,349
Balbi, Bougainville (Solomon Is.)	10,170
Ruapehu, New Zealand	9,175
Egmont, New Zealand	8,286
Orohena, Tahiti	7,618
Ulawan, New Britain (Bismarck Arch.)	7,546
Kosciusko, Australia	7,305
Panié, New Caledonia	5,412

LARGEST LAKES AND THEIR AREAS

Lake and Country	Area in sq. miles
Eyre, Australia	3,600
Torrens, Australia	2,230
Gairdner, Australia	1,500
Taupo, New Zealand	238
Te Anau, New Zealand	132
Wakatipu, New Zealand	112

LONGEST RIVERS AND THEIR LENGTHS

River and Country (or Island)	Length in miles
Darling, Australia	1,910
Murray, Australia	1,600
Murrumbidgee, Australia	1,050
Sepik, New Guinea	700
Fly, New Guinea	650
Macquarie, Australia	590
Flinders, Australia	520
Mamberamo, New Guinea	500
Condamine, Australia	495

THE WORLD IN MAPS

This section of twenty-four pages depicts the World,
its physical and political organization, the distribution of its people, its treasures,
and the condition of its communications and climate.

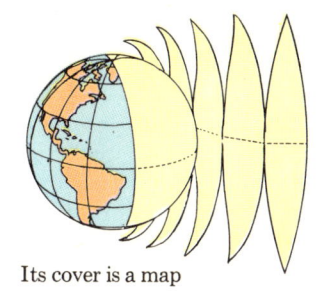

A globe is a model of the earth

Its cover is a map

These gores will cover a globe of the size shown above

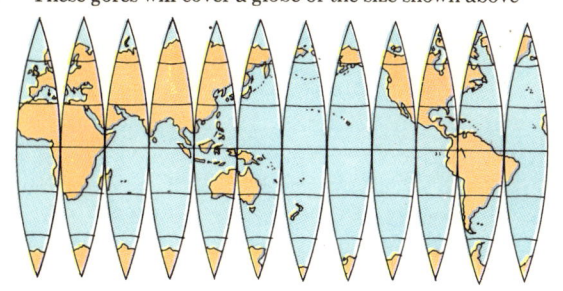

The Americas are moved to left to arrange a compact form for the economic and culture maps

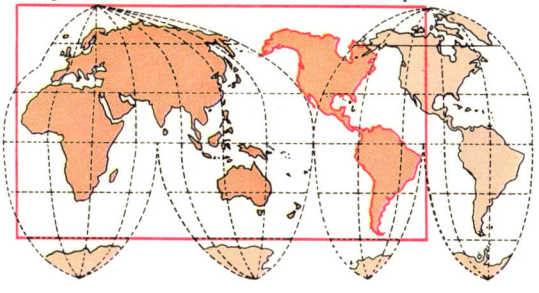

Red line indicates limits of maps on pages 548 and 554

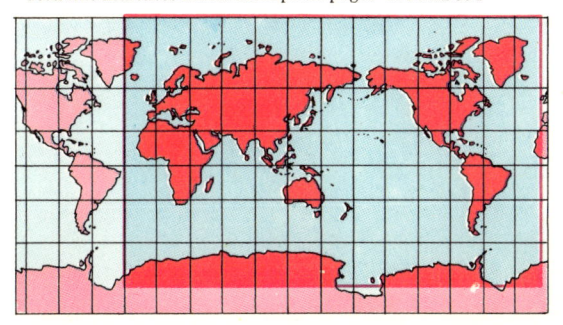

HOW THESE MAPS WERE DERIVED

The first thing to know about maps is that they are all distorted, or out of shape, World maps most of all. This is so because the Earth is a ball. Maps are flat. Producing maps without distortion is just as impossible as wrapping a grapefruit without wrinkling the paper.

The ordinary library or classroom globe is covered with a map which is first printed on paper and then cut into "gores." Gores fit the globe's spherical surface because they are narrow enough to involve little curvature, and they are dampened by the glue so as to be able to conform completely to the globe surface.

A set of unmounted globe gores does not make a satisfactory World map because the geography of the World is cut in too many places. Note that the land mass of Europe and Asia is interrupted five times.

To design a better map for the land masses, we "gather" some of the gores in groups so that each continent is complete. This is the projection used in this section for all the maps depicting distribution of things on land. It is so designed that all land units have the proper relative area.

When it is desirable to show the oceans continuously, as well as the lands, a different projection must be used. In the case of the Physical and Political maps, we use the Miller Cylindrical projection which shows the World as a whole.

On the next two pages are four views of the World which tend to make a visual correction for all distortions.

NORTHERN HEMISPHERE

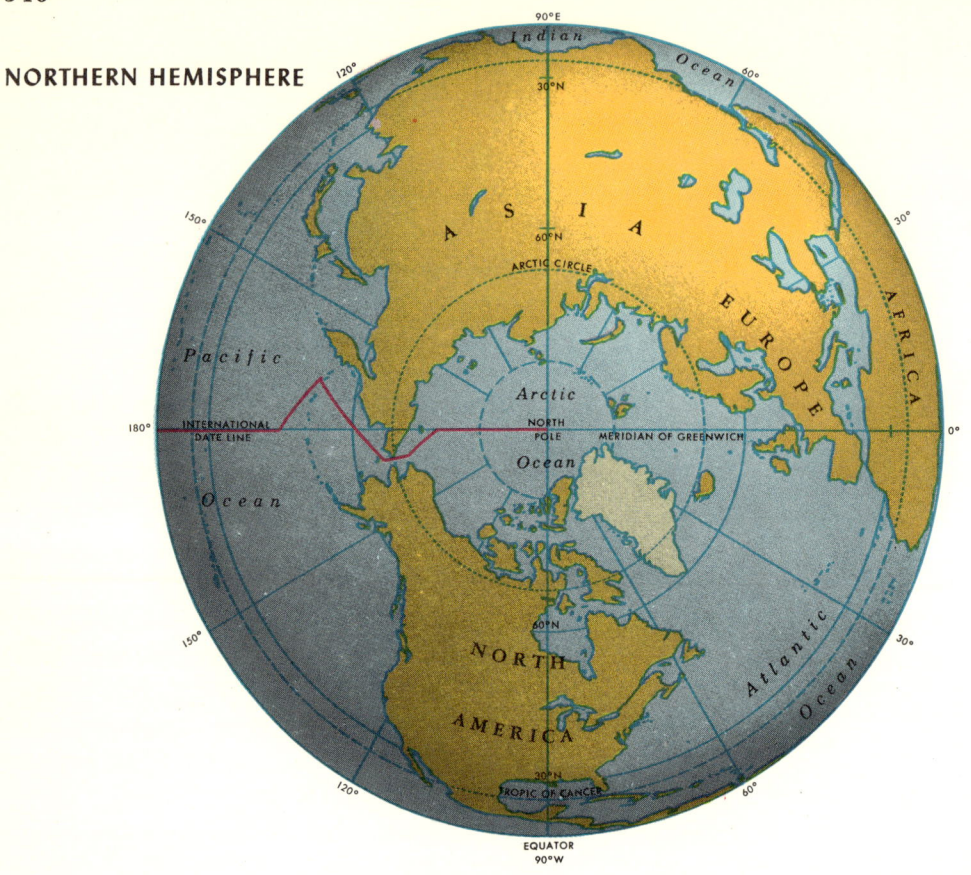

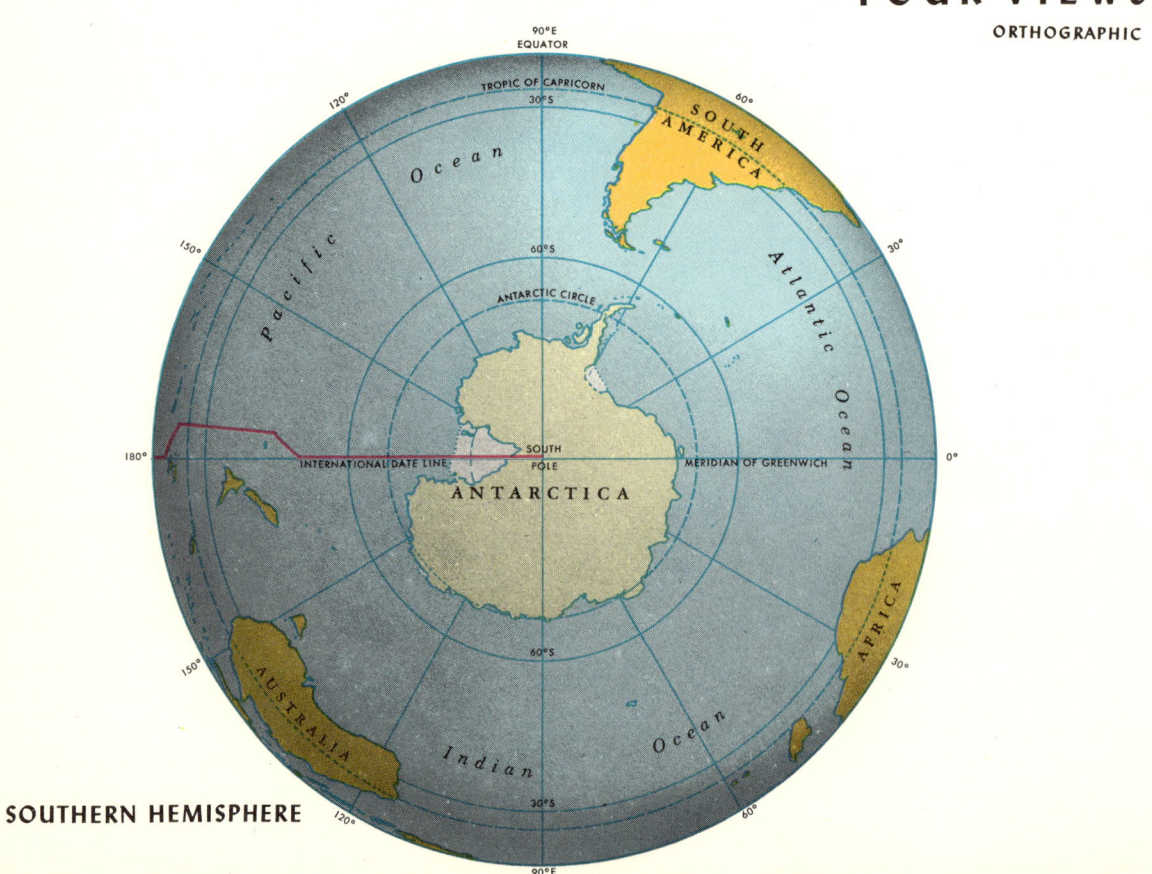

FOUR VIEWS
ORTHOGRAPHIC

SOUTHERN HEMISPHERE

547

WESTERN HEMISPHERE

OF THE WORLD

PROJECTION

EASTERN HEMISPHERE

NORTH POLE
0°
30°
60°
90°
120°
150°
Arctic Ocean
Spitsbergen
Barents Sea
Novaya Zemlya
Kara Sea
Severnaya Zemlya
Laptev Sea
New Siberian Is.
ARCTIC CIRCLE
ICELAND
GULF STREAM
North Sea
Baltic Sea
Rhine
Alps
Danube
Volga
Ural Mts.
Ob
Yenisei
Lena
Siberia
Angara
Lake Baikal
Irtysh
Sea of Okhotsk
Amur
Aral Sea
Black Sea
Caspian Sea
Altai Mts
Gobi Desert
Sea of Japan
Pamirs
Tarim Basin
Mediterranean Sea
Str. of Gibraltar
Atlas Mts.
Euphrates
Tigris
Persian G.
Himalayas
Hwang Ho
Yangtze
China Sea
KUROSHIO CURRENT
Indus
Ganges
Mt. Everest 29,028'
Si Kiang
Ocean
TROPIC OF CANCER
Sahara
Desert
Nile
Red Sea
Arabia
Lake Chad
Niger
Ethiopian Plateau
Arabian Sea
Bay of Bengal
Mekong
South China Sea
PHILIPPINES
35,630'
MICRO
Cape Verde
CEYLON
NORTH EQUATORIAL CURRENT
SOMALI CURRENT
L. Victoria
Congo
EQUATOR
MERIDIAN OF GREENWICH
EQUATORIAL COUNTERCURRENT
SUMATRA
BORNEO
EAST INDIES
NEW GUINEA
MEL
Kilimanjaro 19,565'
L. Tanganyika
Indian
JAVA
Atlantic
BENGUELA CURRENT
Lake Nyasa
Zambezi
MADAGASCAR
SOUTH EQUATORIAL CURRENT
Mauritius
Réunion
Australian Desert
TROPIC OF CAPRICORN
Kalahari Desert
AGULHAS CURRENT
Ocean
Darling
Murray
Cape of Good Hope
TASMANIA
Kerguelen
WEST WIND DRIFT
WEST WIND DRIFT
ANTARCTIC CIRCLE
ANTARCTICA
Richard Edes Harrison 1960

THE WORLD
Physical

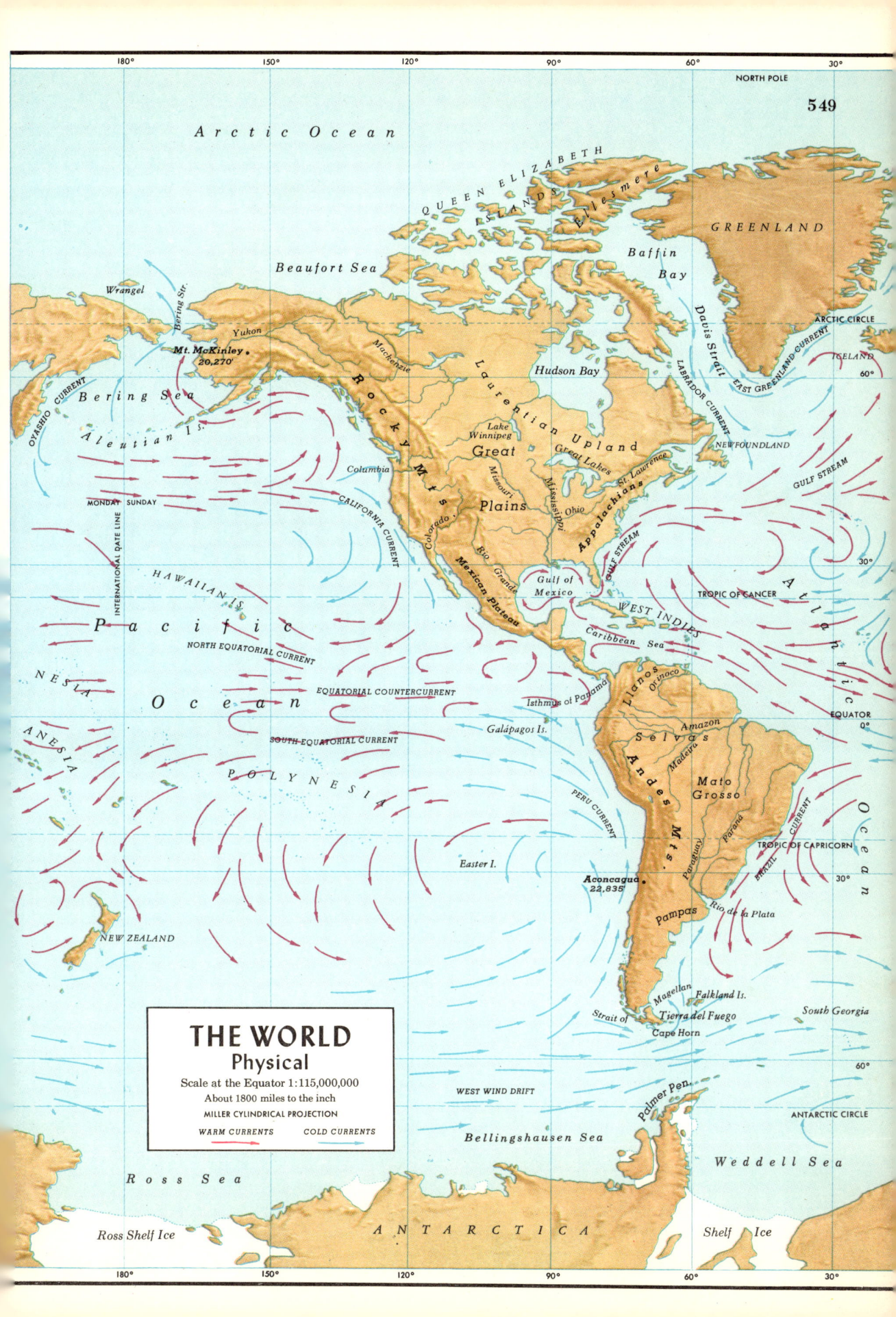

Scale at the Equator 1:115,000,000
About 1800 miles to the inch
MILLER CYLINDRICAL PROJECTION

WARM CURRENTS   COLD CURRENTS

RAINFALL

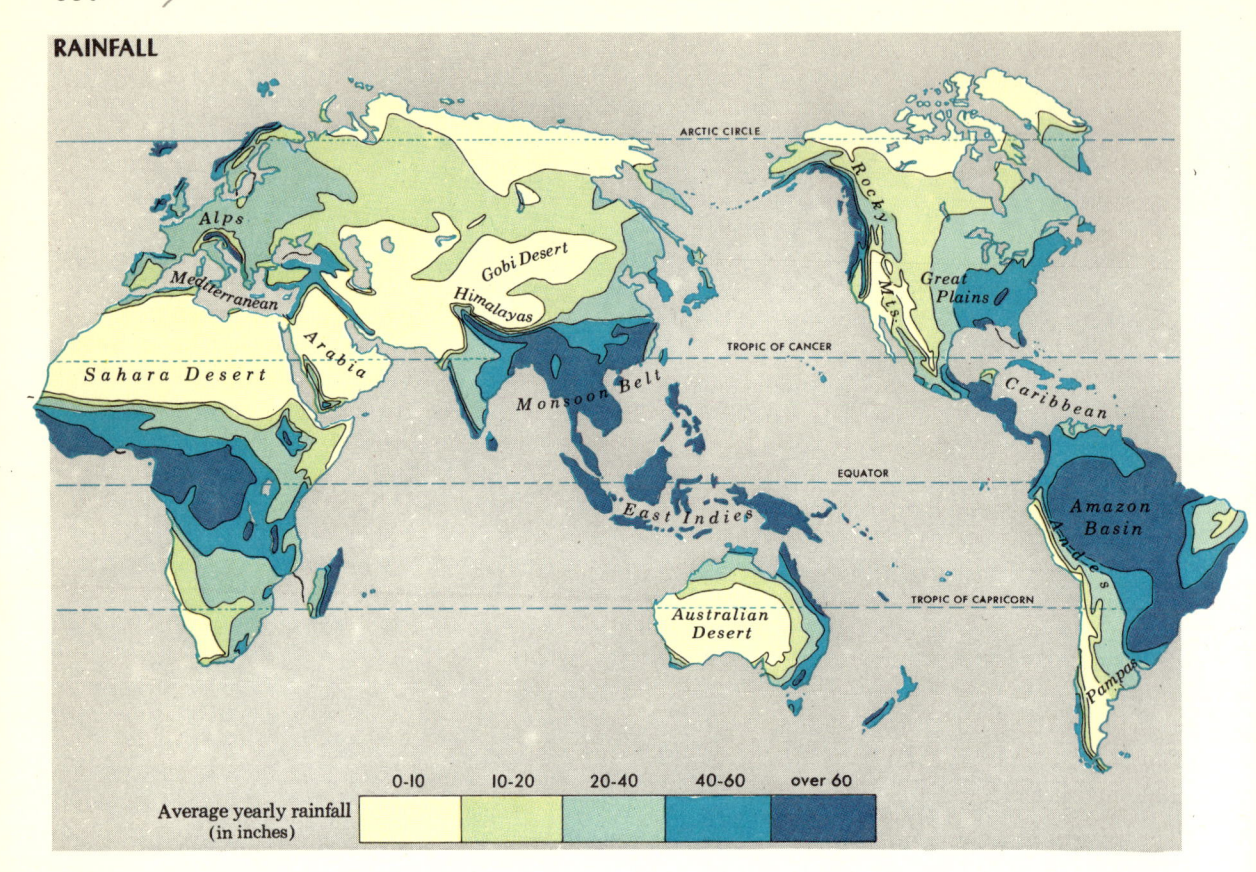

Average yearly rainfall (in inches): 0-10, 10-20, 20-40, 40-60, over 60

TEMPERATURE

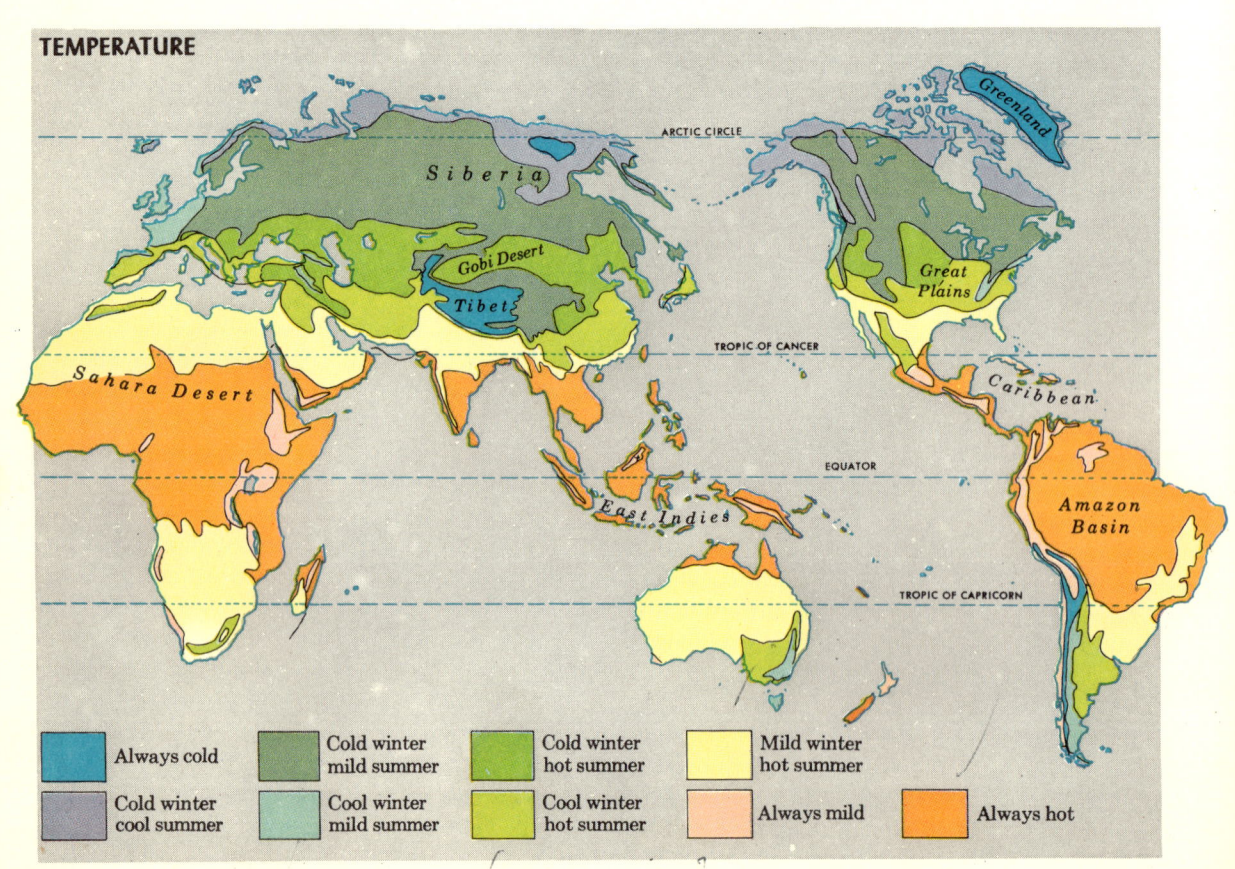

- Always cold
- Cold winter cool summer
- Cold winter mild summer
- Cool winter mild summer
- Cold winter hot summer
- Cool winter hot summer
- Mild winter hot summer
- Always mild
- Always hot

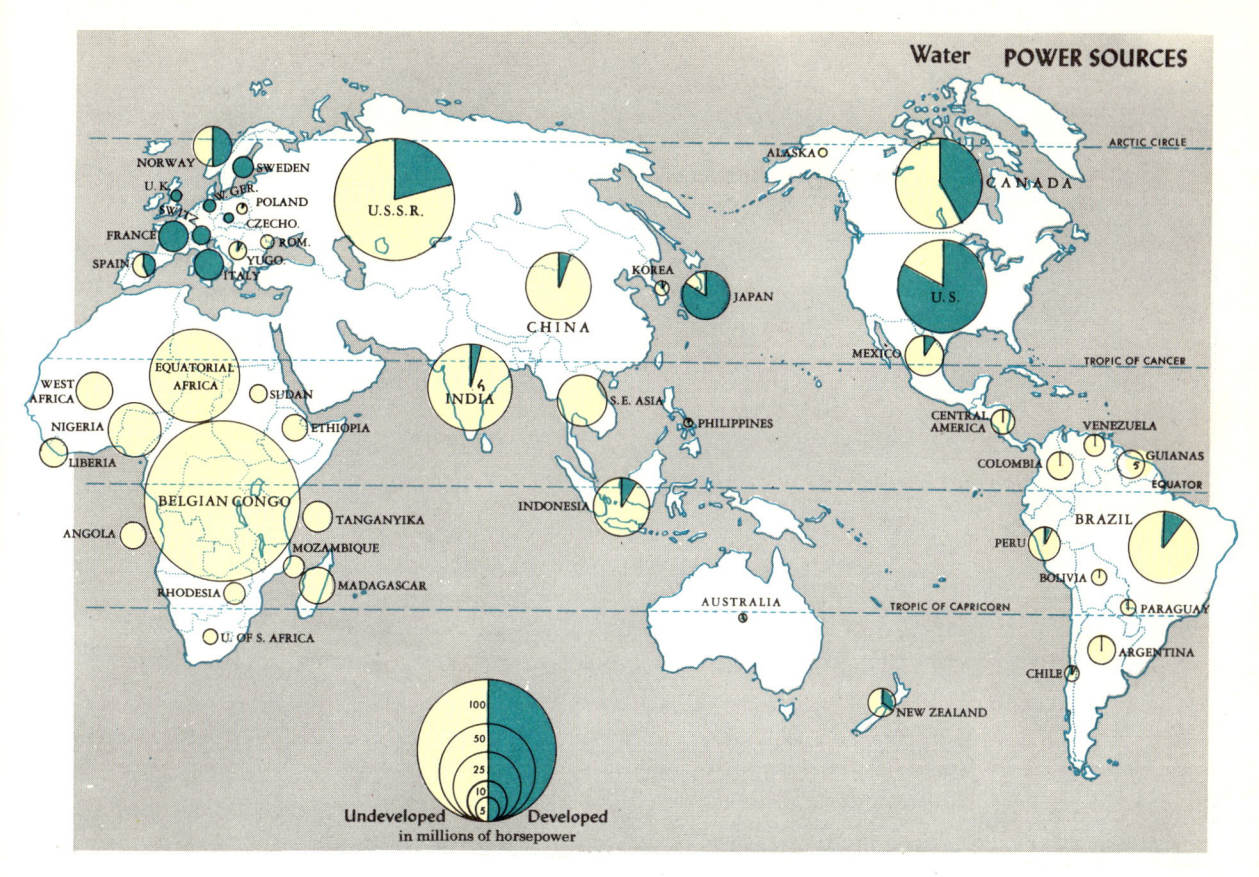

551

Water POWER SOURCES

Undeveloped — Developed
in millions of horsepower

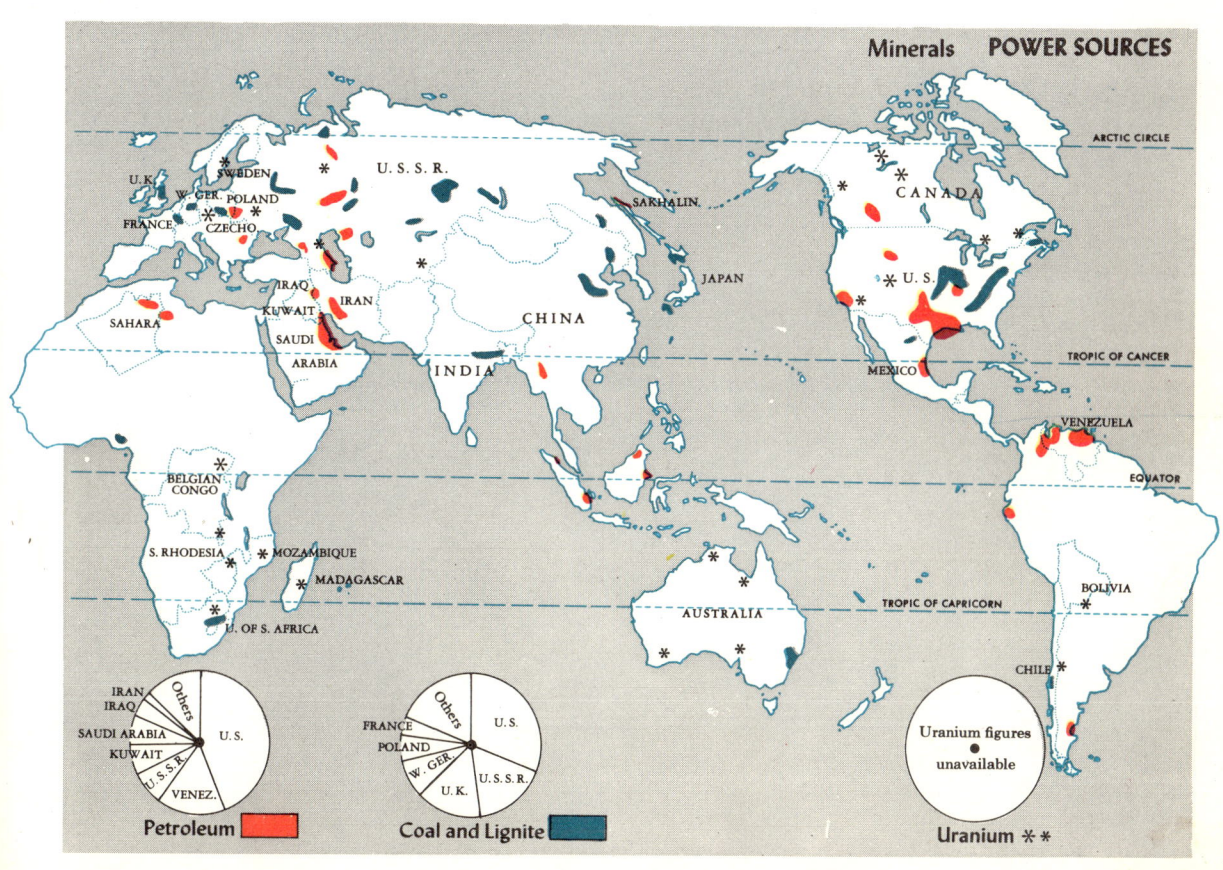

Minerals POWER SOURCES

Petroleum
Coal and Lignite
Uranium

Uranium figures unavailable

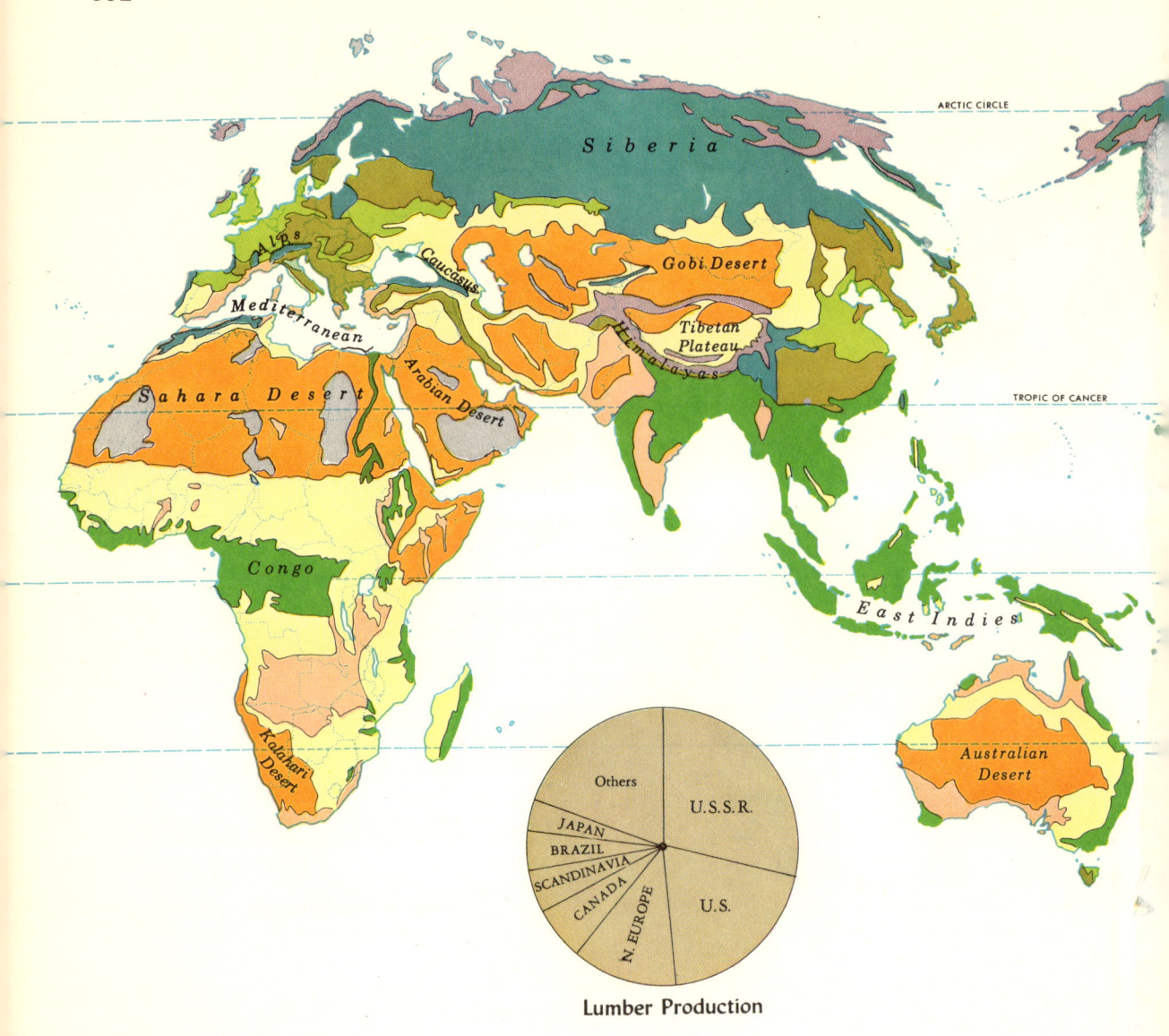

This map of natural vegetation tells an interesting story. If you read the map carefully you can learn much about rainfall, temperature, drainage, and soils, as well as natural vegetation. Vegetation reflects the physical environment.

There are three main types of vegetation: forests, grasslands, and deserts. The number of individual species which make up any of these groups is unbelievably large. Yet, as your map shows, it is possible to locate some very distinctive plant regions.

Climate is the most important of the natural conditions that affect vegetation. Over large areas, the particular sort of plants found is mainly determined by temperature and moisture. Nevertheless, there are exceptions.

Plants may sometimes be found growing under conditions that appear to favor another type of vegetation. For example, desert plants thrive in many places that have enough rainfall to support a grassland vegetation. In such places the soil is usually porous. This means that rain soaks rapidly into the soil. So, in spite of the ample rains, only hardy, drought-resistant desert plants can survive.

At one time forests covered one fourth of the earth. But forests, like other natural

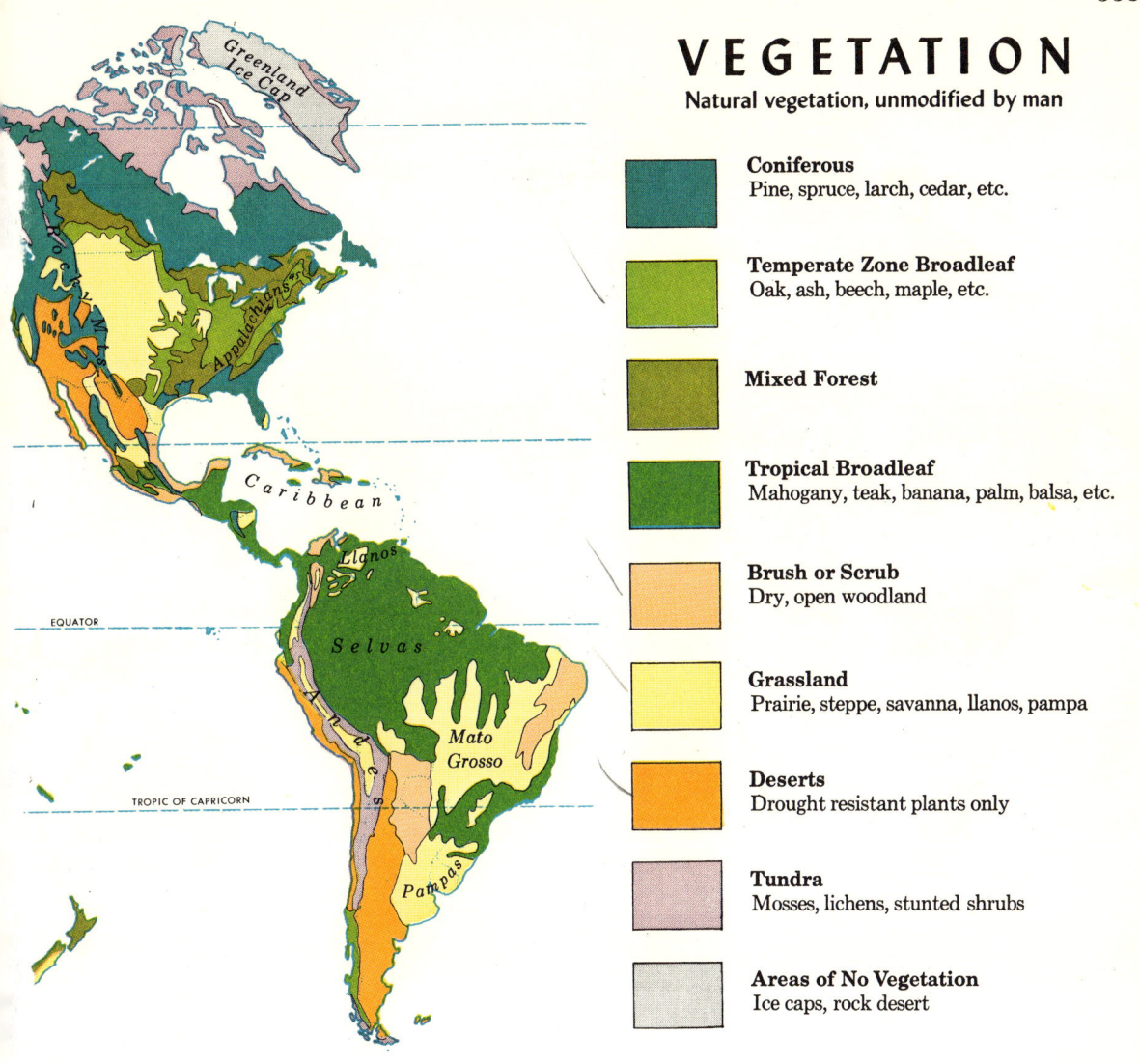

VEGETATION
Natural vegetation, unmodified by man

- **Coniferous** — Pine, spruce, larch, cedar, etc.
- **Temperate Zone Broadleaf** — Oak, ash, beech, maple, etc.
- **Mixed Forest**
- **Tropical Broadleaf** — Mahogany, teak, banana, palm, balsa, etc.
- **Brush or Scrub** — Dry, open woodland
- **Grassland** — Prairie, steppe, savanna, llanos, pampa
- **Deserts** — Drought resistant plants only
- **Tundra** — Mosses, lichens, stunted shrubs
- **Areas of No Vegetation** — Ice caps, rock desert

vegetation regions, have been greatly altered by man. Today forests cover less than one sixth of the earth, because of unwise exploitation without thought of the future.

Forests have some special climatic requirements. They are generally limited to places where summer temperatures average at least 50 degrees. The amount of rainfall needed for forests varies with temperature conditions. In places where it is cool the year around, water does not evaporate rapidly. In such places 15 inches of rainfall each year is enough to support a forest. But in the warm climate of the tropics a forest may need 90 to 150 inches of rain.

Grass represents a stage of natural vegetation that lies between forests and deserts in its rainfall requirements. Grassland formations are typically the result of semi-arid conditions. Grasslands may be covered by short or tall grass.

Originally, grasslands covered one third of the earth. But because the soils that form under grass are often fertile, most prairies have been plowed and planted to crops and the original vegetation has been destroyed.

Deserts, of course, occur where there is little rainfall and where the rate of evaporation is high. About one sixth of the earth is covered by desert land.

KEY TO AFRICA
1. SENEGAL REP.
2. VOLTAIC REP.
3. TOGO
4. DAHOMEY REP.
5. BR. CAMEROONS
6. CONGO REP.
7. CABINDA (PORT.)
8. FR. SOMALILAND
9. UGANDA (BR.)
10. RUANDA-URUNDI (BEL.)
11. NYASALAND
12. SWAZILAND (BR.)
13. BASUTOLAND (BR.)

KEY TO EUROPE
1. EAST GERMANY
2. LUXEMBOURG
3. SWITZERLAND
4. ALBANIA

KEY TO ASIA
1. JORDAN
2. LEBANON
3. ISRAEL
4. KUWAIT (BR.)
5. BAHREIN (BR.)
6. QATAR (BR.)
7. TRUCIAL OMAN (BR.)
8. YEMEN
9. SIKKIM
10. BHUTAN
11. CAMBODIA
12. BRUNEI (BR.)
* UNITED ARAB REPUBLIC

THE WORLD
Political

Scale at the Equator 1:115,000,000
About 1800 miles to the inch
MILLER CYLINDRICAL PROJECTION

THE WORLD'S LARGEST CITIES

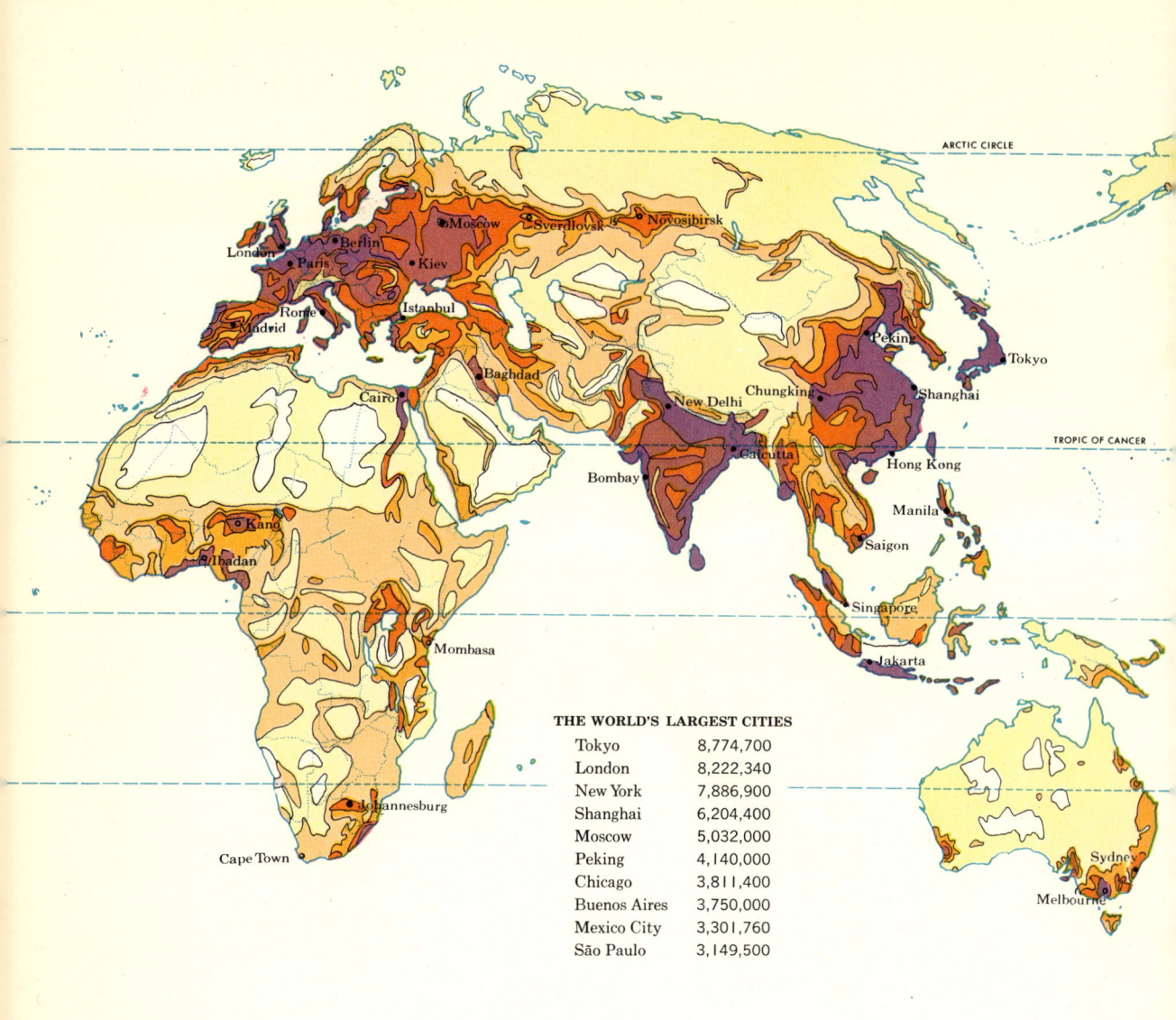

Tokyo	8,774,700
London	8,222,340
New York	7,886,900
Shanghai	6,204,400
Moscow	5,032,000
Peking	4,140,000
Chicago	3,811,400
Buenos Aires	3,750,000
Mexico City	3,301,760
São Paulo	3,149,500

Nearly three billion people live on the earth today. The number of people is growing rapidly. At the end of every eight days the world's population has increased by one million persons. By the end of the year 2000, the world's population will number over six billion—more than twice the population of the earth today.

This map shows that most parts of the earth are almost uninhabited. Other vast areas are only sparsely peopled. Yet, in still other places, great numbers of people appear crowded together. It is quite obvious that people are very unevenly distributed over the surface of the earth.

More than half of the world's population is found in southeastern Asia. Yet this portion of the earth represents but one tenth of the habitable world. Another one fifth of the people of the earth live in Europe, which includes less than one twentieth of the earth's habitable area. On the other hand, the Antarctic continent, with an area of more than five million square miles, has no permanent residents at all. Here the climate is too severe for permanent settlement.

The map shows three principal centers of population. One is southeastern Asia. The second is the industrialized areas of western, southern, and central Europe. The

POPULATION

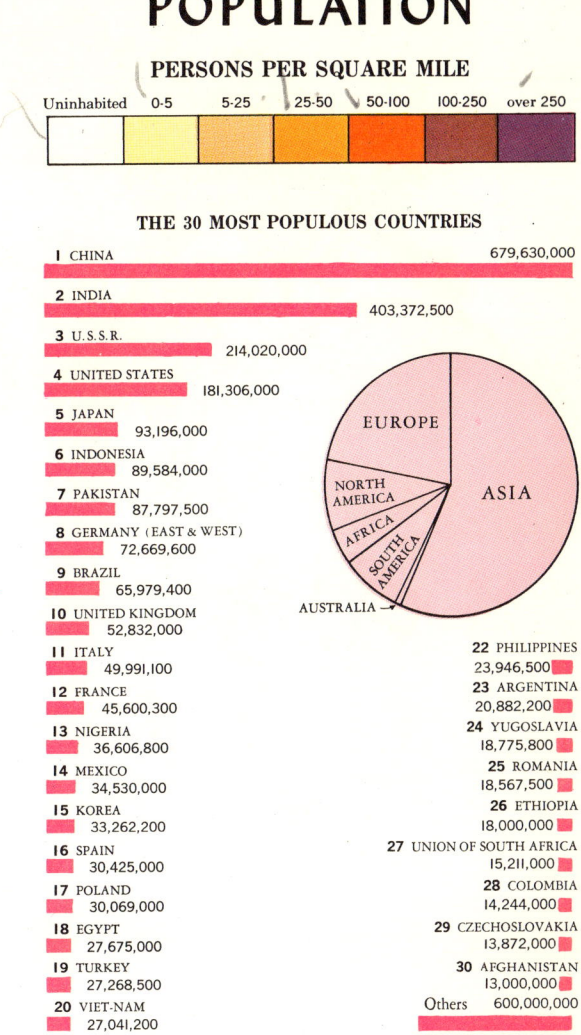

PERSONS PER SQUARE MILE

Uninhabited | 0-5 | 5-25 | 25-50 | 50-100 | 100-250 | over 250

THE 30 MOST POPULOUS COUNTRIES

#	Country	Population
1	CHINA	679,630,000
2	INDIA	403,372,500
3	U.S.S.R.	214,020,000
4	UNITED STATES	181,306,000
5	JAPAN	93,196,000
6	INDONESIA	89,584,000
7	PAKISTAN	87,797,500
8	GERMANY (EAST & WEST)	72,669,600
9	BRAZIL	65,979,400
10	UNITED KINGDOM	52,832,000
11	ITALY	49,991,100
12	FRANCE	45,600,300
13	NIGERIA	36,606,800
14	MEXICO	34,530,000
15	KOREA	33,262,200
16	SPAIN	30,425,000
17	POLAND	30,069,000
18	EGYPT	27,675,000
19	TURKEY	27,268,500
20	VIET-NAM	27,041,200
21	THAILAND	24,591,400
22	PHILIPPINES	23,946,500
23	ARGENTINA	20,882,200
24	YUGOSLAVIA	18,775,800
25	ROMANIA	18,567,500
26	ETHIOPIA	18,000,000
27	UNION OF SOUTH AFRICA	15,211,000
28	COLOMBIA	14,244,000
29	CZECHOSLOVAKIA	13,872,000
30	AFGHANISTAN	13,000,000
	Others	600,000,000

third is the industrial sections of North America.

The most heavily populated areas of Asia are the river valleys and fertile plains, where good soil and water for irrigation are available. This is so because the great bulk of Asia's people still earn their living directly from the land, although there is a growing amount of industry. They naturally tend to concentrate where conditions are best for farming.

The centers of population in Europe and North America have quite a different basis of support. Here the greatest numbers of people are concentrated where mineral resources and power resources are available, or where the opportunities for trade and commerce are greatest.

It is very unlikely that the problem of overcrowding will be solved by sending large numbers of people to the less crowded or empty areas of the earth.

People today, as in the past, move from areas lacking in opportunity toward areas where greater opportunities are available. This means that the most densely populated areas will become even more densely populated in the future. The regions lacking economic opportunity will gradually become even more sparsely settled.

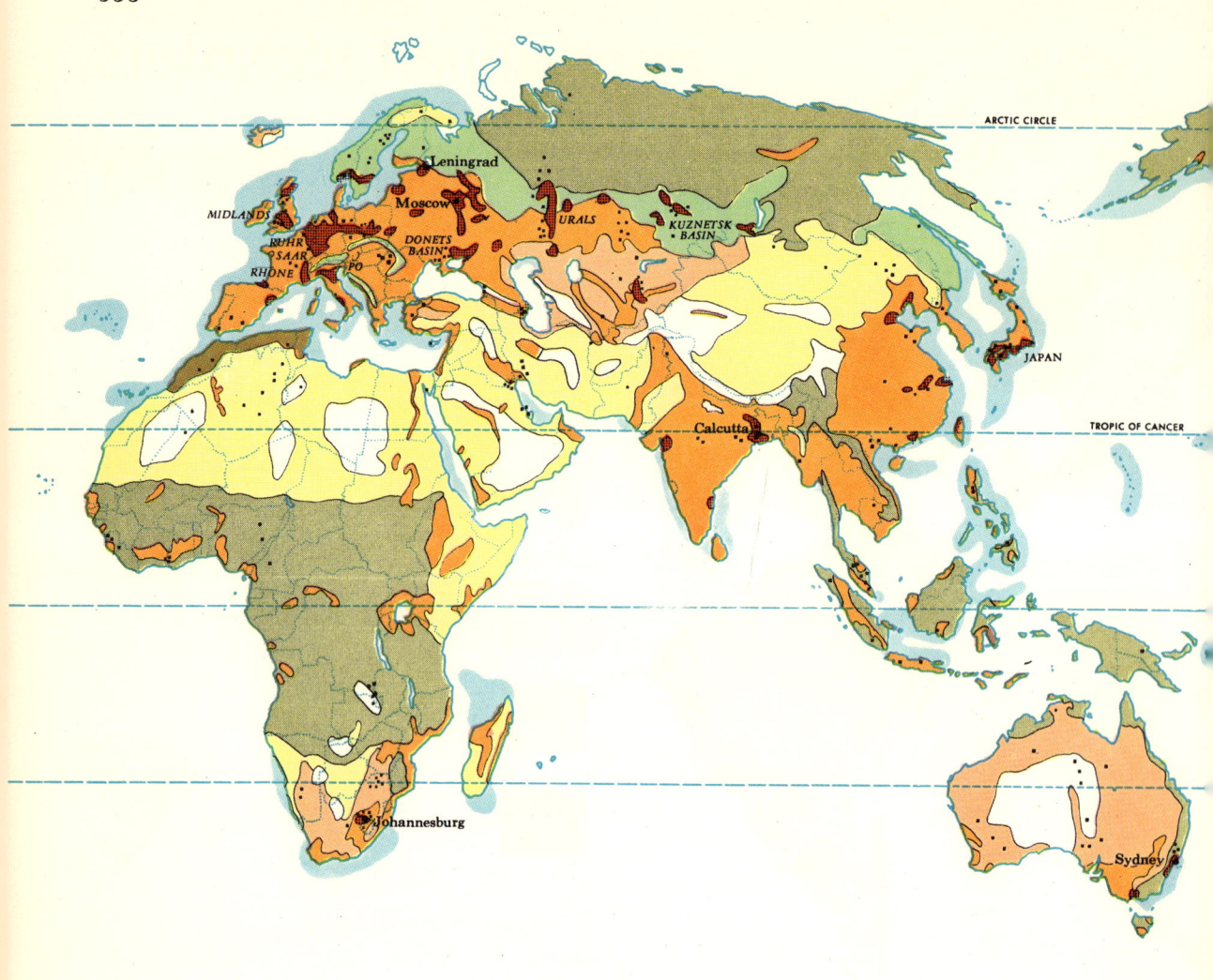

People have a great variety of ways of earning a living. This map shows you how these ways are distributed over the earth.

People who live by hunting and fishing are few in number. Because food taken by hunting and fishing spoils quickly, primitive people who earn their living in this way must consume their catch quickly. It is difficult for them to maintain a steady supply of food. Such people are often subject to periods of famine.

Nomadic herding represents another primitive method of earning a living. Nomadic herders are wanderers. They must keep their flocks moving, ever seeking new pastures. Since it takes a large area of pasture land to support a single animal, groups that follow this way of life are typically few in numbers.

Stock raising also involves the grazing of animals—usually cattle, goats, horses, or sheep. But stock raising implies a permanent home and controlled grazing land. Stock raising today is often a highly specialized way of earning a living.

Agriculture can support many people on a small area of land. In parts of India, China, and Japan, a square mile of farmland may support over 1,000 people. Here average farm size is very small. Most of the

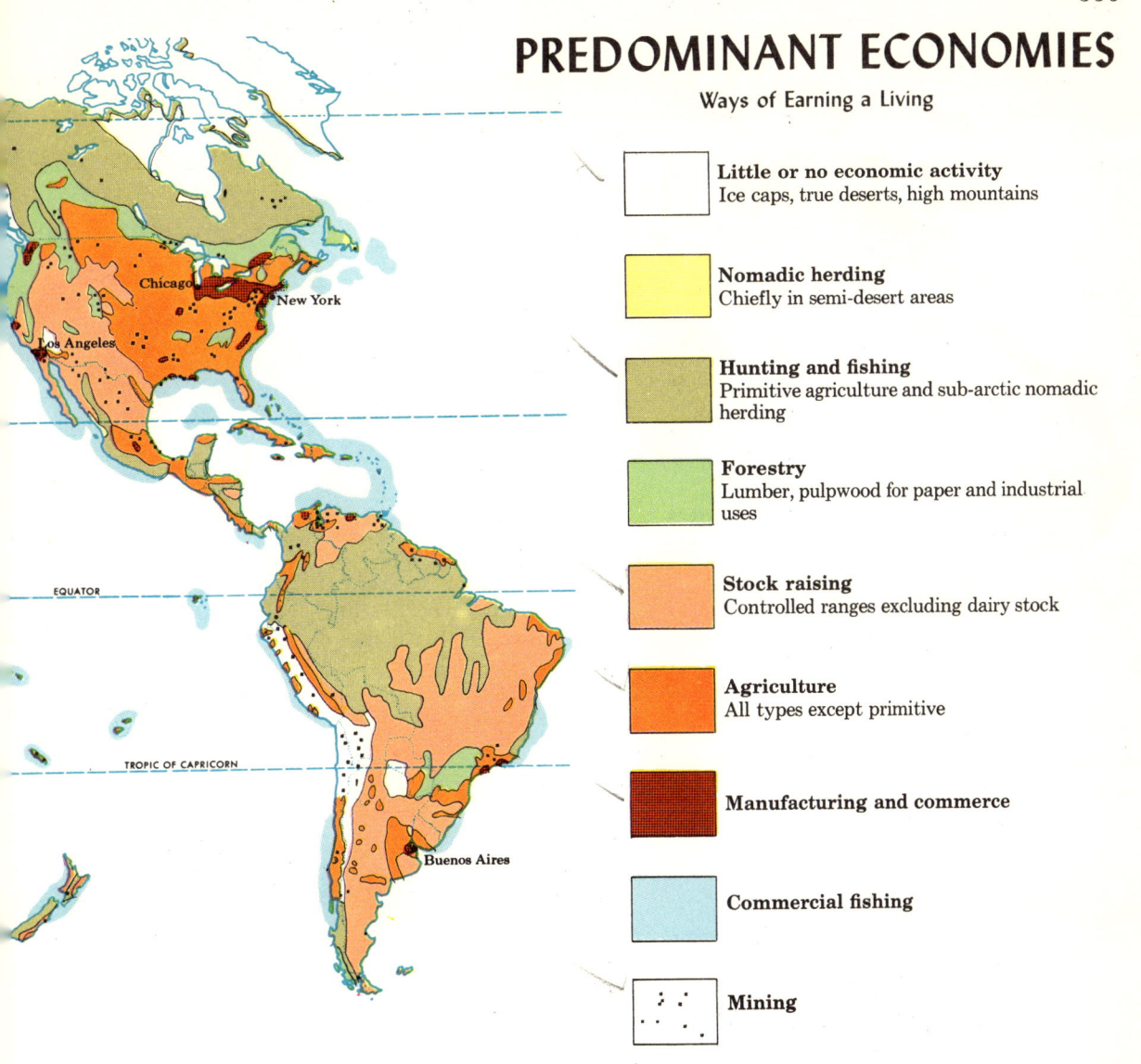

PREDOMINANT ECONOMIES
Ways of Earning a Living

Little or no economic activity
Ice caps, true deserts, high mountains

Nomadic herding
Chiefly in semi-desert areas

Hunting and fishing
Primitive agriculture and sub-arctic nomadic herding

Forestry
Lumber, pulpwood for paper and industrial uses

Stock raising
Controlled ranges excluding dairy stock

Agriculture
All types except primitive

Manufacturing and commerce

Commercial fishing

Mining

---

crop is consumed locally. In contrast to this are the huge wheat farms of the Canadian prairies, the Midwest of the United States, or the Argentine Pampa. Here one farmer may be able to produce enough grain to feed several thousand people.

Forestry, like modern farming and ranching, is often a complex business calling for great skill. Foresters today are careful in cutting and in replanting to assure continued forest growth and production.

Mining is also associated with the needs of a machine civilization. Minerals are often discovered in isolated places. It is here, of course, that the mining communi-

ties must develop. But the products of the mining communities soon find their way to the centers of population, where they are converted to manufactured goods.

Commercial fishermen may travel hundreds of miles from their home ports to fishing areas. And today quick freezing and canning make fish available to people who live thousands of miles from the sea.

Manufacturing and commerce are of great and growing importance. Millions who were formerly farmers now find work in mills, factories, and offices. Such activities usually take place in the world's rapidly growing cities.

AGRICULTURAL PRODUCTS — Wheat, Barley

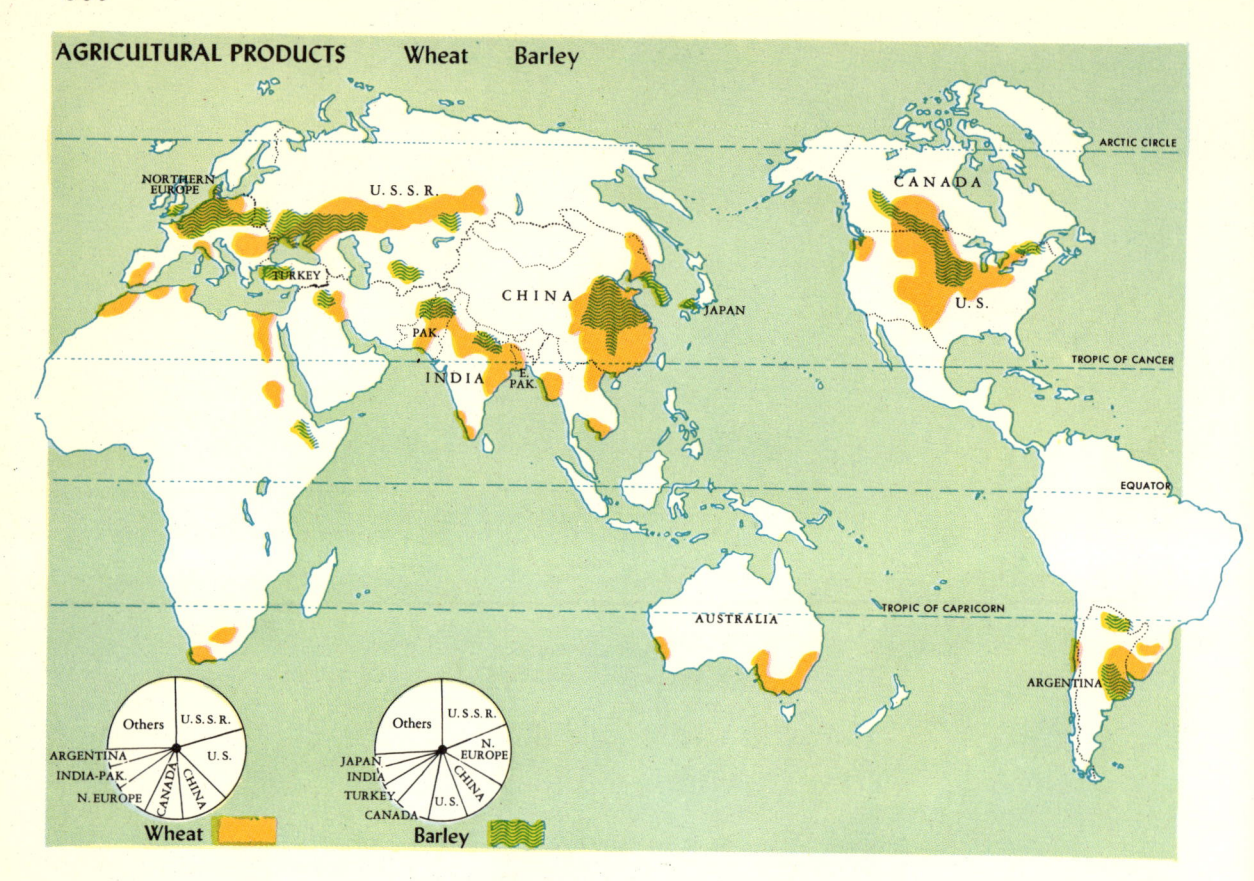

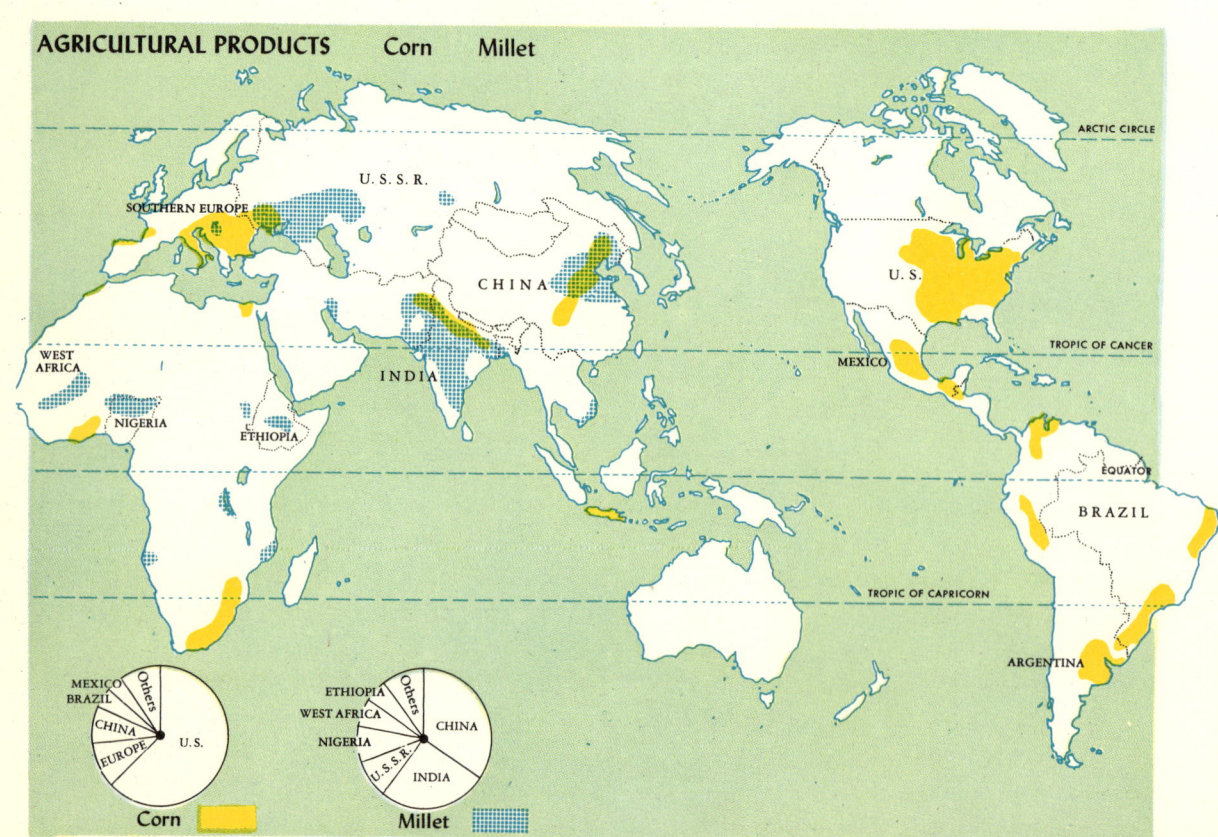

AGRICULTURAL PRODUCTS — Corn, Millet

AGRICULTURAL PRODUCTS
Oats Rye Rice

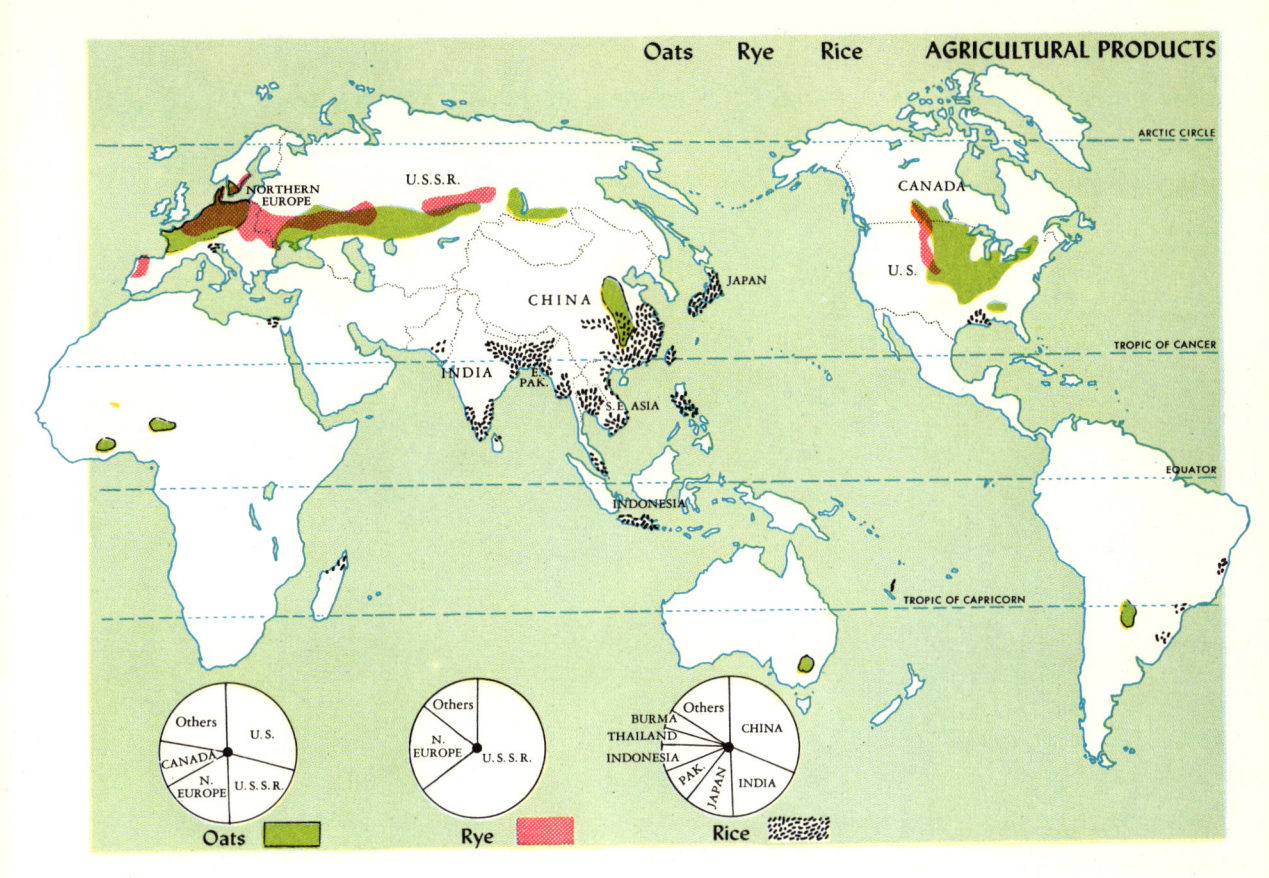

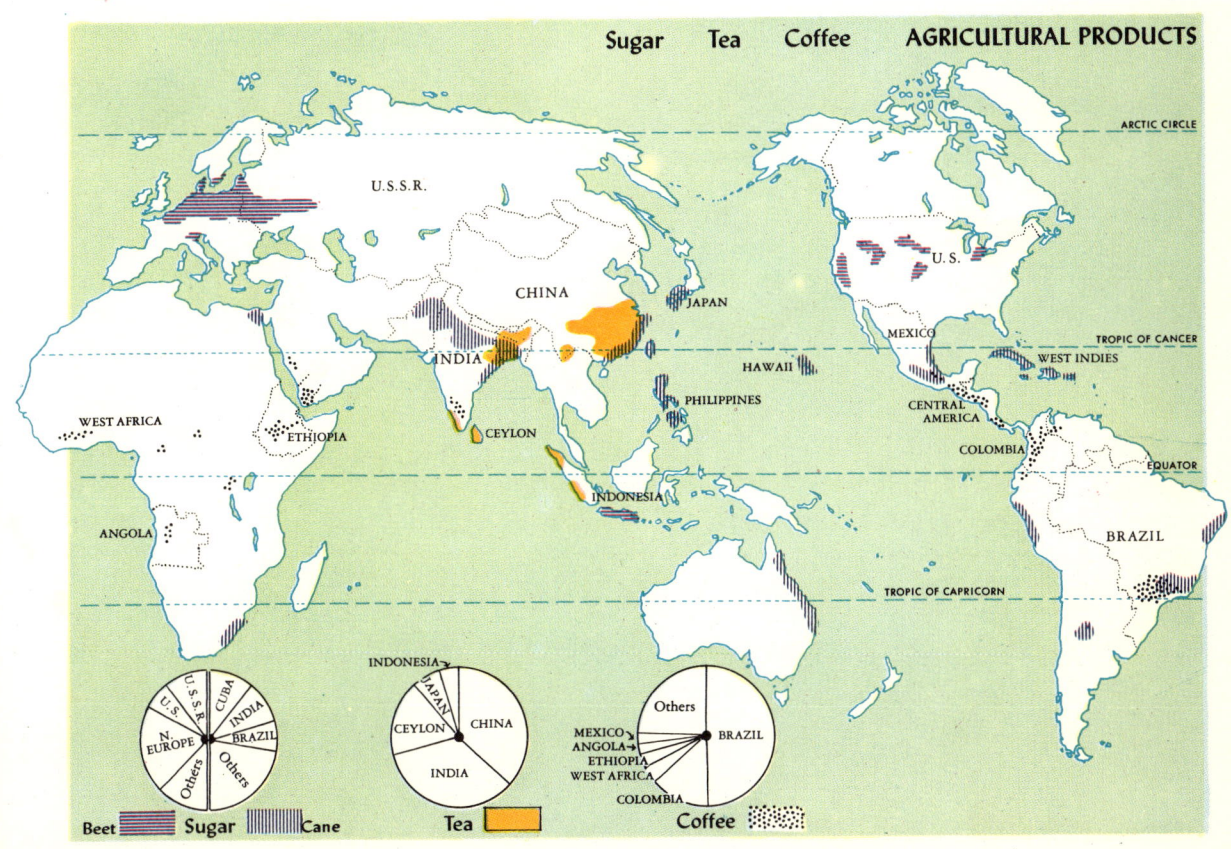

AGRICULTURAL PRODUCTS
Sugar Tea Coffee

FIBERS   Cotton   Flax   Silk

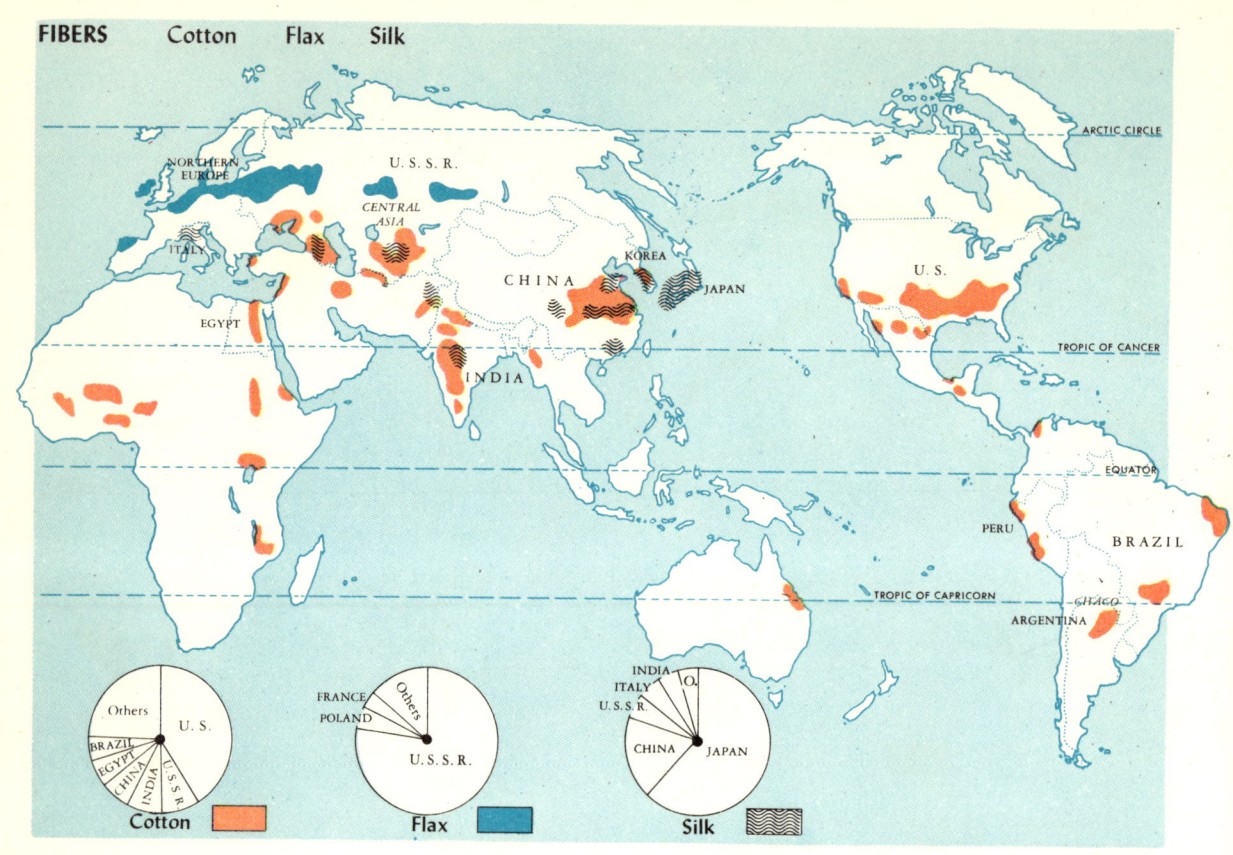

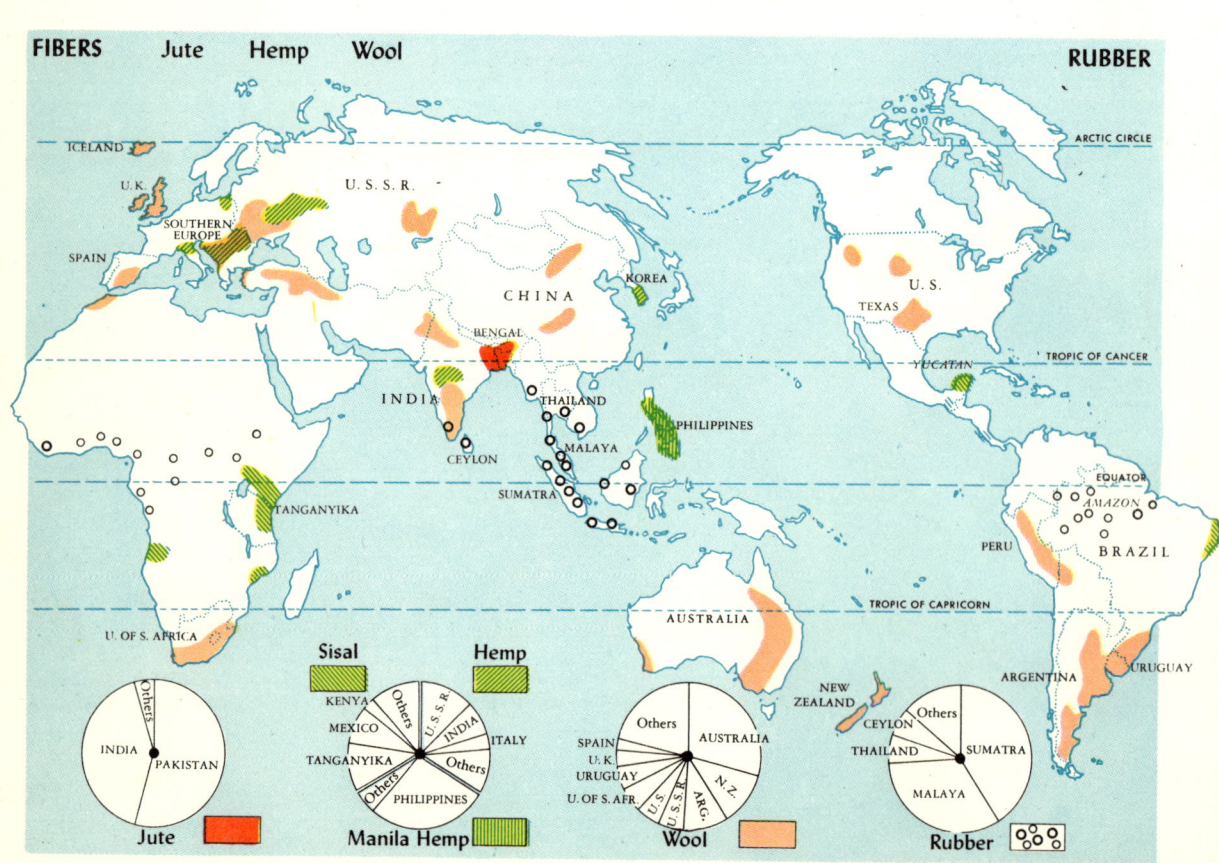

FIBERS   Jute   Hemp   Wool   RUBBER

LIVESTOCK

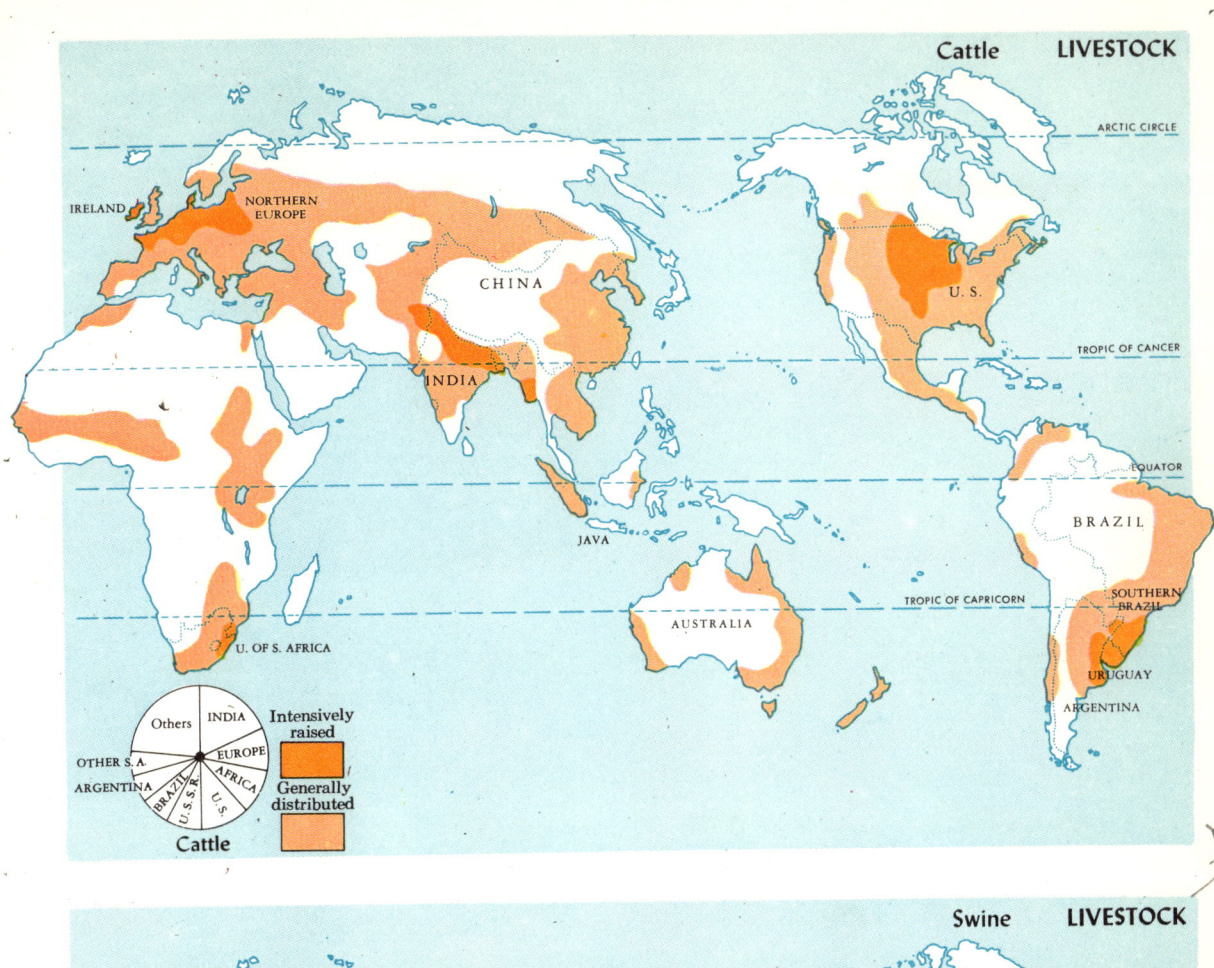

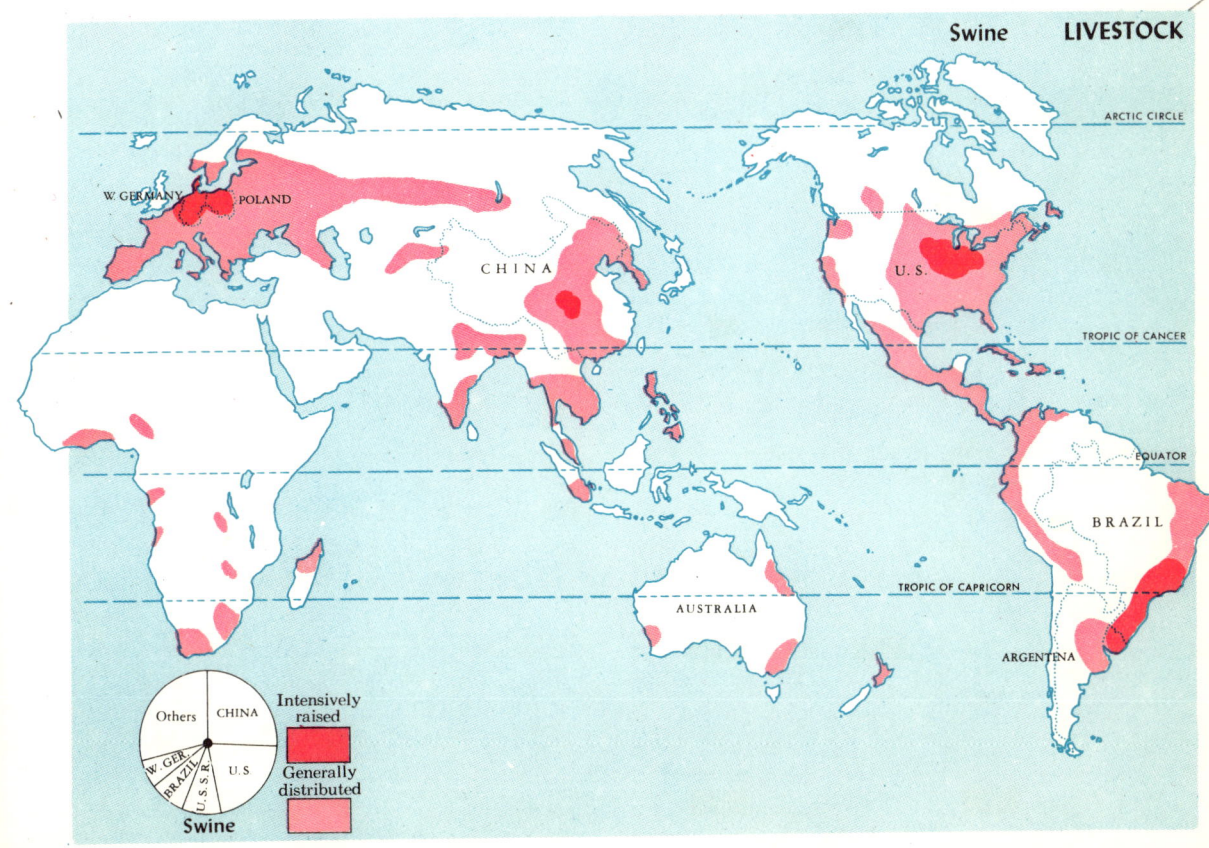

Cattle

564

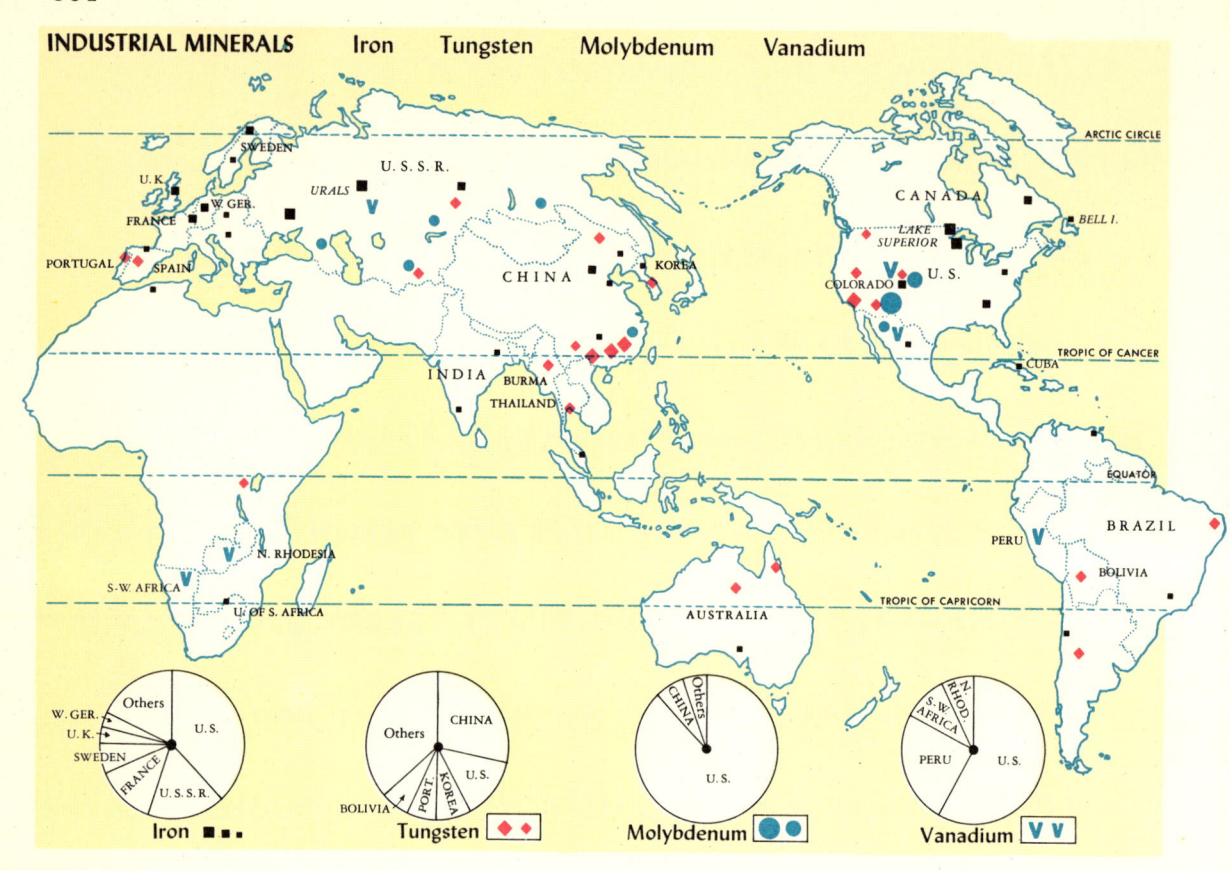

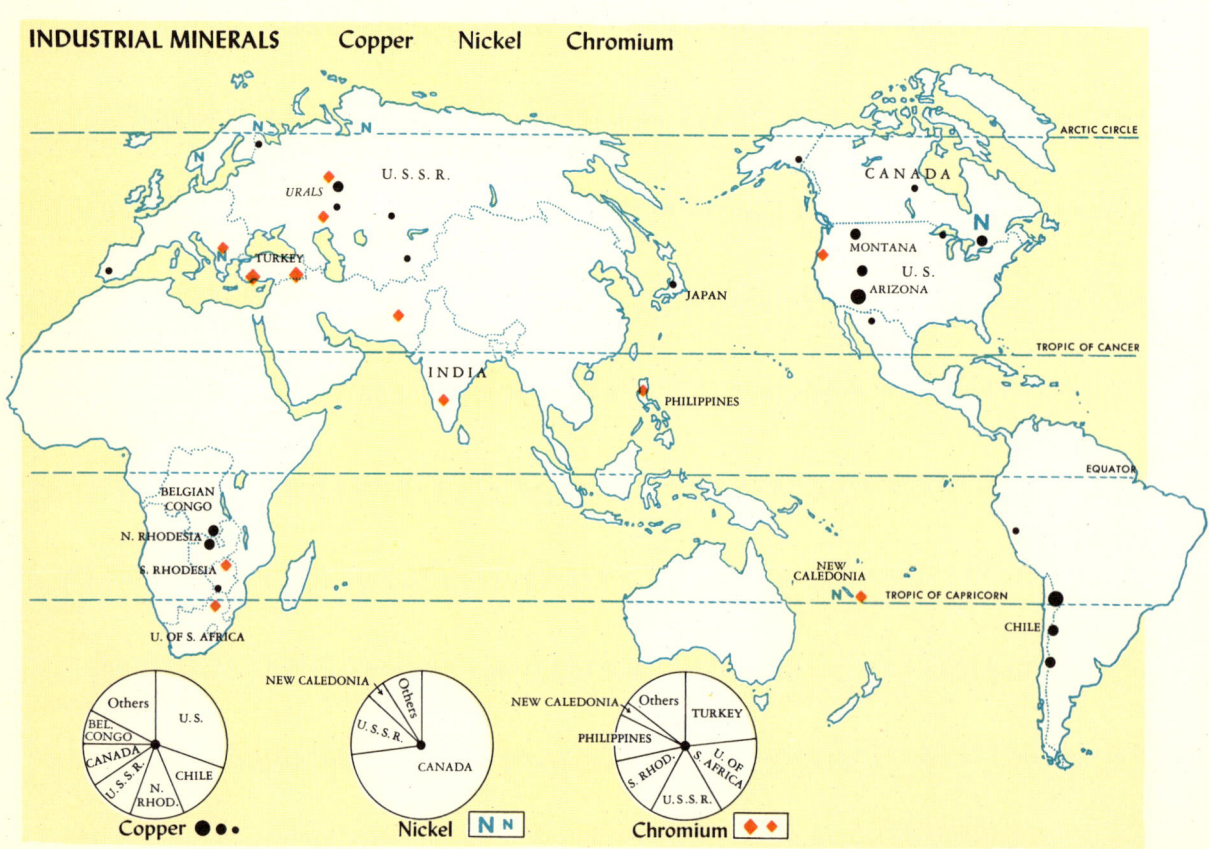

INDUSTRIAL MINERALS   Iron   Tungsten   Molybdenum   Vanadium

INDUSTRIAL MINERALS   Copper   Nickel   Chromium

565

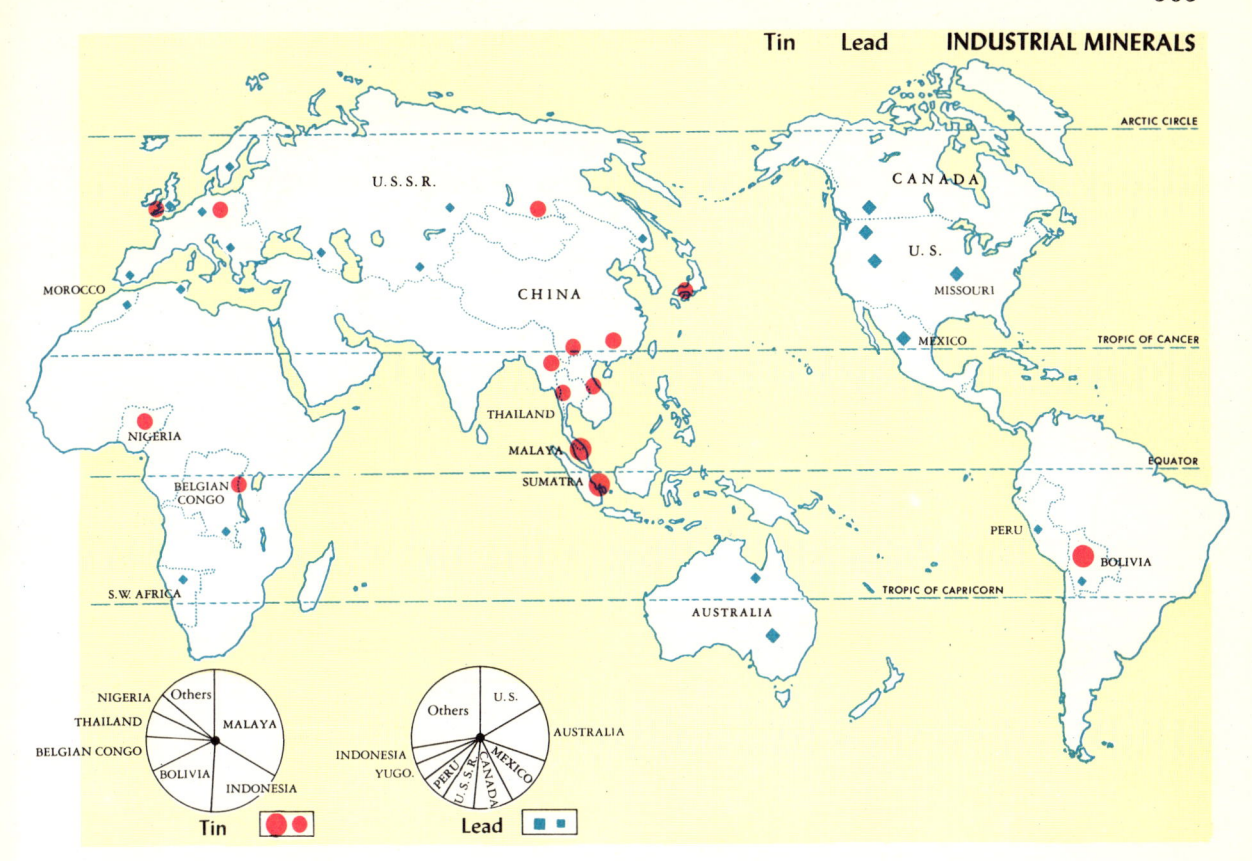

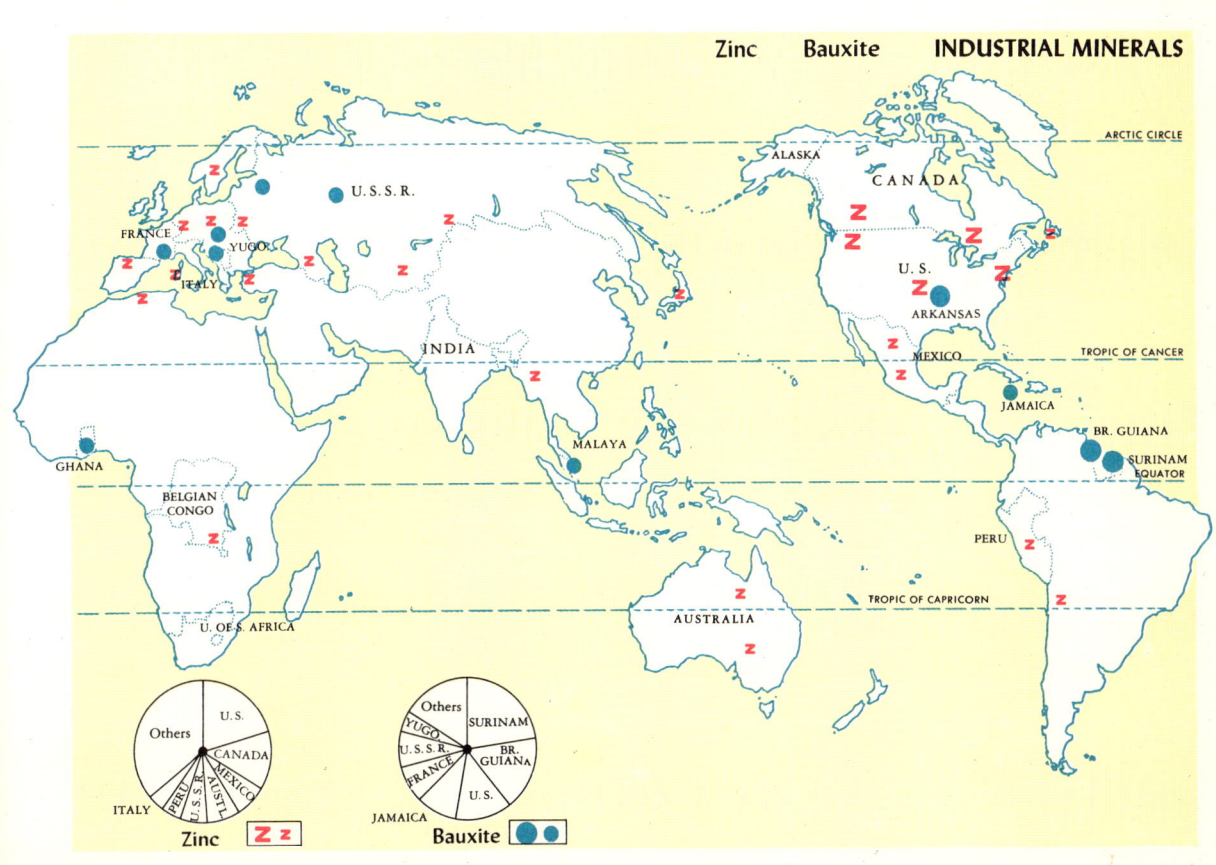

INDUSTRIAL MINERALS — Tin, Lead

INDUSTRIAL MINERALS — Zinc, Bauxite

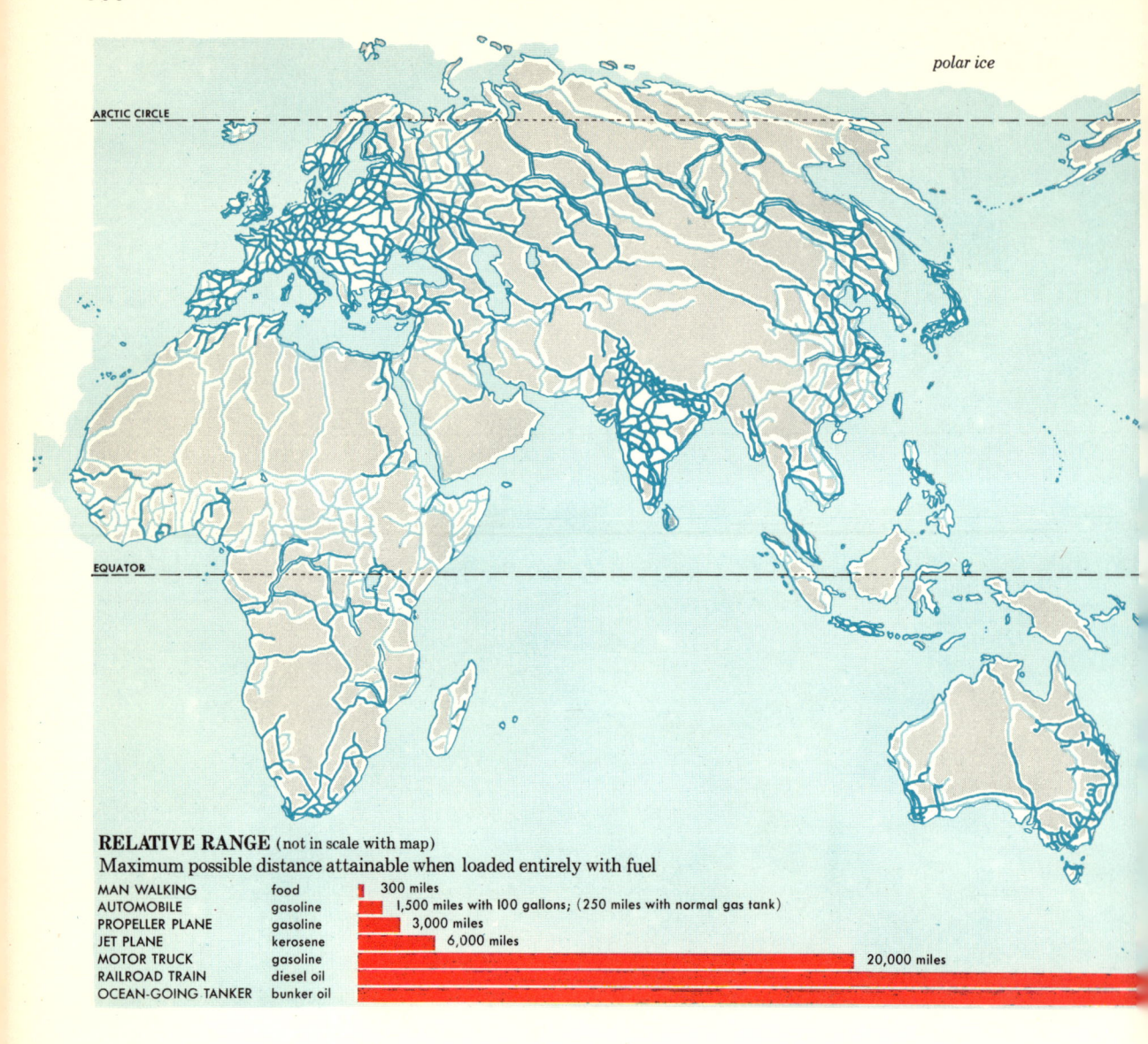

RELATIVE RANGE (not in scale with map)
Maximum possible distance attainable when loaded entirely with fuel

MAN WALKING	food	300 miles
AUTOMOBILE	gasoline	1,500 miles with 100 gallons; (250 miles with normal gas tank)
PROPELLER PLANE	gasoline	3,000 miles
JET PLANE	kerosene	6,000 miles
MOTOR TRUCK	gasoline	20,000 miles
RAILROAD TRAIN	diesel oil	
OCEAN-GOING TANKER	bunker oil	

Before the development of mechanized transportation, both freight and passenger traffic were difficult, expensive, and slow. To move goods, man depended on animals on land and on wind power at sea. Sometimes he depended on human muscle. Human porters carried heavy loads on their heads or backs, and goods were often transported in barges rowed by hand. When people traveled, those who could afford it rode on animals or in animal-drawn carts or coaches; the others walked.

Under these conditions, there was very little interchange of goods. People were forced to supply all of their own needs locally. They grew all their own food and made their own manufactured articles. Only the richest people could afford to buy imported goods. High transportation costs raise the cost of imported goods.

But modern man has railroads, steamships, airplanes, and automobiles and trucks in which to carry his goods and reach other people and places around the world. An efficient transportation system enables people to exchange goods more cheaply and in greater volume. Everybody benefits.

The maps on these pages show you the most important rail and highway routes of the world. The maps on the following two

TRANSPORTATION

Accessibility via Land and Water Transport

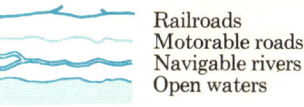

Railroads
Motorable roads
Navigable rivers
Open waters

Areas more than 25 miles from road, railroad or water transport

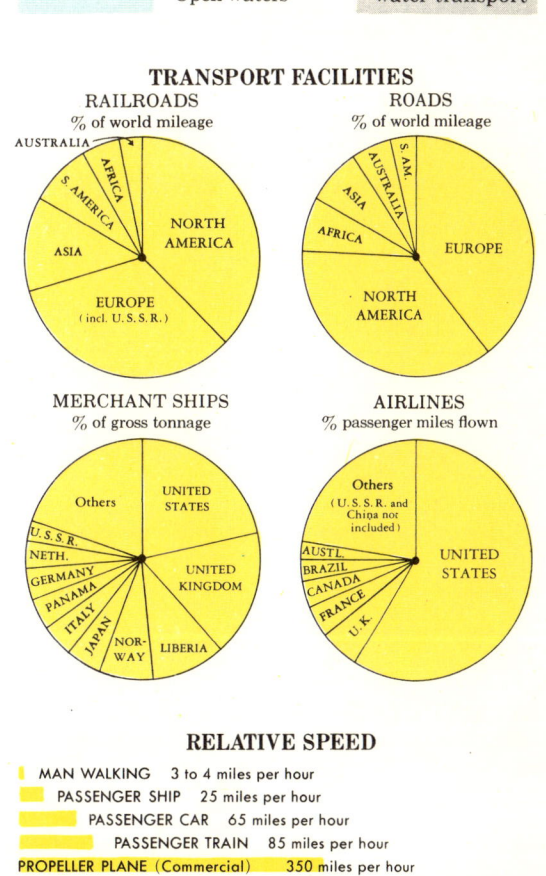

TRANSPORT FACILITIES

RAILROADS — % of world mileage
AUSTRALIA, AFRICA, S. AMERICA, ASIA, EUROPE (incl. U.S.S.R.), NORTH AMERICA

ROADS — % of world mileage
S. AM., AUSTRALIA, ASIA, AFRICA, EUROPE, NORTH AMERICA

MERCHANT SHIPS — % of gross tonnage
Others, U.S.S.R., NETH., GERMANY, PANAMA, ITALY, JAPAN, NORWAY, LIBERIA, UNITED KINGDOM, UNITED STATES

AIRLINES — % passenger miles flown
Others (U.S.S.R. and China not included), AUSTL., BRAZIL, CANADA, FRANCE, U.K., UNITED STATES

RELATIVE SPEED

MAN WALKING	3 to 4 miles per hour
PASSENGER SHIP	25 miles per hour
PASSENGER CAR	65 miles per hour
PASSENGER TRAIN	85 miles per hour
PROPELLER PLANE (Commercial)	350 miles per hour
JET PLANE	600 miles per hour

See next page for air and water routes

85,000 miles
110,000 miles

---

pages show the world's principal air and sea transportation routes.

Land routes try to follow the shortest and easiest path between two points. Great rivers, lakes, swamps, mountains, and hills are physical barriers that sometimes alter the most direct route. Construction costs are high in such difficult terrain. Deserts and other sparsely settled areas are also avoided. Little or no freight can be expected in such places. Generally, the greater the density of population, the more dense is the network of railways and highways.

The United States has more paved highways than any other nation has. Western Europe also has a dense road network. The Soviet Union ranks next to the United States in total road mileage, but few roads in the U.S.S.R. have a paved surface. Except for Japan, the nations of Asia are poorly served by highways. And in tropical Africa and South America rivers often take the place of roads as the chief means of transportation.

The world's total rail mileage is over 800,000 miles. Nearly one third of this mileage is in the United States. As with roads, the U.S.S.R. ranks second. Other leading nations in total rail mileage are Canada, India, Germany, Australia, France, Argentina, Brazil, and Great Britain.

WORLD AIR and WATER ROUTES

- Major air routes
- Major shipping routes

(all distances given in statute miles)

WORLD TIME ZONES

Countries using Greenwich Time; one hour zones: odd / even

Countries and areas not using Greenwich Time

Greenwich Time; half after the hour

INDEX

Page numbers followed by asterisks (°) refer to maps; *italic* page numbers indicate illustrations.

Abadan, Iran: oilcracking plant, 4-*323*
Abidjan, Ivory Coast, 5-*440*
Abipone Indians, 2-110
Abyssinia, *see* Ethiopia
Acapulco, Mexico, 1-75
Accra, Ghana: Arch of Independence, 5-*479;* cargo canoes, 5-*441;* climate, 5-406°; water rationing, 5-*440*
Aconcagua, Mt., Argentina, 2-156°: height, 2-192
Addis Ababa, Ethiopia: Coptic cathedral, 5-*401;* population, 5-480; street scene, 5-*414*
Adelaide, Australia: population, 6-544
Aden, Gulf of, SW Asia, 4-292°, 4-314°, 5-437°
Aden Protectorate, Arabian Peninsula, 4-308°, 4-314°
Adirondack Mts., N. Y., 1-43°
Admiralty Islands, Melanesia, 6-484°
Adriatic Sea, 3-239°
Aegean Sea, 3-239°
Afghanistan, 4-292°, 4-308°, 4-315°: area, 4-384; climate, 4-301; population, 4-384
Africa, 5-387°: agriculture, 5-408; airlines, 5-419; animals, 5-395; area, 5-386; Central, 5-436°; cities, description, 5-413; cities, population, 5-480; climate, 5-407; coastline, 5-386; continental limits, 5-386; countries, area and population, 5-480; desert countries, 5-427; Eastern Highlands, 5-448; Equatorial, 5-445; exploration, 5-412; future, 5-474; game reserves, 5-397, 5-451; geographical variety, 5-388; geological history, 5-390; lakes, principal, area, 5-480; literacy rate, 5-475; mountains, highest, 5-480; nationalism, 5-477; Negro empires, ancient, 5-440; Northern, 5-420°, 5-421; peoples, 5-399, 5-401°; political subdivisions, 5-418°; population, 5-386, 5-400; population density, 5-400°; railroads, 5-419; rainfall average, 5-406°; religious groups, 5-399; rivers, 5-390; rivers, principal, length, 5-480; Southern, 5-454, 5-456°; temperature average, 5-406°; transportation, 5-419; trust territories, 5-418; vegetation; 5-389°; West, 5-440
Afrikaners, U. of S. Africa, 5-458
Agricultural products, worldwide, 6-560°
Ahaggar Mts., Sahara Desert, 5-427
Air routes, worldwide, 6-568°
Alabama, 1-39°, 1-58°
Alaska, 1-38°: description, 1-70; population density, 2-171; walrus herd, 6-*537*
Albania, 3-206°, 3-251°: agriculture, 3-252; area, 3-288; language, 3-204, 3-249; population, 3-288
Albert, Lake, Africa, 5-437°, 5-452: area, 5-480
Albert Edward, Mt., New Guinea: height, 6-544
Alberta, prov., Can., 1-24°: agriculture, 1-33; cattle ranch, 1-*35;* coal mining, 1-32; wheat harvest, 1-*34*
Aleutian Islands, 1-38°
Alexandria, Egypt: ancient, 5-413; description, 5-434; docks, 5-*416;* population, 5-480
Algeria, 5-418°, 5-420°: Arab shepherd, 5-*388;* area, 5-480; land and people, 5-425; population, 5-480
Algiers, Algeria: climate, 5-406°; harbor, 5-*426;* population, 5-480
Alice Springs, Australia: cattle herding, 6-*507;* railroad, 6-503
Alkmaar, Netherlands, 3-*230*
Allegheny Mts., Pa., 1-43°
Allegheny River, Pa., 1-43°
Alma-Ata, U.S.S.R., 3-*265*
Alps, mts., Europe, 3-222: Bridal Veil Falls, 3-*228;* Italian, 3-239; water power, Italy, 3-247
Altai Mountains, Asia, 4-293°, 4-350
Altiplano, Bolivian, 2-184
Altyn Tagh, mts., Asia, 4-293°: river source, 4-297
Aluminum: Canada, 1-*36;* Indonesia, 4-377; southern U. S., 1-61; Surinam, 2-131; U.S.S.R., 3-282; *see also* Bauxite
Amadeus, Lake, Australia, 6-501°
Amazon River, South America, 2-167°, 2-171°: Andes tributaries, 2-142; description, 2-102; freighters, 2-*170;* length, 2-192; navigable distance, 2-102
Amazon River basin, 2-171°: agriculture, 2-117; animal life, 2-106; climate, 2-170; countryside, 2-170; Indians, 2-113, 2-171; land and people, 2-170; rainforests, 2-*101;* rubber industry, 2-173
American Indians, 1-11: corn, 1-51; food plants, 1-7
American Manufacturing Belt, 1-18
Amsterdam, Netherlands, 3-*209*: diamond center, 3-237
Amundsen, Roald, 6-541
Amur River, U.S.S.R., 3-261°: length, 3-288; valley, 3-285
Anambas Islands, SE Asia, 4-341°
Anatolian Plateau, Turkey: wheat raising, 4-*297*
Anchang, China: steel mill, 4-*363*
Andaman Islands, Bay of Bengal, 4-293°
Andaman Sea, 4-293°, 4-341°
Andes Mts., South America, 2-*98,* 2-99°, 2-156°: agriculture, 2-*117,* 2-146; animal life, 2-108; Bolivian, 2-183°, 2-184; Chilean, 2-142; countries of, 2-141; description, 2-100, 2-141; northern chains, 2-129; people, 2-144; plant life, 2-105; volcanoes, 2-*100*
Andorra, 3-223°, 3-238°: description, 3-228
Angara River, U.S.S.R., 3-284: power dam, 3-*285*
Ango Ango, Belgian Congo, 5-445
Angola (Port.), Africa, 5-418°, 5-456°, 5-470: area and population, 5-480
Anguilla, isl., Caribbean Sea, 1-87°
Ankara, Turkey, 4-309
Annam, region, Indochina, 4-341°
Annapolis-Cornwallis Valley, Nova Scotia, 1-35
Antarctica, 6-533°: animal life, 6-536; Arctic Regions, compared with, 6-534; area, 6-534; Australian claims, 6-496; average elevation, 6-535; climate, 6-540; mineral resources, 6-541; mountain ranges, 6-541; New Zealand claims, 6-496; penguin colony, 6-*536;* plant life, 6-536; scientific research, 6-542; seasons, 6-534; United Nations administration, 6-543; whaling, 6-541
Antigua, isl., Caribbean Sea, 1-87°
Antilles, isls., Caribbean Sea, 1-87°
Antioquia, Colombia, 2-135: coffee, 2-137
Antofalla, Mt., Argentina, 2-192
Apartheid, 5-454
Apatite: U.S.S.R., 3-282
Appalachian Highlands, 1-42
Appenines, mts., Italy, 3-239°
Arabia, *see* Saudi Arabia
Arabian Sea, 4-292°
Arabs: Africa, distribution, 5-401°; ethnic group, Africa, 5-399; African settlement, 5-421; shepherd, 5-*400*
Araguaia River, Brazil, 2-167°: length, 2-192
Aral Sea, U.S.S.R., 3-260°, 4-292°: area, 3-288; river mouth, 4-299
Araucanian Indians, 2-110, 2-*113,* 2-144
Arawak Indians, 2-*111*
Arctic Ocean, 4-295°, 6-532°: navigability, 6-543; Russian ship routes, 3-272
Arctic Regions, 6-532°: animal life, 6-536; Antarctica, compared with, 6-534; fur trade, 6-539; military bases, 6-543; mineral resources, 6-543; people, 6-538; plant life, 6-536; seal hunting, 6-538; seasons, 6-534; transportation, 6-538; tundra, 1-*7,* 6-*537*
Argentina, 2-99°, 2-156°: agriculture, 2-117; animal life, 2-108; Antarctic research, 6-542; area, 2-192; capital, 2-123; climate, 2-115; Humid Pampa, 2-103; Indians, 2-110; industry, 2-163; lake district, 2-*157;* land and people, 2-158; pampa, 2-*160;* Paraguayan war, 2-182; population, 2-192; racial composition, 2-112; railroads, 2-121
Argentino, Lake, Argentina, 2-156°: area, 2-192
Arizona, 1-38°, 1-64°: copper smelter, 1-*67;* cotton plantation, 1-*65*
Arkansas, 1-39°, 1-58°
Arkansas River, U.S., 1-50°, 1-58°, 1-64°: length, 1-96
Armenians, U.S.S.R., 3-270
Aroostook River, Maine, 1-43°
Aruba, isl., Caribbean Sea, 1-87°
Asbestos: Argentina, 2-158
Asia, 4-308°: agriculture, 4-381; air routes, 4-309°; ancient civilizations, 4-307; area and extent, 4-296; cities, 4-310, 4-384; climate, 4-300; colonialism, 4-379; communism, 4-382; countries, area and population, 4-384; democracy, 4-379; deserts, 4-350; disease, 4-380; earthquakes, 4-370; Eastern, 4-351°, 4-356; education, 4-380; foreign aid, 4-379; geography, 4-290; highways, 4-309°; Holy Lands, 4-324; industrialization, 4-381; Interior, 4-350, 4-351°; island chains, 4-368°, 4-369°, 4-370; lakes, largest, 4-384; languages and dialects, 4-304, 4-380; Mongol conquest, 4-353; mountains and plateaus, 4-297, 4-350, 4-384; nationalism, 4-379; natural resources, 4-382, 4-383; Northern, 4-294°; peoples, 4-*306,* 4-*307;* population, 4-290; population density, 4-302°; population growth, 4-380; racial types, 4-302; railroads, 4-309°; rainfall, 4-301°; religions, 4-303; river systems, 4-297; seas and oceans, 4-296; Southeastern, 4-340, 4-341°; Southern, *see* Indian peninsula; Southwestern, *see* Near East; temperatures, 4-300°; transportation, 4-309; United Nations aid, 4-379, 4-381; vegetation, 4-296°; volcanoes, 4-370; world trade, 4-383
Asunción, Paraguay: presidential palace, 2-*186*
Aswan Dam, Egypt, 5-*432*
Asyut, Egypt: population, 5-480
Atacama Desert, Chile, 2-*100,* 2-142°: copper mine, 2-*118;* description, 2-143; mineral resources, 2-152
Athabasca, Lake, Saskatchewan, Can., 1-24°, 1-32: area, 1-96
Athens, Greece: climate, 3-200°; Parthenon, 3-*211;* population, 3-288
Atitlán, Lake, Guatemala, 1-*80*
Atlantic Ocean: flow into Mediterranean, 3-245
Atlas Mts., Algeria, 5-387°
Atolls, landform, Oceania, 6-483°: formation of, 6-523
Atomic power: Europe, 3-259; U.S.S.R., 3-286
Atrato River, Colombia, 2-*134*
Auckland, New Zealand: description, 6-498; industry, 6-519; population, 6-544
Austin, Lake, Australia, 6-484°, 6-508
Australia, 6-484°, 6-501°: aborigines, 6-*490,* 6-491, 6-500; agriculture, 6-504; air routes, 6-503°; animal life, 6-*488,* 6-*489;* animal pests, 6-509; Antarctic claims, 6-496; Antarctic research, 6-542; area, 6-544; average elevation, 6-501; capital, 6-498; cities, largest, 6-496, 6-544; climate, 6-495; common trees, 6-503; Commonwealth of, 6-496; Commonwealth of Nations, 6-496; drought, 6-508; European settlement, 6-500, 6-502; foreign trade, 6-513, 6-531; geological age, 6-500; geological relationship to Africa, 5-390; highlands, 6-501; highways, 6-503°; Holden automobile plant, 6-*512;* industry, 6-512; lakes, largest, 6-544; mineral resources, 6-510; New Zealand, compared with, 6-514; Nullarbor Plain, 6-*502;* plant pests, 6-509; oil, 6-531; orchards and vineyards, 6-505; "outback," 6-505; population, 6-544; population density, 6-502°; population distribution, 6-496; railroads, 6-503°; rainfall, 6-495°; rivers, longest, 6-544; sheep ranching, 6-505; soils, 6-502, 6-508; sugar production, 6-505; temperature, 6-494°; tourism, 6-531; vegetation, 6-502°; water supply, 6-508; western plateau, 6-*500;* wheat production, 6-504; wool production, 6-506
Austria, 3-195°, 3-206°, 3-223°: agriculture, 3-233; area, 3-288; capital, 3-212; description, 3-228; oil production, 3-237; population, 3-288
Autobahn, Germany, 3-*259*
Aymara Indians, 2-102, 2-110, 2-*113,* 2-184
Azerbaijan Union Republic, U.S.S.R., 3-270
Azores, isls., Portugal, 3-239
Aztec Indians, 1-71

Babuyan Islands, Philippines, 4-368°
Baffin Bay, 6-532°
Baffin Island, Can., 1-25°, 6-532°
Baghdad, Iraq: description, 4-313; main square, 4-*311;* population, 4-384
Bahama Islands, 1-58°, 1-87°, 1-88
Bahia State, Brazil, 2-174
Bahrein, isl., Persian Gulf, 4-292°, 4-314°: oil, 4-322
Baikal, Lake, U.S.S.R., 3-261°, 4-295°, 4-308°: area, 3-288; peoples, 3-270
Baku, U.S.S.R., 3-282
Balbi, Mt., Bougainville (Solomon Islands): height, 6-544
Balearic Islands, Spain, 3-238°, 3-239
Bali, isl., Indonesia, 4-369°: terraced rice paddies, 4-*371*
Balkhash, Lake, U.S.S.R., 3-260°, 4-292°, 4-308°: area, 3-288; river mouth, 4-299
Baltic Sea, 3-214°, 3-251°
Bamboo: Asia, southeast, 4-342
Baltimore, Maryland, 1-96
Bananas: Caribbean, 1-*92;* Central America, 1-85; Colombia, 2-*138;* Ecuador, 2-147
Banda Sea, Indonesia, 4-369°
Banks Island, Canada, 1-24°, 6-532°
Bantus, African people, 5-399: Basutoland invasion, 5-472; U. of S. Africa, 5-458
Barbados, isl., Caribbean Sea, 1-87°
Barbarians, ancient, 3-203
Barbary Coast, Africa, 5-421: U.S. invasion, 5-425
Barbuda, isl., Caribbean Sea, 1-87°
Barcelona, Spain, population, 3-288
Barents Sea, 3-260°, 6-532°
Barley: world production, 6-560°
Barranquilla, Colombia, 2-140: population, 2-192
Barth, Heinrich, 5-412
Bashkirs, people, U.S.S.R., 3-268
Bass Strait, Australia, 6-*500,* 6-501°
Basutoland, Africa, 5-418°, 5-456°, 5-471: origin, 5-472
Bata shoe factory, Czechoslovakia, 3-257
Batan Islands, Philippines, 4-368°
Batavia, *see* Jakarta
Bathurst Island, Can., 1-25
Batlle y Ordóñez, José, 2-165, 2-190
Bauxite: worldwide sources, 6-565°; *see also* Aluminum
Beaufort Sea, Alsk.-Can., 1-24°
Beaverlodge, Saskatchewan, Can., 1-*30*
Bechuanaland, Africa, 5-418°, 5-456°, 5-471: medical treatment, 5-*472*
Bedouins, 5-427: Libyan, 5-424
Belém, Brazil, 2-*172,* 2-*173*
Belgian Congo, 5-418°, 5-437°: area, 5-480; capital, 5-445; land and people, 5-445; mineral resources, 5-446; population, 5-480; village scenes, 5-*447*
Belgium, 3-195°, 3-206°, 3-223°: agriculture, 3-232; area, 3-288; description, 3-228; fishing, 3-225; landform, 3-222; population, 3-288; railways, 3-207
Belgrade, Yugoslavia, 3-*205*
Belle Ile, France, 3-222°
Belo Horizonte, Brazil, 2-179, 2-188: population, 2-192; Rio de Janeiro highway, 2-*176*
Benares, India: bathing in Ganges, 4-*304*
Benelux, 3-222
Bengal, Bay of, S Asia, 4-293°
Benghazi, Libya, 5-425
Benin, Bight of, Africa, 5-436°

Berbers: Africa, distribution, 5-401°; horsemen, 5-400; village, 5-421
Bering Sea, 1-70, 3-261°, 4-295°, 6-532°
Berkshire Mts., Conn.-Mass., 1-43°
Berlin, Germany: Hansa section, West, 3-259; Kurfürstendamm, 3-209; population (East and West), 3-288
Bhutan, S Asia, 4-308°, 4-327°: description, 4-326; industrialization, 4-338
Biafra, Bight of, 5-436°
Big Ben clock, London, 3-208
Big Horn Mts., Wyo., 1-64°
Bilharziasis, African disease, 5-433
Birhan, Mt., Ethiopia: height, 5-480
Birmingham, Alabama, 1-61, 1-62
Birmingham, England: population, 3-288
Biscay, Bay of, France, 3-223°, 3-225, 3-238°
Bismarck Archipelago, Melanesia, 6-484°: area, 6-544; land formation, 6-482; people, 6-492; population, 6-544
Bitterroot Range, mts., Ida.-Mont., 1-64°
Black Forest, Germany, 3-223°, 3-224°, 3-227
Black Sea, 3-251°, 4-294°: Caucasian coast, 3-267
Blackburn, Mt., Alaska, 1-96
Blanco, Cape, Calif., 1-64°
Block Island, Rhode Island, 1-43°
Blue Mts., Jamaica, 1-88
Blue Mts., Maine, 1-43°
Blue Mts., Oregon, 1-64°
Bogotá, Colombia, 2-126: description, 2-126, 2-132; population, 2-192
Bohemian Forest, W Europe, 3-223°
Bojador, Cape, Africa, 5-412, 5-420°
Bokhara, U.S.S.R., 3-275
Bolivia, 2-99°, 2-183°: agriculture, 2-184; area, 2-192; Indians, 2-110, 2-182, 2-184; land and people, 2-184; mineral resources, 2-185; miners, 2-185; mountain passes, 2-105; population, 2-192; territorial wars, 2-152, 2-182
Bolshevik Party, Russia, 3-265
Bombay, India: air service, 4-309; description, 4-311; population, 4-384; street scene, 4-311
Bon, Cape, Africa, 5-420°
Bona, Mt., Alaska, 1-96
Borneo, Indonesia, 4-293°, 4-308°, 4-369°: comparative size, 4-374; Dyak "long house," 4-375; former Dutch possession, 4-373; headhunters, 4-374; see also Indonesia
Bornholm, isl., Sweden, 3-214°
Bosnia, Yugoslavia, 3-257
Bosporus, strait, Turkey, 3-195°
Boston, Massachusetts, 1-46: Common, 1-17; population, 1-96
Botany Bay, Australia, 6-501°: introduction of sheep, 6-506
Brahmaputra River, Asia, 4-327°, 4-350°: length, 4-384; source, 4-299
Brahmaputra River basin, 4-326: agriculture, 4-334
Brasília, Brazil, 2-179, 2-188
Brazil, 2-99°, 2-167°: agriculture, 2-168, 2-175, 2-181; Amazon country, 2-170; area, 2-192; capital, 2-123; capital, new, 2-179; central highlands, 2-176°; climate, 2-168; coffee plantation, 2-118; eastern, 2-176°; electric power, 2-174, 2-178; European immigrants, 2-181; geological relationship to Africa, 5-390; German colonists, 2-180; highlands, see Brazilian Highlands; Indians, 2-110; language and people, 2-166; mineral resources, 2-118, 2-176, 2-180; Negroes, 2-112; northeast, 2-173°; nuts, 2-173; Paraguayan war, 2-182; plantation worker, 2-111; population, 2-192; rubber industry, 2-172; southern, 2-180°; transportation routes, 2-121; U.S. Civil War refugees, 2-172; Viceroyalty of, 2-119
Brazilian Highlands, 2-99°, 2-101, 2-167°, 2-168
Brazos River, Texas, 1-58°
Brazza, Pierre Savorgnan de, 5-412
Brazzaville, Republic of the Congo, 5-447: population, 5-480
Bridgetown, Barbados, West Indies, 1-89

Brisbane, Australia: population, 6-544
Bristol Bay, Alaska, 1-38°
Bristol Channel, England, 3-222°
British Columbia, prov., Can., 1-24°: agriculture, 1-35; coal mining, 1-32; fisheries, 1-27; forestry, 1-28
British Commonwealth, see Commonwealth of Nations
British East Africa, 5-449
British Guiana, 2-99°, 2-128°: area, 2-192; bauxite production, 2-118; description, 2-131; Hindu settlement, 2-121; population, 2-192
British Honduras, 1-80°, 1-81: area and population, 1-96
British Somaliland, Africa, 5-437°
Brittany, France: agricultural products, 3-231; people, 3-202
Broken Hill, New South Wales, Australia: lead and zinc mines, 6-510
Bruce, James, 5-412
Brunei, Br. prot., Borneo, 4-308°, 4-369°
Brussels, Belgium: population, 3-288
Bucharest, Romania: population, 3-288
Buckingham Palace guards, London, 3-202
Budapest, Hungary, 3-249: population, 3-288
Buenos Aires, Argentina, 2-122: description, 2-123; harbor, 2-163; horse ranch, 2-161; population, 2-192; sunflower harvest, 2-162
Buenos Aires, Lake, South America, 2-142°: area, 2-192
Buffalo, New York, 1-54
Bulawayo, Southern Rhodesia, 5-468
Bulgaria, 3-206°, 3-251°: agriculture, 3-252; alphabet, 3-204; area, 3-288; industry, 3-256; language, 3-204; mountain village, 3-250; population, 3-288; rose distillation plant, 3-256; rug-weavers, 3-257; wheat harvest, 3-252
Burma, 4-293°, 4-308°, 4-341°: agriculture, 4-344; animal life, 4-343; area, 4-384; climate, 4-301, 4-342; peoples, 4-340; plant life, 4-342; population, 4-384; primitive tribes, 4-349; religion, 4-340; rice, 4-301; teak, 4-349
Buryat Mongols, people, U.S.S.R., 3-270
Bushmen, African, 5-399, 5-404
Buxton Village, British Guiana, 2-130
Byelorussia, U.S.S.R.: agriculture, 3-276; collective farm, 3-278; peasant home, 3-271; people, 3-268

Cabot Strait, Can., 1-25°
Cacao: Africa, 5-410; Brazil, 2-175; nut harvest, 5-442; Venezuela, 2-136
Caillié, René, 5-412
Cairo, Egypt: climate, 5-406°; cotton warehouse, 5-434; houses, 5-433; mosque, 5-414; population, 5-480; pyramids, 5-431; street scene, 5-401; textile mill, 5-434
Calcutta, India: air service, 4-309; description, 4-312; Jain temple, 4-330; population, 4-384
Calder Hall, England, atomic plant, 3-258
California, 1-38°, 1-64°: coastline, 1-5; farmland, 1-63; history, 1-65; population growth, 1-70
California, Gulf of, 1-72°
Cambodia, 4-293°, 4-308°, 4-341°: area and population, 4-384; see also Indochina
Cameroon, Africa, 5-418°, 5-436°: area and population, 5-480; village class, 5-478
Cameroon, Mt., Cameroon, 5-387°: height, 5-480
Campeche, Gulf of, Mexico, 1-72°
Camphor: Formosa, 4-365
Canada, 1-23, 1-24°: agriculture, 1-33; area, 1-96; Atlantic Provinces, 1-27, 1-32; borders, 1-23; cattle ranches, 1-35; climate, 1-8°; coal mining, 1-32; fisheries, 1-26; foreign trade, 1-37; forest products, 1-28; French settlers, 1-11; fur farming, 1-29; Heartland, 1-33; industry, 1-36; largest

city, 1-21; Laurentian Upland, 1-6; manufacturing belt, 1-18; mineral resources, 1-30; oil drilling, 1-32; Pacific fisheries, 1-26; Pacific forests, 1-29; population, 1-96; Prairie Provinces, 1-34; pulp and paper, 1-29; transportation, 1-15°
Canadian River, Tex.-Okla., 1-58°
Canal Zone, Panama, 1-80°, 1-86°
Canary Islands (Sp.), Africa, 3-239, 5-420°: mountain craters, 5-394
Canaveral, Cape, Florida, 1-58°
Canberra, Australia, 6-497°: description, 6-498; population, 6-544
Canton, China: houseboats, 4-361; population, 4-384
Canton Island, Oceania, 6-483
Cão, Diogo, 5-412
Cape Cod, see Cod, Cape; also Good Hope, Horn, etc.
Cape Province, U. of S. Africa, 5-460
Cape Town, U. of S. Africa, 5-416: climate, 5-406°; description, 5-460; population, 5-480
Cape Verde Islands (Port.), 5-394
Caracas, Venezuela, 2-126, 2-191: description, 2-126, 2-132; highway, 2-140; population, 2-192
Carib Indians, 2-110
Caribbean Islands, 1-87°: climate, 1-88; economy, 1-90; slavery, 1-12
Caribbean Sea, 1-87°
Cariboo Mts., Br. Col., Can., 1-24°
Caribou Mts., Alberta, Can., 1-24°
Carnauba wax, 2-174
Caroline Islands, Micronesia, 6-484°: area, 6-544; people, 6-492; population, 6-544
Caroní River, Venezuela, 2-135
Carpathian Mountains, E Europe, 3-251°
Carpentaria, Gulf of, 6-484°, 6-501°
Carrara marble, 3-248
Carstenz, Mt., New Guinea: height, 6-544
Cartagena, Colombia, 2-140
Carthage: conquest by Rome, 5-421; founding, 5-413; ruins, 5-424
Casablanca, Morocco, 5-422: population, 5-480
Casbah, North African, 5-414
Cascade Range, mts., Ore.-Wash., 1-64°
Caspian Sea, U.S.S.R.-Iran, 3-260°, 4-294°: area, 3-288; fishing boats, 3-265; river mouth, 4-299
Caste system: India, 4-306, 4-330
Catalina Island, Calif., 1-64°
Catskill Mts., N.Y., 1-43°
Cattle: world distribution, 6-562°
Cauca River, Colombia, 2-129
Caucasus Mts., U.S.S.R., 3-260°: cultural groups, 3-270; Russian border, 3-263
Caxias, Portugal, 3-205
Cayenne, French Guiana, 2-131
Cayman Islands, Caribbean Sea, 1-87°
Celebes, Indonesia, 4-293°, 4-308°, 4-369°: former Dutch possession, 4-373; see also Indonesia
Celebes Sea, 4-293°, 4-369°
Celtic peoples, 3-202
Central African Republic, 5-418°, 5-437°
Central America, 1-80°: climate, 1-8°; Indians, 1-83; Negroes, 1-12; plantations, 1-84; transportation, 1-15°
Central Massif, mts., France, 3-223°, 3-224
Cerro Bolívar, Venezuela, 2-132
Cerro de Pasco, Peru, 2-151
Ceylon, 4-292°, 4-308°, 4-327°: area, 4-384; independence, 4-326; industrialization, 4-338; people, 4-330; population, 4-384; population density, 4-327; religion, 4-330; rice farming, 4-298; rubber, 4-346; tea, 4-335
Chacao Strait, Chile, 2-142°
Chaco, see Gran Chaco
Chad, Lake, Central Africa, 5-437°: area, 5-480
Champlain, Lake, N.Y.-Vermont, 1-43°
Chattahoochie River, U.S., 1-58°
Chelyabinsk, U.S.S.R., 3-284
Chelyuskin, Cape, U.S.S.R., 3-261°, 3-267
Cheops, Great Pyramid of, Egypt, 5-434
Chesapeake Bay, Maryland-Virginia, 1-43°, 1-58°: oyster farming, 1-46

Chester, England, 3-210
Cheyenne River, U.S., 1-50°
Chiang Kai-shek, 4-364
Chibcha Indians, 2-110
Chicago, Illinois, 1-18: meat-packing plant, 1-54; population, 1-96
Chichicastenango, Guatemala, 1-83
Chicle, 1-79
Chile, 2-99°, 2-142°: agriculture, 2-117, 2-149; Antarctic research, 6-542; area, 2-192; Atacama Desert, 2-100; capital, 2-125; climate, 2-115; description, 2-143; Indians, 2-110; lake district, 2-143; mineral resources, 2-118; mining and industry, 2-152; people, 2-144; population, 2-192; roads, 2-121; War of 1879, 2-152; wheat harvest, 2-118
Chiloé, isl., Chile, 2-104
Chimborazo, Mt., Ecuador, 2-192
China, Communist, 4-293°, 4-308°, 4-351°: agriculture, 4-358; ancestor worship, 4-307; area, 4-384; capital, 4-310; civil war, 4-364; civilization, 4-356; communes, 4-358; deforestation, 4-362; deserts, 4-356; farming methods, 4-359; farmland, 4-298; fishing, 4-360; floods, 4-357; Great Wall, 4-357; industry, 4-362; inventions, 4-307, 4-356; Japanese occupation, 4-363; junk, 4-360; largest city, 4-310; mineral resources, 4-363; Ming Tombs dam project, 4-362; monsoons, 4-358; mountains, 4-356; navigable waterways, 4-360; official language, 4-306; population, 4-384; population density, 4-356; railroads, 4-363; rice paddies, 4-357; river systems, 4-357; sampan, 4-360; soil erosion, 4-363; tenant farming, 4-358; transportation, 4-309; U.S.S.R. aid, 4-363; village life, 4-358; war with Japan, 4-364
China, Nationalist, see Formosa
China Sea, 4-293°, 4-351°, 4-368°
Chinese Turkestan, see Sinkiang
Chiriqui, Gulf of, Central America, 1-80°
Cho Oyu, Mt., Asia: height, 4-384
Chone, Ecuador, 2-147
Christchurch, New Zealand: population, 6-544
Chromium: U.S.S.R., 3-284; world-wide sources, 6-564°
Chukchi Sea, 3-261°
Chungking, China: population, 4-384
Chuquicamata, Chile, 2-152
Church of the Holy Sepulchre, Jerusalem, Jordan, 4-325
Chuvashes, people, U.S.S.R., 3-268
Cities: growth, 1-18
Clapperton, Hugh, 5-412
Cleveland, Ohio, 1-20: population, 1-96
Climate: causes, 1-9; effect on vegetation, 6-552; worldwide, 6-550°
Cloves: Zanzibar, 5-453
Coal: world supply, 6-551°
Coast Ranges, mts., U.S., 1-64°
Coats Land, Antarctica, 6-533°
Cobalt: Belgian Congo, 5-446
Cochabamba, Bolivia, 2-185
Cochin China, region, Indochina, 4-341°
Coconut palm: Oceania, 6-526
Cod, Cape, Massachusetts, 1-43°: origin of name, 1-46
Coffee: Africa, 5-411; Brazil, 2-177; Caribbean, 1-92; Central American, 1-84; Colombian plantation, 2-137; Ecuador, 2-148; Indonesia, 4-374; processing, 2-178; Venezuela, 2-136; world production, 6-561°
Colhué, Lake, Argentina, 2-192
Collective farms: Eastern Europe, 3-254; U.S.S.R., 3-277
Colombia, 2-99°, 2-128°: agriculture, 2-138; area, 2-192; capital, 2-126; coastal area, 2-127; emerald mine, 2-134; Indians, 2-110; industry, 2-132; Negroes, 2-112; oil deposits, 2-135; population, 2-192; transportation, 2-139
Colorado, 1-38°, 1-64°
Colorado River, Argentina, 2-156°
Colorado River, U.S., 1-58°, 1-64°: length, 1-96
Columbia River, U.S., 1-64°: length, 1-96
Columbus, Christopher, 1-81: South America exploration, 2-119

Commonwealth of Nations: African members, 5-418°; Asian members, 4-326; Australia, 6-496; capital, 6-496; Caribbean members, 1-88; New Zealand, 6-496
Communes, Chinese, 4-358
Communism: Africa, 5-478; Asia, 4-382
Communist China, see China, Communist
Concepción, Chile, 2-153
Condamine River, Australia, 6-501°: length, 6-544
Congo, Belgian, see Belgian Congo
Congo, Republic of the, 5-418°, 5-437°
Congo River, Africa, 5-437°: basin, 5-439; course, 5-391; description, 5-445; discovery, 5-412; length, 5-480; steamer, 5-445
Connecticut, 1-39°, 1-43°
Connecticut River, U.S., 1-43°
"Continental" island, landform, Oceania, 6-487
Cook, Mt., New Zealand, 6-514: height, 6-544
Cook Islands, Polynesia, 6-485°: area, 6-544; landform, 6-483; population, 6-544
Cook Strait, New Zealand, 6-514°
Copenhagen, Denmark, 3-203: climate, 3-200°; fish market, 3-216; Town Hall square, 3-209
Copper: Bolivia, 2-185; Canada, 1-31; Chile, 2-143, 2-152; oldest mine, 3-220; Peru, 2-150; worldwide sources, 6-564°
Copra: Oceania, 6-526; Philippines, 4-373
Coral atolls: formation of, 6-523
Coral Sea, Oceania, 6-484°
Corcovado, Gulf of, Chile, 2-142°
Córdoba, Argentina, 2-158: population, 2-192
Corinth, Greece, Isthmus of, 3-239
Cork harvest, Spain, 3-242
Corn: discovery of, 1-7; Southern U.S., 1-57; world production, 6-560°
Corn Belt, U.S., 1-51
Cornwall, England: countryside, 3-224; people, 3-202
Corocoro, Bolivia, 2-185
Coronado Bay, Central America, 1-80°
Corsica, isl., France, 3-238°
Cortés, Hernando, 1-71
Corumbá, Brazil, 2-179
Costa Rica, 1-80°, 1-81: area and population, 1-96; coffee plantation, 1-84
Cotton: world production, 6-562°
Couscous, Moroccan dish, 5-422
Crete, isl., Mediterranean, 3-239
Crimea, U.S.S.R., 3-260°: coastline, 3-267
Croatia, Yugoslavia, 3-251°
Cuba, 1-87°: area and population, 1-96; capital, 1-22; sugar cane, 1-91
Cuiaba, Brazil, 2-168
Culiacán, Mexico, 1-78
Cumberland Sound, Can., 1-25°
Curaçao, isl., Caribbean Sea, 1-87°
Cuzco, Peru, 2-144
Cyclades, isls., Greece, 3-239°
Cyprus, isl., Mediterranean, 4-314°
Cyrenaica, region, Libya, 5-420°, 5-425
Cyrillic alphabet, 3-204
Czechoslovakia, 3-206°, 3-251°: agriculture, 3-252; area, 3-288; collective farm, 3-254; industry, 3-257; language, 3-249; population, 3-288; stamp collectors, 3-205

Dahomey, Republic of, Africa, 5-418°, 5-436°
Dairen, China: population, 4-384
Dakar, Senegalese Republic, 5-413: open-air market, 5-408; population, 5-480
Dalai Lama, 4-352
Dalmatia, Yugoslavia, 3-251°
Damascus, Syria, 4-319
Danube River, Europe, 3-223°, 3-251°: Austria, 3-199; course, 3-197, 3-250; length, 3-288
Dardanelles, strait, Turkey, 3-195°
Darling River, Australia, 6-501°: length, 6-544
Dates (food): Africa, 5-410; Iraq, 4-318
Death Valley, Calif., 1-64°
Deccan Plateau, Indian peninsula, 4-327°

Degtyarka, U.S.S.R., 3-284
Delaware, 1-39°, 1-43°, 1-49
Delphi, Greece, 3-199
Denmark, 3-195°, 3-206°, 3-214°: agriculture, 3-218; area, 3-288; cheese warehouse, 3-218; fishing, 3-216; industry, 3-221; language, 3-215; population, 3-288; silversmiths, 3-221
Deserts: driest, 2-143; worldwide, 6-552°
Des Moines River, Iowa, 1-50°
Detroit, Michigan, 1-19, 1-56°: population, 1-96
Devil's Island, French Guiana, 2-127
Dhahran, Saudi Arabia: American community, 4-323
Dhows: Zanzibar, 5-453
Dia, Bartholomeu, 5-412
Diamonds: Belgian Congo, 5-446; Brazil, 2-179; British Guiana, 2-131; U. of S. Africa, 5-468; West Africa, 5-443
Djezira-el-Maghrib, North Africa, 5-421
Dnieper River, U.S.S.R., 3-260°: course, 3-263; Dnieproptrovsk dam, 3-282; Kiev, 3-275; length, 3-288
Dniepropetrovsk, U.S.S.R., 3-282
Dniester River, U.S.S.R., 3-263
Dodecanese Islands, Aegean Sea, 3-239°
Dogger Bank, North Sea, 3-225
Dome of the Rock, Jerusalem, Jordan, 4-325
Dominican Republic, 1-87°: area and population, 1-96
Donegal Bay, Eire, 3-222°
Donets Basin, U.S.S.R., 3-280
Doubtful Sound, New Zealand, 6-515
Dover, Strait of, 3-223°
Drakensburg Mts., Africa, 5-456°
Dry Pampa, Argentina, 2-160
Dubrovnik, Yugoslavia, 3-249
Duluth, Minnesota, 1-55
Dunedin, New Zealand: population, 6-544
Durban, U. of S. Africa, 5-461: Indians, 5-405; population, 5-480
Dutch Guiana, see Surinam
Dyaks, people, Borneo, 4-374

Eannes, Gil, 5-412
East African plateau, 5-448
East African Rift, 5-389
East China Sea, see China Sea
East Germany, see Germany, East
East Indies, 4-373
East Siberian Sea, 3-261°
Easter Island, Polynesia, 6-493
Eastern Hemisphere, 6-547°
Ebro River, Spain, 3-241
Economies, world, 6-558°
Ecuador, 2-99°, 2-142°: agriculture, 2-147; area, 2-192; capital, 2-125; description, 2-141; Indians, 2-110; mining and industry, 2-150; mountain farming, 2-146; peoples, 2-144; population, 2-192; volcanoes, 2-141°
Edward, Lake, Africa, 5-452
Egmont, Mt., New Zealand: height, 6-544
Egypt (United Arab Republic), 5-418°, 5-420°: agriculture, 5-432; ancient cities, 5-413; area, 5-480; desert village, 5-427; first steel plant, 5-477; industry, 5-434; land and people, 5-431; population, 5-480; population growth, 5-434; pyramids, 5-434
Eire (Ireland), 3-195°, 3-206°, 3-223°: agriculture, 3-202; area, 3-288; independence, 3-227; landform, 3-222; peat bog, 3-202; people, 3-202; population, 3-288
El Salvador, 1-80°, 1-81: area and population, 1-96; coffee plantation, 1-84
Elba, isl., Italy, 3-248
Elbe River, Europe, 3-223°, 3-251°: length, 3-288
Elbrus, Mt., U.S.S.R., 3-288
Elburz Mountains, Asia, 4-292°: river source, 4-297
Elgon, Mt., Kenya, 5-387°: height, 5-480
Elisabethville, Belgian Congo: copper smelter, 5-446
Ellice Islands, Polynesia, 6-485°, 6-521°: area, 6-544; landform, 6-483; population, 6-544
Emeralds: Colombia, 2-134
Emi Koussi, Mt., Republic of Chad, 5-387°: height, 5-480

Enderby Land, Antarctica, 6-533°
England, see Great Britain
English Channel, 3-222°: formation, 3-224
Equator: climatic effect, 1-8
Erie, Lake, U.S.-Can., 1-50°: area, 1-96
Erie Canal, N.Y., 1-43°
Eskimos, people, Arctic Regions, 1-12, 6-538: fur trade, 6-539; introduction of rifle, 6-539
Esmeraldas, Ecuador, 2-150
Espírito Santo, state, Brazil, 2-176°
Estonian Union Republic, U.S.S.R., 3-204, 3-270
Ethiopia, 5-418°, 5-437°: area, 5-480; capital, 5-414; highlands, 5-389; land and people, 5-448; mountain range, 5-448; population, 5-480
Etna, Mt., Italy, 3-239°, 3-288: orange grove, 3-244; volcanic building stone, 3-248
Euphrates River, SW Asia, 4-314°: length, 4-384; see also Tigris-Euphrates River
Eurasia, 3-194, 4-294°: land mass, 4-296
Europe, 3-195°, 4-294°: airlines, 3-207°; automobiles, 3-207; cities, descriptions, 3-208; cities, population, 3-288; climate, 3-200; coastline, 3-194; continental limits, 3-194; countries, area and population, 3-288; Eastern, 3-249, 3-251°; future, 3-258; hydroelectric power, 3-198; influence of water, 3-194; lakes, principal, 3-288; languages, 3-202; mountains, 3-194, 3-288; natural resources, 3-197; Northern, 3-213, 3-214°; peoples, 3-202; political boundaries, 3-206°; population, 3-194; population distribution, 3-204°; ports, 3-207; racial mixtures, 3-204, 3-288; railroads, 3-207°; rainfall, 3-201°; rivers, 3-197, 3-288; roads, 3-207°; Southern, 3-238°, 3-239; tariffs, 3-258; temperature, mean, 3-200°; transportation, 3-207; United States of, 3-259; vegetation, 3-198°; Western, 3-222°, 3-234
Evenki, people, U.S.S.R., 3-270
Everest, Mt., Asia, 4-350°: height, 4-384
Eyre, Lake, Australia, 6-501°, 6-508: area, 6-544

Fairbanks, Alaska, 1-70
Fairweather, Mt., Alaska, 1-96
Faiyum, region, Egypt, 5-433
Falkland Islands (Br.), South America, 2-99°, 2-104, 2-156°
Falster, isl., Denmark, 3-214°
Falun, Sweden, 3-220
Fazendas, Brazilian, 2-176
Fellaheen, Egyptian, 5-433
Fernando Po (Sp.), isl., Africa, 5-436°: cacao source, 5-410; description, 5-394
"Fertile Crescent," region, Near East, 4-318
Fez, Morocco, 5-422
Fezzan, region, Libya, 5-420°, 5-425
Fiat factory, Italy, 3-258
Fibers: world production, 6-562°
Fiji Islands, Melanesia, 6-485°, 6-521°: area, 6-544; capital, 6-499; hut building, 6-492; people, 6-492; population, 6-544; sugar plantations, 6-529
Finger Lakes, N.Y., 1-43°
Finland, 3-195°, 3-206°, 3-214°: area, 3-288; dairy farm, 3-219; forestry, 3-216; industry, 3-221; lake country, 3-213; language, 3-204, 3-215; population, 3-288
Finland, Gulf of, 3-214°
Fiordland, New Zealand, 6-516
Finno-Ugrian language, 3-270
Flattery, Cape, Wash., 1-64°
Flax: world production, 6-562°
Flinders River, Australia, 6-501°: length, 6-544
Florence, Italy, 3-247
Flores, isl., Indonesia, 4-369°
Flores Sea, Indonesia, 4-369°
Florida, 1-39°, 1-58°: beach, 1-7; citrus farm, 1-57; phosphate mining, 1-60
Fly River, New Guinea: length, 6-544
Foggara, desert water source, 5-428
Fonseca, Gulf of, Central America, 1-80°
Foraker, Mt., Alaska, 1-96

Forests: worldwide, 6-552°
Formosa (Nationalist China), 4-293°, 4-308°, 4-351°: area and geography, 4-364, 4-384; agriculture and industry, 4-365; camphor production, 4-365; capital, 4-364; climate, 4-364; co-operative school, 4-383; flax field, 4-365; Japanese control, 4-364; population, 4-364, 4-384; sugar cane harvest, 4-365
Fort Lamy, Chad Republic, 5-411
Foxe Channel, Can., 1-25°
France, 3-195°, 3-206°, 3-223°: agriculture, 3-231; Alsatian plain, 3-226; Antarctic research, 6-542; area, 3-288; colonial possessions, 3-235; dairy farmer, 3-205; description, 3-227; fishing, 3-225; grape harvest, 3-231; landform, 3-222; mining and industry, 3-237; population, 3-288; shipyard, 3-235; steel mill, largest, 3-236
Franklin, District of, Can., 1-24°
Fraser River, Br. Col., Can., 1-24°, 1-35
Franz Josef Land, U.S.S.R., 3-260°, 6-532°
French Community States, Africa, 5-418°: area, 5-480; Madagascar, 5-457; population, 5-480
French Equatorial Africa, 5-387°, 5-447
French Guiana, 2-99°, 2-128°: area, 2-192; description, 2-130; population, 2-192
French Somaliland, Africa, 5-437°
French West Africa, 5-387°, 5-443
Friendly Islands, see Tonga Islands
Frobisher Bay, Can., 1-25°
Frunze, U.S.S.R., 3-275
Fujiyama, Mt., Japan, 4-290
Fulani, African people, 5-440
Fundy, Bay of, Can., 1-25°

Gabon Republic, Africa, 5-418°, 5-436°
Gaillard Cut, Panama Canal, 1-86
Gairdner, Lake, Australia, 6-501°: area, 6-544
Galápagos Islands, South America, 2-104
Galilee, Sea of, 4-324
Galveston, Texas, 1-61
Gama, Vasco da, 5-412
Gambell, St. Lawrence Island, 6-538
Gambia (Br.), Africa, 5-418°, 5-436°, 5-442
Ganges River, Asia, 4-308°: Hindu pilgrims, 4-304; length, 4-384; source, 4-299, 4-329
Ganges River basin, 4-326: agriculture, 4-334
"Garden of Eden," 5-401
Gary, Indiana, 1-55
Gaspé Peninsula, Que., Can., 1-25°
Gatun Lake, Panama Canal, 1-86
Gauchos, 2-113: Argentine, 2-155; Uruguayan, 2-164
Geelong, Australia: population, 6-544
Genesee River, N.Y., 1-43°
Genghis Khan, 4-353
Genil River, Spain, 3-243
Genoa, Italy, 3-247: development, 3-208
George, Lake, N.Y., 1-43°
Georgetown, British Guiana, 2-131
Georgia, 1-39°, 1-58°: granite quarry, 1-62
Georgian Union Republic, U.S.S.R.: goat farm, 3-277; people and language, 3-270
Germanic languages, 3-203
Germany, East (German Democratic Republic), 3-195°, 3-206°, 3-223°: agriculture, 3-233; area, 3-288; chemical plant, 3-234; description, 3-228; fishing, 3-225; industry, 3-237; landform, 3-222; population, 3-288
Germany, West (German Federal Republic), 3-195°, 3-206°, 3-223°: agriculture, 3-233; area, 3-288; description, 3-228; fishing, 3-225; landform, 3-222; mining and industry, 3-237; population, 3-288; schoolroom, 3-203; superhighways, 3-207; Volkswagen factory, 3-236
Gezira, the, Sudanese region, 5-443
Ghadamès, Libya, 5-425
Ghana, 5-418°, 5-436°: agriculture, 5-442; ancient empire, 5-440; area, 5-480; cacao crop, 5-410; capital, 5-440; educational puppet show, 4-478; mineral resources, 5-443; native

houses, 5-402; Parliament, 5-402; political rally, 5-479; population, 5-480; Supreme Court, 5-441
Gibraltar (Br.), S Europe, 3-238°: ownership, 3-239; Rock of, 3-240
Gibraltar, Strait of, 3-238°, 5-420°: current flow, 3-245; width, 5-389
Gibson Desert, Australia, 6-501°
Gila River, Ariz., 1-64°
Gilbert Islands, Micronesia, 6-485°, 6-521°: area, 6-544; landform, 6-483; population, 6-544
Glasgow, Scotland: development, 3-208; population, 3-288
Gloucester, Massachusetts, 1-47
Gobi Desert, Asia, 4-293°: prehistoric animals, 4-353; size, 4-350; Yumen oilfields, 4-363
Godwin Austen, Mt., India: height, 4-384
Goias, state, Brazil, 2-176°: description, 2-179
Gold: Alaska, 1-70; Australia, 6-510; Canada, 1-30; Belgian Congo, 5-446; Brazil, 2-179; British Guiana, 2-131; New Zealand, 6-519; U. of S. Africa, 5-466; U.S.S.R., 3-285
Gold Coast, see Ghana
Golden Gate Bridge, San Francisco, 1-19
Gondwanaland, ancient continent, 5-390
Good Hope, Cape of, Africa, 5-394, 5-456°
Gorky, U.S.S.R., 3-274, 3-282
Gosnold, Captain, 1-46
Göteborg, Sweden, 3-216, 3-220
Gran Chaco, South America, 2-99°, 2-103, 2-156°, 2-183°: Argentina, 2-159; Bolivian, 2-185; climate, 2-115; war for possession, 2-183
Grand Banks, Atlantic Ocean, 1-25°, 1-26
Grand Canyon, Ariz., 1-64°
Grasse, France, 3-231
Grasslands, worldwide, 6-552°
Great Barrier Reef, Australia, 6-484°, 6-501°
Great Basin, Nevada, 1-64°
Great Bear Lake, Can., 1-24°, 1-32: area, 1-96
Great Britain, 1-195°, 3-206°, 3-222°: African explorers, 5-412; agriculture, 3-230; Antarctic research, 6-542; area, 3-288; atomic power plant, 3-258; climate, 3-200; colonial possessions, 3-235; composition, 3-227; country scene, 3-197; fishing, 3-225; geological history, 3-224; landform, 3-222; population, 3-288; mining and industry, 3-236
Great Dividing Range, mts., Australia, 6-501°: first crossing, 6-502
Great Erg, Sahara Desert, 5-427, 5-428°
Great Escarpment, Brazil, 2-168
Great Khingan Mountains, Asia, 4-293°
Great Lakes, U.S.-Can., 1-39°: area, 1-96; ore boats, 1-55
Great Sandy Desert, Australia, 6-501°: size, 6-495
Great Salt Lake, Utah, 1-64°
Great Slave Lake, Can., 1-24°, 1-29: area, 1-96
Great trek, South Africa, 5-462
Great Victoria Desert, Australia, 6-501°: size, 6-495
Greater Antilles, Caribbean Sea, 1-87°
Greater Sunda Islands, Indonesia, 4-369°
Greece, 3-195°, 3-206°, 3-239°: agriculture, 3-242; area, 3-288; climate, 3-201; industry, 3-246; landform, 3-239; merchant fleet, 3-240, 3-246; mountain village, 3-241; population, 3-288; sponge divers, 3-245
Greece, ancient: African cities, 5-413; city-states, 3-198; original inhabitants, 3-204
Greek Orthodox Church, U.S.S.R., 3-269
Green Mts., Vermont, 1-4, 1-43°
Green River, Utah-Wyo., 1-64°
Greenland, 6-532°: comparative size, 4-374; Eskimos, 6-539; titanium mine, 6-543
Grenada, isl., Caribbean Sea, 1-87°, 1-90
Guadalcanal, isl., Solomon Islands, 6-487
Guadalquivir River, Spain, 3-238°, 3-241

Guadeloupe, isl., Caribbean Sea, 1-87°
Guam (U.S.), isl., Micronesia, 6-484°, 6-521°
Guanajuato, Mexico, 1-74
Guano, 2-109: Oceania, 6-528; Peru, 2-149
Guaraní Indians, 2-110, 2-182: village, 2-186
Guatemala, 1-80°, 1-81: area and population, 1-96; education, 1-82; people, 1-13; village scenes, 1-83
Guayaquil, Ecuador, 2-150: population, 2-192
Guayaquil, Gulf of, Ecuador, 2-142°
Guernsey, isl., English Channel, 3-223°
Guiana Highlands, South America, 2-99°, 2-100, 2-128°, 2-129: Brazil, 2-168; mineral deposits, 2-135
Guianas, South America, 2-128°, 2-130: coastline, formation, 2-127; highlands, see Guiana Highlands; Hindu population, 2-130; Negroes, 2-112; transportation routes, 2-121; see also British Guiana, French Guiana, Surinam
Guiara Falls, Argentina, 2-159
Guinea, 5-418°, 5-436°: area and population, 5-480
Guinea Coast, Africa, 5-442
Guinea, Gulf of, Africa, 5-436°: coastline, 5-440
Gulf of Mexico, see Mexico, Gulf of; also Honduras, Gulf of, etc.
Gum arabic: Africa, 5-411

Haarlem, Netherlands, 3-232
Hainan, isl., China, 4-293°, 4-308°, 4-351°
Haiti, 1-87°: area and population, 1-96; description, 1-87; people, 1-12
Hamburg, Germany: development, 3-208; population, 3-288
Hamilton, New Zealand: population, 6-544
Hamilton, Ontario, 1-37
Hamites, ethnic group, Africa, 5-399
Hamun-i-Helmand, Lake, SW Asia: area, 4-384
Haparanda, Sweden: climate, 3-200°
Hardanger Fiord, Norway, 3-215
Harney Lake, Oregon, 1-64°
Hatteras, Cape, N. Carolina, 1-58°
Havana, Cuba, 1-22°: population, 1-96
Hawaii, 1-38°, 1-69: landform, 6-487; Mauna Loa, 6-486; people, 6-493; sugar plantations, 6-529
Hawkes Bay, prov., New Zealand: sheep raising, 6-517
Hejaz, Saudi Arabia, 4-314°
Hemispheres, 6-546°
Hemp: world production, 6-562°
Heron Island, Australia, 6-501
Hieroglyphics, Egyptian, 5-431
High Maluti, mts., Basutoland, 5-409
Himalaya Mountains, Asia, 4-293°, 4-350: river source, 4-297; source of Ganges, 4-329
Hindi, language, India, 4-306
Hindu Kush, mts., Asia, 4-292°: river source, 4-297
Hispaniola, isl., Caribbean Sea, 1-87°
Hobart, Australia: population, 6-544; zinc refinery, 6-510
Hokkaido Island, Japan, 4-295°, 4-368°
Holland, see Netherlands
Hollywood, California, 1-68
Holy Lands, 4-324
Honduras, 1-80°, 1-81: area and population, 1-96; mountain road, 1-81
Honduras, British, see British Honduras
Honduras, Gulf of, 1-80°
Hong Kong, Br. col., China, 4-312°: air service, 4-309; description, 4-311; houseboats, 4-361; population, 4-384
Honolulu, Hawaii, 1-69
Honshu Island, Japan, 4-295°, 4-368°: rice fields, 4-372; tea growing, 4-373
Hood, Mt., Oregon, 1-64°
Horn, Cape, South America, 2-142°
Hottentots, African, 5-399: village hut, 5-404

Houston, Texas, 1-16: chemical plants, 1-60; population, 1-96
Howard Island, Oceania, 6-483
Huascarán, Mt., Peru, 2-142°: height, 2-192
Hudson Bay, Can., 1-25°
Hudson River, N.Y., 1-43°
Humid Pampa, Argentina, 2-160
Hungary, 3-206°, 3-251°: agriculture, 3-252; area, 3-288; industry, 3-257; language, 3-204, 3-249; locomotive factory, 3-256; population, 3-288; textile mill, 3-257
Huron, Lake, North America, 1-50°: area, 1-96
Hutt, New Zealand: population, 6-544
Hwang Ho (Yellow) River, Asia, 4-351°: length, 4-384; source, 4-299
Hyderabad, India: population, 4-384

Ibadan, Nigeria: population, 5-480
Iberian peninsula, 3-239
Ice age: Northern Europe, 3-213; U.S.S.R., 3-263
Iceland, 3-195°, 3-206°, 3-214°: agriculture, 3-218; area, 3-288; children, 3-203; fishing, 3-216; language, 3-215; population, 3-288; whaling, 3-217
Idaho, 1-38°, 1-64°: potato farm, 1-65
Idenburg, Mt., New Guinea: height, 6-544
Igarka, U.S.S.R., 3-285
Igorots, people, Philippines, 4-372, 4-374
Iguassú Falls, Brazil, 2-102
Iguazú Falls, Argentina, 2-159
Ijssel, Lake, Netherlands, 3-222
Illampú, Mt., Bolivia, 2-183°: height, 2-192
Illimani, Mt., Bolivia, 2-183°: height, 2-192
Illinois, 1-39°, 1-50°: corn field, 1-51
Illinois River, Ill., 1-50°
Inca Indians, 2-110: empire, 2-144
Incahuasi, Mt., Argentina, 2-192
India, 4-292°, 4-308°, 4-327°: area, 4-384; Bhakra Dam, 4-337; brick making, 4-339; caste system, 4-306, 4-330; cattle hides, 4-334; Colombo Plan, 4-336; Community Development Program, 4-336; dam building, 4-338; education, 4-338; farm village, 4-332; Five Year Plans, 4-339; geological relationship to Africa, 5-390; handloom weaving, 4-339; Hinduism, 4-306; home industry, 4-338; independence, 4-326; industrialization, 4-336; iron and steel production, 4-339; languages and dialects, 4-304, 4-306; largest city, 4-312; mineral resources, 4-338; people, 4-331; plowing field, 4-333; Point Four Program, 4-336; population, 4-384; rainfall, 4-300; religions, 4-304, 4-330; rice harvest, 4-328; Tata Steel Works, 4-339; transportation, 4-309; United Nations aid, 4-336; wheat harvest, 4-333
Indian Ocean, 4-308°
Indian Peninsula, 4-292°, 4-327°: agriculture, 4-332; animal life, 4-328; climate, 4-327; land mass, 4-326; peoples, 4-330; plant life, 4-328; population density, 4-327; rainfall, 4-327; religions, 4-330; river systems, 4-326; tenant farming, 4-332; see also Ceylon; India; Pakistan
Indiana, 1-39°, 1-50°, 1-51
Indians, American, see American Indians
Indochina, 4-341°: agriculture, 4-344; animal life, 4-343; climate, 4-342; independence from France, 4-340; peoples, 4-340; plant life, 4-342; primitive tribes, 4-340; religion, 4-340; see also Cambodia; Laos; Vietnam
Indonesia, Republic of, 4-293°, 4-308°, 4-369°: agriculture, 4-374; area, 4-384; capital, 4-312; chief products, 4-373; climate, 4-371; earthquakes, 4-370; industrialization, 4-377; landform, 6-482; land mass, 4-373; natural resources, 4-377; population, 4-384; population density, 4-374; settlement, 6-490;

typhoons, 4-371; volcanoes, 4-370
Indus River, Asia, 4-315°, 4-327°: length, 4-384; source, 4-299
Indus River basin, 4-326
Industrial Revolution: effect on European cities, 3-210; Western Europe, 3-222
Inner Mongolia, see Mongolia, Inner
Ionian Sea, 3-239°
Iowa, 1-39°, 1-50°, 1-51
Iquitos, Peru, 2-102
Iran, 4-292°, 4-308°, 4-314°: agriculture, 4-319; area, 4-384; language and people, 4-316; oil, 4-322, 4-382; population, 4-384; religion, 4-316
Iraq, 4-292°, 4-308°, 4-314°: agriculture, 4-318; area, 4-384; capital, 4-313; date production, 4-318; "Fertile Crescent," 4-318; language and people, 4-316; oil, 4-322, 4-382; population, 4-384; religion, 4-316; sharecropping, 4-318
Ireland, see Eire
Irish Sea, 3-222°
Irkutsk, U.S.S.R., 3-275: power dam, 3-284
Iron: worldwide sources, 6-564°
Iron Knob, South Australia: iron ore mining center, 6-511
Irrawaddy River, Asia, 4-341°: length, 4-384; source, 4-299
Israel, 4-292°, 4-308°, 4-314°: agriculture, 4-320; area, 4-384; citrus exports, 4-320; desert farmland, 4-303; "Fertile Crescent," 4-318; kibbutzim, 4-320; language and people, 4-316; population, 4-384; soil conservation, 4-320; wheat harvest, 4-320
Istanbul, Turkey, 4-310
Italy, 3-195°, 3-206°, 3-239°: agriculture, 3-242; area, 3-288; capital, 3-211; climate, 3-201; industry, 3-247; landform, 3-239; merchant fleet, 3-246; mineral resources, 3-248; motor scooter factory, 3-248; population, 3-288; wheat field, 3-245
Ivory Coast, Rep. of the, Africa, 5-418°, 5-436°
Ixtacihuatl, Mt., Mexico, 1-96

Jacquí River, Brazil, 2-181
Jakarta, Indonesia: description, 4-312; population, 4-384; street scene, 4-313
Jamaica, West Indies, 1-87°: rainfall, 1-88
James River, U.S., 1-50°
Jamshedpur, India: Tata Steel Works, 4-339
Japan, 4-293°, 4-308°, 4-368°: agriculture, 4-372; Antarctic research, 6-542; area, 4-384; capital, 4-310; climate, 4-371; "cottage industry," 4-376; earthquakes, 4-370; fish industry, 4-372; Formosa occupation, 4-364; highest mountain, 4-290; imports and exports, 4-376; industrialization, 4-376; Korean occupation, 4-366; Manchuria occupation, 4-363; population, 4-372, 4-384; shipbuilding, 4-377; tea growing, 4-373; transportation, 4-309; typhoons, 4-371; volcanoes, 4-370; war with China, 4-364
Japan, Sea of, 4-293°, 4-368°
Java, Indonesia, 4-293°, 4-308°, 4-369°: agriculture, 4-374; former Dutch possession, 4-373; prehistoric man, 4-307; see also Indonesia
Java Sea, 4-293°, 4-369°: fishing boat, 4-375
Jericho, Jordan: watering wells, 4-316
Jersey, isl., English Channel, 3-223°
Jerusalem (new city), Israel, 4-325
Jerusalem (old city), Jordan: description, 4-325; Garden of Gethsemane, 4-325; Mount of Olives, 4-324
Jesselton, British North Borneo: cowboys, 4-375
Johannesburg, U. of South Africa, 5-417: African compounds, 5-467; climate, 5-406°; Europeans, 5-405; gold mines, 5-466; population, 5-480; town hall, 5-465
Johnson Island, Oceania, 6-483
Jordan, 4-292°, 4-308°, 4-314°:

area, 4-384; language and people, 4-316; population, 4-384; religion, 4-316
Jos Plateau, Nigeria, 5-*442*
Juan de Fuca Strait, U.S.-Can., 1-64°
Jungles, *see* Rainforests
Juniata River, Pa., 1-43°
Jura Mts., W Europe, 3-223°
Juruá River, Brazil, 2-167°: length, 2-192
Jute: Brazil, 2-173; Pakistan, 4-334; world production, 6-562°

K2, mt., *see* Godwin Austen, Mt.
Kabul, Afghanistan: Afghani men, 4-*302*
Kaieteur Falls, British Guiana, 2-129
Kalahari Desert, Africa, 5-456°: Bechuanaland, 5-471; compared to Sahara, 5-388; Orange River, 5-393
Kalgoorlie, Western Australia: gold mining, 6-510
Kalinin, U.S.S.R., 3-274
Kalmyks, people, U.S.S.R., 3-270
Kamchatka Peninsula, U.S.S.R., 3-261°, 4-295°
Kanchenjunga, Mt., Asia: height, 4-384
Kano, Nigeria, 5-413: airport, 5-*476*
Kansas, 1-38°, 1-50°, 1-51
Kansas City, Missouri, 1-55
Kanye, Bechuanaland, 5-*471*
Kapok: Indonesia, 4-373
Kara Sea, 3-260°
Karachi, Pakistan: population, 4-384
Karaganda, U.S.S.R., 3-275, 3-284
Karakoram Mountains, Asia, 4-292°, 4-296°: river source, 4-297
Karelia, U.S.S.R., 3-270
Kariba Dam, Rhodesia, 5-*469*
Karnak, Egypt: temple hieroglyphics, 5-*431*
Karroo, region, South Africa, 5-*473*
Kasai River, Africa, 5-437°: length, 5-480
Kashmir, 4-327°: houseboats, 4-*326*; marketplace, 4-*305*
Katanga, region, Belgian Congo, 5-*446*
Kauai, Hawaii, 1-38°, 1-69
Kaysersberg, France, 3-*231*
Kazakh Union Republic, U.S.S.R.: area and people, 3-269; industry, 3-284
Keewatin, District of, Can., 1-24°
Kennebec River, Maine, 1-43°
Kent, England, 3-*229*
Kentawai Islands, Indonesia, 4-369°
Kentucky, 1-39°, 1-58°
Kenya, 5-418°, 5-437°: 5-480; capital, 5-449; game reserves, 5-451; land and people, 5-449; native village, 5-*450;* population, 5-480
Kenya, Mt., Kenya, 5-387°, 5-389: height, 5-480
Khabarovsk, U.S.S.R., 3-285
Khangai Mountains, Asia, 4-293°
Kharkov, U.S.S.R., 3-275, 3-280
Khartoum, Egypt, 5-*391*
Khevsurs, people, U.S.S.R., 3-270
Kibbutzim, Israeli, 4-320
Kiev, U.S.S.R.: description, 3-275; industry, 3-282
Kikuyu, African people, 5-449
Kilimanjaro, Mt., 5-387°, 5-389, 5-392: farming region, 5-451; height, 5-480
Kimberley, U. of S. Africa, 5-468
King, Mt., Canada, 1-96
Kingston, Jamaica, 1-88
Kirghiz Union Republic, U.S.S.R.: cotton field, 3-*277*; people, 3-269
Kiruna, Sweden, 3-220
Kitimat, British Columbia, 1-*36*
Klyuchevskaya, Mt., U.S.S.R., 3-288
Knysna, U. of S. Africa, 5-*458*
Kodiak Island, Alaska, 1-38°
Koko Nor, Lake, China: area, 4-384
Kola Peninsula, U.S.S.R., 3-282
Kola trees: Africa, 5-410
Komsomolsk, U.S.S.R., 3-275, 3-285
Korea, North, 4-293°, 4-308°, 4-351°: area and population, 4-384; *see also* Korean Peninsula
Korea, South, 4-293°, 4-308°, 4-351°: area and population, 4-384; capital, 4-*313*, 4-*367*; United Nations aid, 4-367; *see also* Korean Peninsula
Korean Peninsula, 4-293°: agriculture and industry, 4-366; climate and geography, 4-366;

Japanese occupation, 4-366; Korean War, 4-367; mountain village, 4-*366;* population density, 4-367; soil erosion, 4-367
Kosciusko, Mt., Australia, 6-501°: height, 6-544
Krapf, Johann, 5-412
Krivoi Rog, U.S.S.R., 3-280
Kruger National Park, U. of S. Africa, 5-*465*
Ksar, Sahara oasis, 5-*430*
Kublai Khan, 4-353
Kuibyshev, U.S.S.R., 3-274, 3-282
Kunlun Mountains, Asia, 4-293°, 4-350
Kurile Islands, NE Asia, 4-295°
Kuwait, Arabian Peninsula, 4-308°, 4-314°: Arab rug merchant, 4-*303;* oil, 4-322
Kuznetsk Basin, U.S.S.R., 3-284
Kyoto, Japan: population, 4-384
Kyushu Island, Japan, 4-293°, 4-368°: rice growing, 4-372; steel industry, 4-376
Kyzl Kum Desert, U.S.S.R., 3-260°

La Paz, Bolivia, 2-*124*: description, 2-125, 2-184; population, 2-192
Labrador, Canada, 1-25°: fisheries, 1-26
Ladoga, Lake, U.S.S.R., 3-260°: area, 3-288
Lagos, Nigeria: population, 5-480
Laguna district, Mexico, 1-79
Lanai, Hawaii, 1-38°
Lancaster Sound, Can., 1-25°
Land rotation: Brazil, 2-168.
Lander, Richard, 5-412
Laos, 4-292°, 4-308°, 4-341°: area and population, 4-384; *see also* Indochina
Lapland, N Europe: agriculture, 3-218; people and language, 3-*203*, 3-*215*
Laptev Sea, 3-261°
Latacunga, Ecuador, 2-*111*
Latin, influence of, 3-204
Latvian Union Republic, U.S.S.R., 3-270
Launceston, Australia: population, 6-544
Laurentian Mountains, Can., 1-*6*
Lead: Australia, 6-510; worldwide sources, 6-565°
Lebanon, 4-292°, 4-308°, 4-314°: agriculture, 4-321; area, 4-384; climate, 4-321; language and people, 4-316; population, 4-384; religion, 4-316
Leech Lake, Minn., 1-*50°*
Leeward Islands, Caribbean Sea, 1-87°
Leiden, Netherlands, 3-232
Lena River, U.S.S.R., 3-261°: course, 3-263; gold source, 3-285; length, 3-288; source, 4-297
Lenin, V. I., 3-265: tomb, 3-*268*
Lenin, U.S.S.R., 3-288
Leningrad, U.S.S.R.: building construction, 3-*282;* description, 3-274; industry, 3-*282;* population, 3-288; port, 3-275
Leopold II, Lake, Central Africa, 5-437°: area, 5-480
Léopoldville, Belgian Congo, 5-*446*: disease control, 5-475; population, 5-480; street scene, 5-*416*
Lesser Antilles, Caribbean Sea, 1-87°
Lesser Sunda Islands, Indonesia, 4-369°
Lewis Range, Mts., Mont., 1-64°
Leyte, isl., Philippines, 4-368°
Lhasa, Tibet, 4-350: The Potala, 4-*352*
Liberation Province, Egypt, 5-*477*
Liberia, 5-418°, 5-436°: agriculture, 5-442; area and population, 5-480; harbor scene, 5-*443;* rubber worker, 5-*410;* village scene, 5-*440*
Libya, 5-418°, 5-420°: area, 5-480; co-capitals, 5-425; description, 5-424; population, 5-480
Liechtenstein, 3-223°, 3-228
Lignite: world supply, 6-551°
Ligurian Sea, 3-238°
Lima, Peru, 2-*125*: description, 2-126, 2-153; mountain railroad, 2-150; population, 2-192
Limestone: Australia, 6-511
Limpopo River, Africa, 5-456°: length, 5-480
Lisbon, Portugal: climate, 3-200°; harbor, 3-*210;* river, 3-241

Lithuanian Union Republic, U.S.S.R., 3-270
Little America, Antarctica, 6-533°
Liverpool, England, 3-208
Livestock: world distribution, 6-563°
Livingstone, David, 5-412
Livingstone, Northern Rhodesia, 5-468
Llanos (plains), South America, *see* Orinoco Llanos
Llanquihue, Lake, Chile, 2-192
Llullaillaco, Mt., Chile, 2-142°: height, 2-192
Loa, Rio, Chile, 2-143
Lofoten Islands, Norway, 3-214°
Logan, Mt., Can., 1-24°: height, 1-96
London, England: climate, 3-200°; docks, 3-*236*; population, 3-288; Westminster Bridge, 3-*208*
Long Island, N.Y., 1-43°: duck farm, 1-*49*
Long Island Sound, 1-43°
Los Angeles, California: freeway, 1-*16*; industry, 1-67; population, 1-96
Louisiana, 1-39, 1-58°: bayou, 1-*5*; mineral resources, 1-60
Lourenço Marques, Mozambique, 5-*470*
Lower California, Mexico, 1-72°
Loyalty Islands, Melanesia, 6-485°, 6-521°
Lucania, Mt., Can., 1-24°: height, 1-96
Lumber: worldwide production, 6-552°
Luxembourg, 3-195°, 3-206°, 3-223°: agriculture, 3-232; area and population, 3-288; steel industry, 3-*237*
Luzon, isl., Philippines, 4-368°: headhunters, 4-372

Macchu Picchu, Peru, 2-*145*
Macdonald, Lake, Australia, 6-501°, 6-508
Macedonian Plain, Greece, 3-244
Mackay, Lake, Australia, 6-501°, 6-508
Mackenzie, District of, Can., 1-24°
Mackenzie River, Canada, 1-24°: length, 1-96
Macquarie River, Australia, 6-501°: length, 6-544
Madagascar, 5-387°, 5-418°: land and people, 5-456
Madeira Islands (Port.), Africa, 3-239, 5-420°: description, 5-394; embroidery, 3-*247;* wine, 3-242
Madeira River, Brazil, 2-167°: length, 2-192
Madras, India: population, 4-384
Madrid, Spain, 3-*210*: population, 3-288
Magdalena River, South America, 2-*128*, 2-*129*: length, 2-192; steamer, 2-*140*
Magdalena River Valley, cattle, 2-*139;* coffee, 2-138; farm land, 2-*116*
Magellan, Ferdinand, 2-119, 2-154
Magellan, Strait of, South America, 2-*103*, 2-142°, 2-154, 2-156°
Magnesite: U.S.S.R., 3-284
Magnitogorsk, U.S.S.R., 3-275, 3-284
Mahogany, Philippine, 4-373
Maine, 1-39°, 1-43°: coastline, 1-*2*; paper mill, 1-*45;* potato farm, 1-*48*
Makalu, Mt., Asia: height, 4-384
Malacca, Strait of, Asia, 4-293°
Malagasy Republic, *see* Madagascar
Malaria: Africa, 5-475
Malay Peninsula, 4-293°, 4-341°
Malaya, Federation of, 4-293°, 4-308°, 4-341°: agriculture, 4-344; animal life, 4-343; area, 4-384; climate, 4-342; Hong Fatt tin mine, 4-*347*; peoples, 4-340; plant life, 4-342; population, 4-384; primitive tribes, 4-349; religion, 4-340; rubber industry, 2-173, 4-*346*; tin production, 4-347
Malayo-Polynesian peoples, Africa, 5-479
Maletsunyane Falls, South Africa, 5-*455*
Malheur Lake, Oregon, 1-64°
Mali Federation, Africa, 5-418°, 5-436°
Malta (Br.), isl., Mediterranean, 3-239
Mamberamo River, New Guinea: length, 6-544

Man, Isle of, England, 3-202, 3-222°
Manaus, Brazil, 2-102, 2-*172*: opera house, 2-*171*
Manchuria, prov., China, 4-295°, 4-351°: description, 4-363; Japanese occupation, 4-363; largest city, 4-313; open-pit coal mine, 4-*363;* steel mill, 4-363
Mandarin, language, China, 4-306
Mandingo, ancient African empire, 5-440
Manganese: Brazil, 2-179; British Guiana, 2-131; U.S.S.R., 3-282
Manhattan Island, 1-*10*: skyline, 1-*16*
Manila, The Philippines: air service, 4-309; bay, 4-*313*; description, 4-312; population, 4-384
Manila hemp, 4-373, 4-*374*
Manioc: Brazil, 2-*173*
Manitoba, prov., Can., 1-24°: agriculture, 1-33
Manitoba, Lake, Canada, 1-24°: area, 1-96
Mao Tse-tung, 4-364
Maoris, people, New Zealand, 6-514: war with settlers, 6-516
Map projections, 6-545
Maquis, African forest, 5-421
Mar Chiquita, Lake, Argentina, 2-192
Maracaibo, Venezuela: population, 2-192
Maracaibo, Lake, Venezuela, 2-103, 2-128°: area, 2-192; oil fields, 2-*132*, 2-*134*
Marajó Island, Brazil, 2-104, 2-*168*
Marco Polo, 4-353
Mariana Islands, Micronesia, 6-484°: area, 6-544; landform, 6-487; people, 6-492; population, 6-544; sugar plantations, 6-529
Marie Byrd Land, Antarctica, 6-533°: highest peaks, 6-541
Marquesas Islands, Polynesia: area and population, 6-544
Marrakech, Morocco, 5-*415*, 5-*422*: population, 5-480
Marshall Islands, Micronesia, 6-485°, 6-521°: area, 6-544; landform, 6-483; people, 6-492; population, 6-544
Martha's Vineyard, isl., Mass., 1-43°
Martinique, isl., Caribbean Sea, 1-87°
Maryland, 1-39°, 1-43°, 1-49
Masai, African people, 5-439
Massachusetts, 1-39°, 1-43°: cranberries, 1-*49*
Matadi, Belgian Congo, 5-445
Maté: Argentina, 2-159
Mato Grosso, plateau, Brazil, 2-99°, 2-167°
Mato Grosso, state, Brazil, 2-176° 2-179
Matterhorn, Mt., Switzerland, 3-*222;* height, 3-288
Mau Mau rebellion, Kenya, 5-449
Maui, Hawaii, 1-38°
Mauna Loa, Mt., Hawaii, 1-69, 6-*486*
Maupiti, Society Islands: netting fish, 6-*524;* watermelon raising, 6-*527*
Mauritanian Islamic Republic, Africa, 5-418°, 5-436°
Maya Mts., Central America, 1-80°
Mayan Indians, 1-73: Guatemalan ruins, 1-82
McKinley, Mt., Alaska, 1-38°: height, 1-96
Mead, Lake, Nev.-Ariz., 1-64°
Mecca, Saudi Arabia, 4-324
Medellín, Colombia, 2-*129:* population, 2-192; textile mill, 2-*135;* transportation routes, 2-140
Medina, Saudi Arabia, 4-325
Mediterranean countries: African, agriculture, 5-411; climate, 3-201; reforestation need, 3-259
Mediterranean Sea, 3-195°, 3-239°, 5-420°: current from Atlantic, 3-245; fishing, 3-246
Mekong River, Asia, 4-341°, 4-351°: length, 4-384; source, 4-299
Melanesia, Oceania, 6-484°: area, 6-544; islands and people, 6-491; population, 6-544
Melbourne, Australia, 6-*497*: description, 6-498; population, 6-544
Memphis, Egypt, 5-413
Mendocino, Cape, Calif., 1-64°
Mendoza, Argentina, 2-158, 2-*159*

Mercedario, Mt., Argentina, 2-192
Mergui Archipelago, SE Asia, 4-341°
Mérida, Cordillera de, South America, 2-132
Merrimack River, New Hampshire, 1-43°
Merseburg, East Germany, 3-234
Meru, Mt., Tanganyika, 5-408
Mesabi Mountains, Minnesota, 1-55
Mesopotamia, Argentine, 2-159
Mesopotamia, region, SW Asia, 4-292°, 4-314°: oldest civilization, 4-307
Messina, Strait of, 3-239°
Mestizos, South American, 2-110
Mexico, 1-72°: agriculture, 1-78; area, 1-96; capital, 1-22; climate, 1-8°; land and people, 1-71; mines and industry, 1-74; population, 1-96; transportation, 1-15°; village life, 1-76
Mexico City, Mexico, 1-22, 1-71: population, 1-96
Mexico, Gulf of, 1-58°, 1-72°: oil reserves, 1-61
Michigan, 1-39°, 1-50°: automobile industry, 1-56
Michigan, Lake, U.S., 1-50°: area, 1-96
Micronesia, Oceania, 6-484°: area, 6-544; islands and people, 6-492; outrigger canoe, 6-492; population, 6-544
Middle East, see Near East
Midwestern U.S., 1-50°: agriculture, 1-51; air view, 1-5, 1-52; industry, 1-54
Milan, Italy: industry, 3-247; population, 3-288
Milk River, Mont., 1-64°
Miller Cylindrical Projection, 6-545
Millet: world production, 6-560°
Milwaukee, Wisconsin, 1-96
Minas Gerais, state, Brazil, 2-174, 2-176°: capital, 2-179
Minch, The, Scotland, 3-222°
Mindanao, isl., Philippines, 4-368°
Mindoro, isl., Philippines, 4-368°
Minerals, worldwide distribution, 6-564°
Minneapolis, Minnesota, 1-54
Minnesota, 1-39°, 1-50°: iron mine, 1-55
Miquelon (Fr.), isl., N. Amer., 1-25°, 3-225
Miraflores Locks, Panama Canal, 1-86
"Missing links," 5-401
Mississippi, 1-39°, 1-58°
Mississippi River, U.S., 1-50°, 1-58°: length, 1-96
Missouri, 1-39°, 1-50°, 1-51
Missouri River, U.S., 1-50°, 1-64°: length, 1-96
Mohawk River, N.Y., 1-43°
Moldau River, Czechoslovakia, 3-212
Moldavia, Romania, 3-251°
Molokai, Hawaii, 1-38°
Molucca Islands, Indonesia, 4-369°
Molucca Sea, Indonesia, 4-369°
Molybdenum: worldwide sources, 6-564°
Mombasa, Kenya, 5-449
Monaco, 3-223°, 3-228
Mongol peoples, U.S.S.R., 3-270
Mongolia, Inner, region, China, 4-293°, 4-351°
Mongolia, Outer (Mongolian People's Republic), 4-308°, 4-351°: Genghis Khan, 4-353; geography, 4-353; herding, 4-354, 4-355; nomadism, 4-354; relations with China and U.S.S.R., 4-355
Monongahela River, W. Va.-Pa., 1-43°
Monsoons: Asia, 4-300; Australia, 6-495; China, 4-358; Indian peninsula, 4-327
Montana, 1-38°, 1-64°
Mont Blanc, mt., France, 3-288
Monte Carlo, Monaco, 3-228
Monterrey, Mexico, 1-75
Montevideo, Uruguay: beach, 2-164; description, 2-124, 2-165; population, 2-192
Montreal, Canada, 1-21: population, 1-96
Moorea, Society Islands, 6-522
Moors, desert people, 5-430
Moosehead Lake, Maine, 1-43°
Morocco, 5-418°, 5-420°: area and population, 5-480; description, 5-422
Morón, Venezuela, 2-134
Moscow, U.S.S.R.: agricultural exhibit, 3-283; description,
3-274; industry, 3-282; kvass vendor, 3-271; Lenin's tomb, 3-268; population, 3-288; St. Basil's Cathedral, 3-270; university, 3-274
Moshesh, Basuto warrior, 5-477
Moshi Mosque, Tanganyika, 5-451
Moslems: Africa, 5-399
Mosquito Gulf, Central America, 1-80°
Mozambique (Port.), Africa, 5-418°, 5-456°, 5-470: area and population, 5-480
Mozambique Channel, Africa, 5-456°
Mukden, China: description, 4-313; industry, 4-363; population, 4-384
Munich, West Germany: population, 3-288
Murano, Italy: glass blower, 3-247
Murray River, Australia, 6-501°: length, 6-544
Murray River Valley, Australia: grape growing, 6-505
Murrumbidgee River, Australia, 6-501°: length, 6-544

Nacimiento, Mt., Argentina, 2-192
Nagana, African disease, 5-460
Nagasaki, Japan: harbor, 4-370; shipyard, 4-377
Nagoya, Japan: population, 4-384
Nahuel Huapí Lake, Argentina, 2-192
Nairobi, Kenya, 5-449; climate, 5-406°; population, 5-480; Royal Technical College, 5-476
Nan Shan, mts., Asia, 4-293°
Nandi, Fiji Islands, 6-523
Nanking, China: population, 4-384
Nantucket Island, Mass., 1-43°
Naples, Italy, 3-247: origin of name, 3-204; population, 3-288; workmen, 3-205
Natal, province, U. of S. Africa, 5-461
Nationalism, African, 5-426, 5-477
Nationalist China, see Formosa
Nauru Island, Micronesia, 6-485°: area, 6-544; landform, 6-483; phosphate, 6-483, 6-529; population, 6-544
Nautilus, U.S.S. 6-543
Navajo Indians, 1-4
Nayarit, Mexico, 1-73
Nazaré, Portugal, 3-241
Ndebele, African people, 5-404, 5-464
Near East, 4-314°: ancient civilization, 4-315; climate, 4-315; date palm, 4-319; geography, 4-318; holy cities, 4-324; Kurdish nomads, 4-321; nomadism, 4-316; oases, 4-319; oil, 4-322; peoples, 4-316; rainfall, 4-316; religion, 4-324; see also individual countries
Nebraska, 1-38°, 1-50°, 1-51
Negev, desert, Israel, 4-320
Negro, Rio, Brazil, 2-167°: length, 2-192
Negro, Rio, Uruguay, 2-165
Negro Africa, 5-436°
Negroes: Africa, 5-399, 5-401°; African empires, 5-440; Ecuador, 2-147; North America, 1-12; South America, 2-112; U. of S. Africa, 5-458, 5-466
Negros, isl., Philippines, 4-368°
Nejd, Saudi Arabia, 4-314°
Nentsi, people, U.S.S.R., 3-270
Nepal, 4-308°, 4-327°: area, 4-384; description, 4-326; industrialization, 4-338; population, 4-384
Netherlands, 3-195°, 3-206°, 3-223°: agriculture, 3-233; area, 3-288; canal barge, 3-230; colonial possessions, 3-235; description, 3-228; fishing, 3-225; mining and industry, 3-237; land reclamation, 3-222; population, 3-288; tulips, 3-232; windmills, 3-225
Neva River, U.S.S.R., 3-274
Nevada, 1-38°, 1-64°
Nevis, isl., Caribbean Sea, 1-87°
New Amsterdam, British Guiana, 2-131
New Bedford, Mass., 1-47
New Britain, Melanesia, 6-484°: landform, 6-487
New Brunswick, prov., Canada, 1-25°: agriculture, 1-35; fisheries, 1-26
New Caledonia, Melanesia, 6-485°, 6-521°: area, 6-544; landform, 6-482, 6-487; people, 6-492; plant life, 6-488; population,
6-544
New Delhi, India: population, 4-384
New England, 1-43°: farmland, 1-49; industry, 1-44; lobstermen, 1-46
New Granada, South America: Viceroyalty of, 2-119
New Guinea, Melanesia, 6-484°: area, 6-544; comparative size, 4-374; landform, 6-482, 6-487; mountains, 6-523, 6-544; oil, 6-531; population, 6-544; Pygmies, 6-490; rivers, 6-544
New Hampshire, 1-39°, 1-43°, 1-48
New Hebrides, Melanesia, 6-485°, 6-521°: area, 6-544; landform, 6-482; people, 6-492; population, 6-544
New Ireland, Melanesia, 6-484°: landform, 6-487
New Jersey, 1-39°, 1-43°: farm, 1-49
New Mexico, 1-38°, 1-64°
New Schwabenland, Antarctica, 6-533°
New South Wales, state, Australia, 6-501°: coal deposits, 6-511; gold mining, 6-510; industry, 6-513; lead and zinc production, 6-510; Merino sheep station, 6-506°; soil, 6-502
New York City: harbor, 1-45; population, 1-96; population history, 1-17; skyline, 1-16
New York State, 1-39°, 1-43°: farm products, 1-48
New Zealand, 6-485°, 6-514°: agriculture, 6-517; air routes, 6-514°; animal life, 6-516; Antarctica, 6-496, 6-542; area and geography, 6-514, 6-544; capital, 6-498; cities, 6-498, 6-544; climate, 6-514; Commonwealth of Nations, 6-496; compared with Australia, 6-514; dairy farming, 6-517; discovery, 6-516; electricity, 6-519; exports, 6-518; farmland, 6-517; fiords, 6-516; foreign trade, 6-531; industry, 6-518; lakes, 6-544; landform, 6-482, 6-487; Maori children, 6-493; Maori wars, 6-516; mineral resources, 6-519; mountains, 6-514, 6-544; pasture land, 6-517; plant life, 6-488, 6-516; population, 6-498, 6-514, 6-515°, 6-544; settlement, 6-516; sheep raising, 6-517; tourism, 6-531; vegetation, 6-515°; wool production, 6-517
Newcastle, New South Wales, Australia: coal mines, 6-511; population, 6-544
Newfoundland, prov., Can., 1-25°: fishing village, 1-26
Niagara Falls, 1-37
Niagara Peninsula, Ontario, 1-35
Nicaragua, 1-80°, 1-81: area and population, 1-96
Nicaragua, Lake, Nicaragua, 1-80°: area, 1-96
Nice, France, 3-225
Nickel: Canada, 1-31; worldwide sources, 6-564°
Niger River, Africa, 5-436°: course, 5-391; discovery, 5-392; length, 5-480
Nigeria, 5-418°, 5-436°: area and population, 5-480; pagan shrine, 5-444; river crossing, 5-438; tin miners, 5-443
Nile River, Africa, 5-420°, 5-437°: Aswan Dam, 5-433; course, 5-391; delta, 5-434; flooding, 5-431; Khartoum confluence, 5-391; length, 5-480; Owen Falls dam, 5-452; Sudd, the, 5-443; valley, 5-431
Niobrara River, Nebraska, 1-50°
Nitrate, Chilean, 2-152
Nizhni Tagil, U.S.S.R., 3-284
Normandy, France, 3-231
North America, 1-3°, 1-14°: Arctic tundra, 1-7, 6-537; cities, leading, 1-17, 1-96; climate, 1-8, 1-9°; compared to South America, 2-104; exploration, 1-11; facts and figures, 1-96; future, 1-94; geography, 1-4; lakes, largest, 1-96; manufacturing belt, 1-18; mountains, highest, 1-96; people, 1-10; population density, 1-10°; rivers, longest, 1-96; settlement, 1-2, 1-11; transportation, 1-15°; vegetation, 1-4°
North Atlantic Drift, 3-200
North Borneo, Br. col., Borneo, 4-308°, 4-369°
North Carolina, 1-39°, 1-58°
North Dakota, 1-38°, 1-50°, 1-53
North Island, New Zealand, 6-514°: dairy farming, 6-517; volcanoes, 6-516
North Korea, see Korea, North; Korean Peninsula
North Pole, Arctic Regions, 6-532°: discovery, 6-541
North Sea, 3-223°: fishing grounds, 3-216; formation, 3-224
North Vietnam, see Vietnam, North
Northeastern U. S., 1-43°: agriculture, 1-48; fisheries, 1-46; industry, 1-44
Northern Ireland, 3-222°; see also Great Britain
Northern Hemisphere, 6-546°
Northern Rhodesia, 5-468
Northern Territory, region, Australia, 6-501°: cattle ranching, 6-507
Northwest Territories, Can., 1-24°
Norway, 3-195°, 3-206°, 3-214°: agriculture, 3-218; Antarctic research, 6-542; area, 3-288; fiords, 3-197; fishing, 3-216; forestry, 3-217; hillside farm, 3-218; language, 3-215; mining and industry, 3-220; population, 3-288
Notre Dame de Paris, 3-208
Nouméa, New Caledonia: population, 6-544
Nova Scotia, prov., Can., 1-25°: apples, 1-35; fisheries, 1-26
Novaya Zemlya, isl., U.S.S.R., 3-260°, 6-532°
Novosibirsk, U.S.S.R., 3-284
Nowa Huta, Poland, 3-255
Nullarbor Plain, Australia, 6-501°
Nyasa, Lake, Central Africa, 5-437°, 5-452: area, 5-480
Nyasaland, 5-469

Oahu, Hawaii, 1-38°
Oases: Damascus, Syria, 4-319; Sahara desert, 5-426
Oats: world production, 6-561°
Ob River, U.S.S.R., 3-260°: course, 3-263; length, 3-288; source, 4-297
Ocean Island, Micronesia, landform, 6-483; phosphate deposits, 6-483, 6-529
Oceania, 6-485°: agriculture, 6-526; animal life, 6-488, 6-527; cities, 6-499; climate, 6-494; copra industry, 6-527; fishing, 6-525, 6-531; "guano islands," 6-528; island types, 6-483; landforms, 6-522; mineral resources, 6-528, 6-530; peoples, 6-490; plant life, 6-488; plantations, 6-529; tourism, 6-531; vegetation, 6-527; white population, 6-493; see also Australia; Melanesia; Micronesia; Polynesia
Oder River, Europe, 3-223°, 3-251°: course, 3-249
Odessa, U.S.S.R., 3-275, 3-282
Ogooué River, French Cameroons, 5-439
Ohio, 1-39°, 1-50°, 1-51
Ohio River, U.S., 1-58°: length, 1-96
Oil: Argentina, 2-158; Australia, 6-531; Austria, 3-237; Bolivia, 2-185; Canada, 1-32; Colombia, 2-134; Europe, 3-197; Indonesia, 4-377; Iran, 4-382; Iraq, 4-382; Mexico, 1-74; Near East, 4-322; New Guinea, 6-531; Peru, 2-151; role in world affairs, 4-322; Romania, 3-257; Saudi Arabia, 4-382; southern U.S., 1-61; Tierra del Fuego, 2-154; U.S.S.R., 3-282; Venezuela, 2-134; western U.S., 1-67; world supply, 6-551°
Oil palm: Africa, 5-410
Ojos del Salado, Mt., South America, 2-142°: height, 2-192
Okeechobee, Lake, Florida, 1-58°
Okhotsk, Sea of, 3-261°, 4-295°, 6-532°
Oklahoma, 1-38°, 1-53, 1-58°
Okovanggo River, Africa, 5-456°: length, 5-480
Olive trees: Southern Europe, 3-243
Oman Protectorate, 4-308°, 4-314°
Omsk, U.S.S.R., 3-275
Onega, Lake, U.S.S.R., 3-260°: area, 3-288
Ontario, prov., Can., 1-25°: forestry, 1-28; mining, 1-31
Ontario, Lake, U.S.—Can., 1-43°: area, 1-96

Oran, Algeria: population, 5-480
Orange Free State, province, U. of S. Africa, 5-463
Orange River, Africa, 5-456°: course, 5-393; length, 5-480
Oregon, 1-38°, 1-64°: farmland, 1-65
Orinoco Llanos, South America, 2-99°, 2-128°: agriculture, 2-104; cattle 2-129, 2-138; oil deposits, 2-134
Orinoco River, South America, 2-101, 2-128°: length, 2-192; llanos, see Orinoco Llanos
Orizaba, Mexico, 1-75
Orizaba, Mt., Mexico, 1-72°: height, 1-96
Orkney Islands, Scotland, 3-223°
Orleans, Isle of, Can., 1-33
Orohéna, Mt., Tahiti, 6-521°: height, 6-544
Oruro, Bolivia, 2-185
Osaka, Japan: population, 4-384
Ostend, Belgium, 3-225
Ostrava, Czechoslovakia: steel mill, 3-255
Outer Mongolia, see Mongolia, Outer
Owen Falls, Uganda, Africa, 5-452
Ozarks, Lake of the, Missouri, 1-50°

Pacific Ocean: area and extent, 6-482; control of islands, 6-496; coral atoll, 6-487; deepest point, 6-522; underwater mountain chains, 6-482; see also Oceania
Päijänne, Lake, Finland, 3-217
Pakaraima Mts., South America, 2-128°
Pakistan, 4-292°, 4-308°, 4-327°: area, 4-384; Colombo Plan, 4-336; dam building, 4-338; education, 4-338; home industry, 4-338; independence, 4-326; industrialization, 4-336; jute production, 4-334; mineral resources, 4-338; Point Four Program, 4-336; population, 4-384; rainfall, 4-328; religion, 4-330; snake-charmer, 4-305; terrace farming, 4-335; United Nations aid, 4-336
Palawan, isl., Philippines, 4-368°
Palmer Peninsula, Antarctica, 6-533°: highest peaks, 6-541
Pamir Mountains, U.S.S.R., 4-292°, 4-350: people, 3-270; plateau, 3-263; river source, 4-297
Pampa, region, South America, 2-99°: Argentine, 2-156°, 2-160
Panama, 1-80, 1-81°: area and population, 1-96
Panama, Gulf of, 1-80°
Panama Canal, 1-86°
Panama hats, 2-147
Pan-American Highway, 2-191
Panay, isl., Philippines, 4-368°
Panié, Mt., New Caledonia: height, 6-544
Papeete, Tahiti: description, 6-499; harbor, 6-499; population, 6-544
Paraguay, 2-99°, 2-183°: area, 2-192; Indians, 2-110, 2-182; land and people, 2-186; mineral resources, 2-187; population, 2-192; territorial wars, 2-182
Paraguay River, South America, 2-167°, 2-183°, 2-186: tributaries, 2-182; valley, 2-103
Paraíba Valley, Brazil, 2-177
Paramaribo, Surinam, 2-131
Paraná, state, Brazil, 2-180°: agriculture, 2-178
Paraná-Paraguay river system, 2-182
Paraná Plateau, Brazil, 2-180
Paraná River, South America, 2-156°, 2-167°: Argentina, 2-159; length, 2-192; valley, 2-103
Paris, France: climate, 3-200°; development, 3-208; Notre Dame cathedral, 3-208; population, 3-288
Park, Mungo, 5-392, 5-412
Parry Islands, Canada, 1-24°, 6-532°
Parthenon, Athens, 3-211
Patagonia, region, Argentina, 2-99°, 2-101, 2-156°, 2-160: glacier, 2-103; sheep ranch, 2-157, 2-161

Patzcuaro, Lake, Mexico, 1-78
Paulo Afonso Falls, Brazil, 2-175
Paz del Rio, Colombia, 2-133
Peace River, Alberta, Can., 1-24°, 1-35: length, 1-96
Peary, Robert E., 6-541
Pecos River, N. Mex.-Tex., 1-58°
Peipus, Lake, U.S.S.R.: area, 3-288
Peking, China: description, 4-310; "Palace of Rest and Culture," 4-313; population, 4-384; prehistoric man, 4-307, 4-356; stadium, 4-382
Peloponnesus, Greece, 3-239
Pelotas, Brazil, 2-181
Pemba (Br.), isl., Africa, 5-437°, 5-453
Pennsylvania, 1-39°, 1-43°: farmland, 1-48
Penobscot River, Maine, 1-43°
Pepper: Indonesia, 4-373
Permafrost, Siberian land, 3-264
Persia, see Iran
Persian Gulf, 4-292°, 4-314°
Perth, Australia: population, 6-544
Peru, 2-99°, 2-142°: agriculture, 2-146; area, 2-192; capital, 2-126; coastal climate, 2-149; description, 2-142; guano deposits, 2-109; Indians, 2-110; mining and industry, 2-150; people, 2-144; population, 2-192; sea birds, 2-149; sugar growing, 2-117; Viceroyalty of, 2-119; war with Chile, 2-152
Petitgrain oil: Bolivia, 2-186
Petroleum, see Oil
Philadelphia, Pennsylvania: Independence Hall, 1-18; population, 1-96
Philippine Sea, 4-368°
Philippines, The, 4-293°, 4-308°, 4-368°: agriculture, 4-372; area, 4-384; barrios, 4-373; climate, 4-371; earthquakes, 4-370; exports, 4-372, 4-377; industrialization, 4-377; language, 4-306, 4-372; largest city, 4-312; Manila hemp, 4-374; population, 4-372, 4-384; primitive peoples, 4-372; religion, 4-372; tenant farming, 4-372; terrace agriculture, 4-291; typhoons, 4-371; volcanoes, 4-370
Phoenicians: African cities, 5-413, 5-421
Phosphate: Nauru Island, 6-483, 6-529; Ocean Island, 6-483, 6-529; southern U.S., 1-60
Pietermaritzburg, U. of S. Africa, 5-461
Pikes Peak, Colo., 1-64°
Pilcomayo River, South America, 2-156°, 2-183°: Argentina, 2-159; length, 2-192
Pineapple: Hawaii, 1-69; U. of S. Africa, 5-460
Pines, Isle of, Caribbean Sea, 1-87°
Pitchblende: Canada, 1-32
Pittsburgh, Pennsylvania, 1-44: population, 1-96
Pizarro, Francisco, 2-126
Plata La, South America: Viceroyalty of, 2-119
Plata, Río de la, South America, 2-103, 2-156°, 2-164
Platinum: Canada, 1-31
Platte River, Nebraska, 1-50°
Ploesti, Romania, 3-257
Po River, Italy, 3-241
Po River Valley, Italy: natural gas, 3-248; rice fields, 3-244; silk-worm industry, 3-243
Pocono Mts., N.J.-Pa., 1-43°
Poland, 3-206°, 3-251°: agriculture, 3-252; area, 3-288; industry, 3-255; language, 3-249; population, 3-288; potato field, 3-250
Polar lands, 6-534: see also Antarctica; Arctic Regions
Polynesia, Oceania, 6-485°, area, 6-544; islands and people, 6-493; population, 6-544; settlement, 6-490; see also New Zealand
Ponce, Puerto Rico, 1-88
Ponte de Fiana, Madagascar, 5-457
Poopó, Lake, Bolivia, 2-103, 2-183°: area, 2-192
Popocatepetl, Mt., Mexico, 1-71, 1-72°: height, 1-96
Population: world increase, 6-556
Population density: world, 6-556°
Port Darwin, Australia, 6-503
Port Kembla, Australia, 6-511: steel plant, 6-512
Port Pirie, Australia, 6-511
Port Radium, Canada, 1-32
Portland, Maine, 1-46
Portland, Oregon, 1-68
Pôrto Alegre, Brazil, 2-181: population, 2-192

Portugal, 3-195°, 3-206°, 3-238°: African explorers, 5-412, 5-470; agriculture, 3-242; area, 3-288; colonial possessions, 3-235; cork harvest, 3-242; fishing, 3-245; industry, 3-247; population, 3-288; South American colonies, 2-119
Portuguese Guinea, Africa, 5-418°, 5-436°
Potash: West Germany, 3-237
Potosí, Bolivia, 2-185
Potrero Cerrado Valley, Costa Rica, 1-81
Powder River, Wyo.-Mont., 1-64°
Power sources, worldwide, 6-551°
Prague, Czechoslovakia, 3-212, 3-250
Pretoria, U. of S. Africa, 5-464: population, 5-480
Prince Edward Island, Can., 1-25°: agriculture, 1-35; fur farming, 1-29
Prince of Wales Island, Can., 1-24°
Principé (Port.), isl., Africa; 5-394
Pringle Bay, U. of S. Africa, 5-454
Providence, Rhode Island, 1-44
Puebla, Mexico, 1-75
Puelche Indians, 2-110
Puerto Ordaz, Venezuela, 2-133
Puerto Rico, 1-87°, 1-88: people, 1-12; rainfall, 1-88; rainforest, 1-7; sugar cane, 1-91; tobacco farm, 1-93
Punta Arenas, Chile, 2-154
Pusan, Korea: population, 4-384
Pygmies, African, 5-399, 5-404
Pygmy Negritos, people, The Philippines, 4-372
Pyramid Lake, Nevada, 1-64°
Pyramids: Egypt, 5-434; Mexico, 1-73
Pyrenees, Mts., S Europe, 3-223°, 3-224, 3-238°, 3-239

Qatar, Arabian peninsula, 4-308°: oil, 4-322
Quebec, prov., Can., 1-25°: agriculture, 1-33; forestry, 1-28
Quebracho trees: Argentina, 2-159; Bolivia, 2-186; lumbering methods, 2-160
Quechua Indians, 2-113
Queen Maud Land, Antarctica, 6-533°
Queensland, state, Australia, 6-501°: soil, 6-502; sugar production, 6-504, 6-505
Quinine: Indonesia, 4-373, 4-374; South America, 4-374
Quito, Ecuador, 2-124: climate, 2-115; description, 2-125; industry, 2-153

Railroads: worldwide, 6-566°
Rabat, Morocco, 5-422
Rainfall: worldwide, 6-550°
Rainforests: African, 5-445; Amazon, 2-170; Asia, 4-291, 4-348; South American, 2-108; worldwide, 6-553°
Rainier, Mt., Wash., 1-64°
Rainmakers, African, 5-409
Rangoon, Burma: air service, 4-309; Buddhist temple, 4-342
Ras Dashan, Mt., Ethiopia, 5-387°: height, 5-480
Rebmann, Johannes, 5-412
Recife, Brazil, 2-166: description, 2-124; population, 2-192; sugar refinery, 2-175
Red Lakes, Minn., 1-50°
Red River, Ark.-La., 1-58°: length, 1-96
Red River, U.S.-Can., 1-50°
Red Sea, 4-292°, 4-314°, 5-437°
Reindeer Lake, Sask., Can., 1-24°
Rhine River, W Europe, 3-223°: castles, 3-226; course, 3-197; drowned valley, 3-225; farming village, 3-233; length, 3-288
Rhode Island, 1-39°, 1-43°, 1-48
Rhodes, Cecil, 5-468
Rhodesia and Nyasaland, Federation of, 5-418°, 5-456°, 5-469: area and population, 5-480
Rhone River, W Europe, 3-223°: course, 3-197; length, 3-288; valley farms, 3-233
Rice: Asia, southeast, 4-344; Burma, 4-301; China, 4-358; Formosa, 4-365; Ganges River basin, 4-334; Japan, 4-372; Korea, 4-366; world production, 6-561°
Rio de Janeiro, Brazil, 2-123, 2-177: Belo Horizonte highway, 2-176; description, 2-123; district, 2-176°; population, 2-192

Rio de Oro, reg., Spanish West Africa, 5-422
Rio Grande, river, U.S.-Mex., 1-58°, 1-72°: length, 1-96
Rio Grande do Sul, state, Brazil, 2-169, 2-180°
Rio Negro, etc., see Negro, Rio
Ritsa, Lake, U.S.S.R., 3-263
River Rouge, Michigan, 1-56
Riviera, France-Italy, 3-199, 3-225
Roads: worldwide, 6-566°
Rocky Mountains, 1-6, 1-40: Canada, 1-24°; U.S., 1-64°
Romance languages, 3-202
Romania, 3-206°, 3-251°: agriculture, 3-252; area, 3-288; industry, 3-257; language, 3-249; population, 3-288
Rome, Italy, 3-211: climate, 3-200°; handicraftsmen, 3-247; population, 3-288; river, 3-241
Rome, ancient: African cities, 5-413; alphabet, 3-204; conquest of Carthage, 5-421; descendants, 3-202; empire, 3-198
Rosario, Argentina, 2-162: population, 2-192
Ross Sea, Antarctica, 6-533°
Ruanda-Urundi (Bel.), Africa, 5-418°, 5-437°
Rubber: Africa, 5-411; Amazon jungle, 2-177, 2-178; Indonesia, 4-373, 4-374; Malay Peninsula, 4-346; world production, 6-562°
Ruapehu, Mt., New Zealand: height, 6-544
Rudolf, Lake, Africa, 5-437°, 5-452: area, 5-480
Russia, see Union of Soviet Socialist Republics
Russian Revolution, 3-265
Russian Soviet Federated Socialist Republic, 3-251°: population, 3-268
Ruwenzori, Mt., Belgian Congo, 5-387°: height, 5-480
Rye: world production, 6-561°
Ryuku Islands, E Asia, 4-293°

Sacramento River, Calif., 1-64°
Saguia el Hamra, Spanish West Africa, 5-422
Sahara Desert, 5-427°: agriculture, 5-411; extent, 5-388; description, 5-427; formation, 5-401, 5-428; highest temperature, 5-407; peoples, 5-430; sand dunes, 5-390; travel routes, 5-429
Saigon, South Vietnam, 4-312
St. Basil's Cathedral, Moscow, 3-270
St. Elias, Mt., Alaska, 1-64°
St. George's, Grenada, West Indies, 1-88
St. John River, U.S.-Can., 1-43°
St. Lawrence Island, Alaska: Eskimo village, 6-538
St. Lawrence River, U.S.-Can., 1-25°, 1-43°: length, 1-96
St. Lawrence Seaway, 1-33, 1-37, 1-55, 1-94: bridge, 1-23
St. Louis, Missouri, 1-20, 1-55: population, 1-96
St. Lucia, isl., Caribbean Sea, 1-87°, 1-89
St. Pierre (Fr.), isl., N Amer., 1-25°: French fishing base, 3-225
St. Stephen's Cathedral, Vienna, 3-212
Sajama, Mt., Bolivia, 2-183°: height, 2-192
Sakhalin, isl., U.S.S.R., 3-261°, 4-295°: mineral deposits, 3-285
Salamanca, Mexico, 1-74
Salisbury, Southern Rhodesia, 5-415, 5-468: population, 5-480
Salmon River, Idaho, 1-64°
Salt mining: southern U.S., 1-60
Salta, Argentina, 2-158
Salton Sea, Calif., 1-64°
Salvador, Brazil, 2-174: population, 2-192
Salween River, Asia, 4-341°, 4-350°: length, 4-384; source, 4-299
Samar, isl., Philippines, 4-368°
Samarkand, U.S.S.R., 3-271, 3-275
Samburu, African people, 5-439
Samoa, isls., Polynesia, 6-485°, 6-521°: area, 6-544; bananas, 6-528; landform, 6-487; outrigger canoe, 6-524; Polynesian family, 6-493; population, 6-544
San Francisco, Calif.: Golden Gate Bridge, 1-19; manufacturing, 1-68; population, 1-96
San Gimignano, Italy, 3-198
San Joaquin River, Calif., 1-64°
San Jorge, Gulf of, Argentina, 2-156°
San Juan, Argentina, 2-158
San Juan, Puerto Rico, 1-88

San Marcos, University of, 2-126
San Marino, 3-239°
San Martín, Lake, South America, 2-142°
San Matías Gulf, Argentina, 2-156°
San Rafael, Argentina, 2-158
Santa Catarina, state, Brazil, 2-180°: Italian colony, 2-181
Santa Cruz, Bolivia, 2-185
Sanford, Mt., Alaska, 1-96
Santarém, Brazil, 2-172: Japanese immigrants, 2-173
Santiago, Chile: description, 2-125; industry, 2-153; population, 2-192
Santos, Brazil, 2-187
São Francisco River, Brazil, 2-167°, 2-174: length, 2-192
São Paulo, Brazil, 2-112: description, 2-123; electric power, 2-178; population, 2-192
São Paulo, state, Brazil, 2-176°: settlement, 2-177
São Tomé (Port.), isl., Africa, 5-394
Saratov, U.S.S.R., 3-274
Sarawak, Br. col., Borneo, 4-293°, 4-308°, 4-369°
Sardinia, isl., Italy, 3-238°: coal, 3-248; fishermen, 3-246
Sarnia, Ontario, 1-37
Saskatchewan, prov., Can., 1-24°, 1-33
Saskatchewan River, Canada, 1-96
Saudi Arabia, 4-292°, 4-308°, 4-314°: agriculture, 4-321; area, 4-384; Bedouins, 4-321; holy cities, 4-324; language and peoples, 4-316; oasis, 4-297; oil deposits, 4-322, 4-379, 4-382; population, 4-384; religion, 4-316
Savannas, African: agriculture, 5-409; countries, resources, 5-442; description, 5-439; landscape, 5-438
Sayan Mountains, Asia, 4-293°
Scandinavia, 3-213°, 3-214°: hydroelectric plant, 3-221; see also Denmark, Finland, Iceland, Norway, Sweden
Schweitzer, Albert, 5-439
Scotland, 3-223°: countryside, 3-224; landforms, 3-224; people, 3-202; wedding procession, 3-202; see also Great Britain
Sea lanes, worldwide, 6-568°
Seattle, Washington, 1-68
Segovia Highland, Venezuela, 2-134
Seine River, France, 3-196, 3-223°: drowned valleys, 3-225; length, 3-288
Sekondi, Ghana, 5-474
Senegal, Republic of the, Africa, 5-418°, 5-436°, 5-442
Senegal River, Africa, 5-412, 5-436°
Seoul, South Korea, 4-367: description, 4-313; population, 4-384
Sepik River, New Guinea: length, 6-544
Serbia, Yugoslavia, 3-251°
Serengeti Plains, Tanganyika, 5-450, 5-451
Seven Islands, Canada, 1-32
Severnaya Zemlya, isl., U.S.S.R., 3-261°, 6-532°
Sevier Lake, Utah, 1-64°
Shanghai, China: description, 4-310; harbor traffic, 4-312; houseboats, 4-361; population, 4-384
Shasta, Mt., Calif., 1-64°
Shatt-al-Arab, region, Iraq: date production, 4-318
Shenyang, China, see Mukden, China
Shikoku Island, Japan, 4-295°, 4-368°: rice growing, 4-372
Shinkolobwe, Belgian Congo, 5-446
Si River delta, 4-358
Siam, see Thailand
Siam, Gulf of, 4-293°, 4-341°
Siberia, U.S.S.R., 3-261°, 4-295°: agriculture, 3-276; climate, 4-301; coldest place, 4-300; collective farm, 3-284; description, 3-284; largest city, 3-284; major cities, 3-275; permafrost, 3-264; railroads, 3-272; rivers, 3-263, 3-284; taiga, 3-262; village, 3-285; wheat field, 3-262
Sicily, 3-239°: lemons, 3-243; mineral resources, 3-248; orange grove, 3-244
Sidi Kacem, Morocco, 5-423
Sierra de Córdoba, Argentina, 2-158
Sierra Leone, Africa, 5-418°, 5-436°: agriculture, 5-442; area, 5-480; cacao trees, 5-411; mineral resources, 5-443; population, 5-480
Sierra Madres, mts., Mexico, 1-72°

Sierra Nevada, mts., Calif.-Nev., 1-64°
Silesia, Poland, 3-251°
Silk: Italy, 3-243; world production, 6-562°
Silver: Chile, 2-152; Mexico, 1-74
Singapore, Malaya: population, 4-384
Sinkiang, prov., China, 4-293°, 4-308°, 4-350°: description, 4-352; oasis, 4-353
Sioux Indians, 1-11
Sisal: African crop, 5-410
Sitkine Mts., Can., 1-24°
Skate, U.S.S., 6-543
Skoda munitions works, Czechoslovakia, 3-257
Slavery, in North America, 1-12
Slavic languages, 3-203: alphabet, 3-204; U.S.S.R., 3-269
Sleeping sickness, 5-409
Slovenia, Yugoslavia, 3-257
Snake River, U.S., 1-64°: length, 1-96
Society Islands, Polynesia, 6-485°, 6-521°: area, 6-544; landform, 6-487; netting fish, 6-524; population, 6-544
Sogne Fiord, Norway, 3-197
Solomon Islands, Melanesia, 6-484°, 6-521°: area, 6-544; landform, 6-482; people, 6-492; population, 6-544
Solomon's Temple, Jerusalem, Jordan, 4-325
Somalia, 5-418°, 5-437°: area and population, 5-480
Somerset Island, Can., 1-25°
Songhai, African people, 5-440
Sorghum: Africa, 5-411
South Africa, see Union of South Africa
South America, 2-99°: agriculture, 2-116, 2-189; airlines,, 2-121°; ancient civilizations, 2-110; animal life, 2-106; area and extent, 2-98; cities, 2-122; cities, major, population, 2-192; class structure, 2-190; climate, 2-114°; compared to North America, 2-104; countries, 2-98; countries, area and population, 2-192; education, 2-190; exploration, 2-119°; future prospects, 2-188; hottest region, 2-115; hydroelectric project, 2-189; Indians, 2-110, 2-113; industry, 2-188; interior countries, 2-182, 2-183°; islands, 2-104; lakes, 2-103, 2-192; mineral resources, 2-118, 2-190; mountain chains, 2-100; mountains, highest, 2-192; northern section, 2-127, 2-128°; plant life, 2-104; population, 2-98; population density, 2-110°; quinine, 2-374; racial mixtures, 2-110; railroads, 2-121°; river systems, 2-101; rivers, longest, 2-192; roads, 2-121°; rubber, 2-374; settlement, history, 2-119, 2-189; southern countries, 2-155, 2-156°; transportation, 2-120°, 2-190; urban population, 2-113; vegetation, 2-104°; west coast, 2-101
South Australia, state, Australia, 6-501°: iron ore mining center, 6-511; limestone, 6-511
South Carolina, 1-39°, 1-58°
South China Sea, see China Sea
South Dakota, 1-38°, 1-50°, 1-53
South Korea, see Korea, South; Korean Peninsula
South Vietnam, see Vietnam, South
South Island, New Zealand, 6-514°: fiord, 6-487; Fiordland, 6-514; mountain chain, 6-514; Roxbrough hydroelectric plant, 6-519
South Pole, Antarctica, 6-533°: discovery, 6-541; lowest temperature recorded, 6-534
Southampton Island, Can., 1-25°
Southern Hemisphere, 6-546°: largest cities, 6-498
Southern Rhodesia, 5-468
Southern U.S., 1-58°: agriculture, 1-57, 1-63; industry, 1-60; largest city, 1-16; slavery, 1-12; soil erosion, 1-59
South-West Africa, 5-418°, 5-456°, 5-470: area and population, 5-480
Soviet Union, see Union of Soviet Socialist Republics
Spain, 3-195°, 3-206°, 3-238°: agriculture, 3-242; area, 3-288; capital, 3-210; colonial possessions, 3-235; fishing, 3-245; grape harvest, 3-241; Inca conquest, 2-144; industry, 3-247; medieval

city, 3-240; population, 3-288; South American colonies, 2-119; waterwheel well, 3-243
Spanish Guinea, 5-418°, 5-436°
Spanish Sahara, Africa, 5-387°
Spanish West Africa, 5-418°, 5-420°, 5-422
Spencer Gulf, Australia, 6-501°
Sphinx, Egyptian, 5-435
Spice Islands, 4-373
Spitsbergen, Norway, 3-220, 6-532°
Sputnik II, satellite, 3-286
Stalin, Joseph, 3-265
Stalin, Mt., U.S.S.R.: height, 3-288
Stalinabad, U.S.S.R., 3-275
Stalingrad, U.S.S.R., 3-275: Volga dam, 3-280; women workers, 3-271
Stalino, U.S.S.R., 3-280
Stalinsk, U.S.S.R., 3-284
Stanley, Henry M., 5-412, 5-446
Steele, Mt., Can., 1-96
Steep Rock Mine, Can., 1-31
Sucre, Bolivia, 2-185
Sudan, 5-418°, 5-437°: agriculture, 5-443; area and population, 5-480; extent, 5-388; native village, 5-402
Sudanese Republic, Africa, 5-418°, 5-436°
Sudbury, Ontario, Can., 1-31
Sudd, the, Sudanese region, 5-443
Suez Canal, 5-434, 5-435, 5-477: opening, 4-296
Sugar: Australia, 6-505; Brazil, 2-174; Caribbean, 1-89; Colombia, 2-136; Formosa, 4-365; Hawaii, 1-69; Indonesia, 4-374; Oceania, 6-529; Philippines, 4-373; world production, 6-561°
Sulfur: Chile, 2-153; southern U.S., 1-60
Sulu Archipelago, Philippines, 4-368°
Sulu Sea, 4-293°, 4-368°
Sumatra, Indonesia, 4-293°, 4-308°, 4-369°: former Dutch possession, 4-373; rubber industry, 2-173; see also Indonesia
Sumbawa, isl., Indonesia, 4-369°
Sunda Islands, Indonesia, 4-369°
Superior, Lake, U.S.-Can., 1-50°: area, 1-96
Surinam (Dutch Guiana), South America, 2-99°, 2-128°: area, 2-192; bauxite deposits, 2-118; bush village, 2-130; description, 2-131; population, 2-192; rice farmer, 2-130; settlement, 2-130
Susquehanna River, Pa., 1-43°
Suva, Fiji Islands: description, 6-499; population, 6-544
Svans, people, U.S.S.R., 3-270
Sverdlovsk, U.S.S.R., 3-284
Swaziland (Br.), Africa, 5-418°, 5-456°, 5-471
Sweden, 3-195°, 3-206°, 3-214°: agriculture, 3-218; area, 3-288; ball-bearing plant, 3-221; chief port, 3-220; fishing, 3-216; forestry, 3-217; language, 3-215; mining and industry, 3-220; population, 3-288; wheat farm, 3-219
Swine: world distribution, 6-562°
Switzerland, 3-195°, 3-206°, 3-223°: agriculture, 3-233; area, 3-288; description, 3-228; hillside farms, 3-232; industry, 3-237; population, 3-288
Sydney, Australia: air distances, 6-500; Bondi Beach, 6-491; description, 6-498; harbor, 6-496; population, 6-544
Syria (United Arab Republic), 4-292°, 4-308°, 4-314°: agriculture, 4-319, 4-321; area, 4-384; climate, 4-321; cottonfield, 4-318; Damascus oasis, 4-319; "Fertile Crescent," 4-318; language and peoples, 4-316; mountain village, 4-317; population, 4-384; religion, 4-316

Table Mountain, South Africa, 5-416
Tacoma, Washington, 1-68
Tadzhik Union Republic, U.S.S.R., 3-370
Tagalog, language, The Philippines, 4-306, 4-372
Tagus River, Portugal, 3-241
Tahiti, isl., Polynesia, 6-521°: capital, 6-499; unloading cattle, 6-529
Tahoe, Lake, Calif., 1-64°
Taichung, Formosa: recruit training center, 4-365

Taipei, Formosa, 4-364
Taiwan, see Formosa
Takla Makan, desert, Asia, 4-350°, 4-356
Tala, Mt., Ethiopia: height, 5-480
Talara, Peru, 2-151
Tampico, Mexico, 1-75
Tana, Lake, Central Africa, 5-437°: area, 5-480; Nile source, 5-391
Tananarive, Madagascar, 5-457
Tanganyika, 5-418°, 5-437°, 5-451: area and population, 5-480; Moshi Mosque, 5-451
Tanganyika, Lake, Africa, 5-437°, 5-452: area, 5-480
Tangier, Africa: ancient name, 5-413; street scene, 5-416
Taormina, Sicily: lacemaking, 3-247
Tapajóz River, Brazil, 2-167°, 2-192
Tarahumara Indians, 1-76
Tariffs, European, 3-258
Tarim River, Sinkiang, 4-353
Tartars, people, U.S.S.R., 3-268
Tashkent, U.S.S.R., 3-275: textile mill, 3-283
Tasman, Abel, 6-516
Tasman Sea, Oceania, 6-485°
Tasmania, state, Australia, 6-501°: aborigines, 6-500; apple orchard, 6-505; climate, 6-495; Commonwealth of Australia, 6-496; hydroelectric power plant, 6-530; limestone, 6-511; zinc refinery, 6-510
Tata Steel Works, India, 4-339
Taupo, Lake, New Zealand: area, 6-544
Taxco, Mexico, 1-77
Te Anau, Lake, New Zealand: area, 6-544
Tea: Ceylon, 4-335; Indonesia, 4-374; Japan, 4-373; Uganda plantation, 5-452; world production, 6-561°
Teak: Burma, 4-349
Tehran, Iran: population, 4-384
Tema, Ghana, 5-440
Temperatures, worldwide, 6-550°
Temple of the Emerald Buddha, Bangkok, Thailand, 4-340
Tennessee, 1-39°, 1-58°
Texas, 1-38°, 1-58°: cattle ranch, 1-59; mineral resources, 1-60
Thailand, 4-293°, 4-308°, 4-341°: agriculture, 4-344; animal life, 4-343; area, 4-384; Buddhist monk, 4-305; canal market, 4-348; climate, 4-342; plant life, 4-342; peoples, 4-340; population, 4-384; primitive tribes, 4-349; religion, 4-340; rice fields, 4-340; river village, 4-299; teak logs, 4-343; water buffalo, 4-343
Thames River, England, 3-236
Thebes, Egypt, 5-413
Thor-Able rocket, 1-95
Thule, Greenland: weather station, 6-539
Tiber River, Italy, 3-241
Tibesti, mts., North Africa, 5-430, 5-436°
Tibet, 4-293°, 4-308°, 4-350°: capital, 4-350; geography, 4-350; religion, 4-352; residence of Dalai Lama, 4-352; transportation 4-309
Tibu, African desert people, 5-430
Tien Shan, mts., Asia, 4-292°, 4-350: river source, 4-297
Tientsin, China: description, 4-310; population, 4-384
Tierra del Fuego, South America, 2-103, 2-104, 2-142°: description, 2-154; Indians, 2-113
Tigris-Euphrates River, Asia, 4-314°: mouth, 4-299; valley, 4-318
Timbuktu, Nigeria, 5-413
Timor, isl., Indonesia, 4-369°
Timor Sea, 4-369°
Tin: Bolivia, 2-185; Indonesia, 4-377; Malay Peninsula, 4-347; Nigeria, 5-443; worldwide sources, 6-565°
Titicaca, Lake, South America, 2-102, 2-103, 2-142°, 2-182, 2-183°: area, 2-192; description, 2-184
Tobacco: Brazil, 2-174; discovery, 1-7; southern U. S., 1-57
Tocantins River, Brazil, 2-167°: length, 2-192
Tocorpuri, Mt., Chile, 2-192
Togo, Africa, 5-418°, 5-436°: area and population, 5-480
Tokelau Islands, Polynesia, 6-485°: area, 6-544; landform, 6-483; population, 6-544

Tokyo, Japan, 4-*313*: air service, 4-309; bicycle factory, 4-*376;* description, 4-310; population, 4-384
Toltec Indians, 1-73
Toluca, Mt., Mexico, 1-96
Tomsk, U.S.S.R., 3-275
Tonga (Friendly) Islands, Polynesia, 6-485°: area and population, 6-544
Tonkin, region, Indochina, 4-341°
Toronto, Canada: harbor, 1-*21;* population, 1-96
Torrens, Lake, Australia, 6-501°, 6-508: area, 6-544
Torreón, Mexico, 1-79
Toubkal, Mt., Morocco: height, 5-480
Transkei, region, U. of S. Africa, 5-*462*
Trans-Siberian Railroad, 3-272
Transvaal, prov., U. of S. Africa, 5-*458,* 5-*463,* 5-464
Trapani, Sicily, 3-*246*
Tres Cruces, Mt., Argentina, 2-192
Trinidad, isl., Caribbean Sea, 1-87°, 2-104
Tripoli, Libya: U. S. invasion, 5-425
Tripolitania, region, Libya, 5-420°, 5-424
Tristão, Nuno, 5-412
Tsavo Reserve, Kenya, 5-451
Tsetse fly, 5-409, 5-439
Tuamotu Islands, Polynesia, 6-521°: area, 6-544; landform, 6-*483;* population, 6-544
Tuaregs, N. African people, 5-*399,* 5-430
Tucson, Arizona, 1-65
Tucumán, Argentina, 2-158
Tula, U.S.S.R., 3-282
Tumac-Humac Mts., South America, 2-*128*°
Tumen River, Asia, 4-366
Tundra: Arctic, 1-7, 6-537; Asia, 4-291; North America, 6-*537*°; worldwide, 6-*553*°
Tungsten: worldwide sources, 6-564°
Tungting, Lake, China, 4-351°: area, 4-384
Tungus, peoples, U.S.S.R., 3-270
Tunis, Tunisia: Moslem quarter, 5-*417;* population, 5-480
Tunisia, 5-*418*°, 5-*420*°: area and population, 5-480; description, 5-*424;* Phoenician colonies, 5-421
Tupi Indians, 2-110
Tupungato, Mt., South America, 2-*142*°: height, 2-192
Turin, Italy: industry, 3-247, 3-*248,* 3-*258*
Turkey, 3-*206*°, 4-292°, 4-308°, 4-314°: agriculture, 4-321; Anatolian Plateau, 4-*297;* area, 4-384; climate, 4-321; language, 3-204; 4-316; largest city, 4-*310*°; peoples, 4-316; population, 4-384; religion, 4-316
Turkmens, people, U.S.S.R., 3-269
Turko-Tartars, people, U.S.S.R., 3-269
Turk-Sib Railroad, U.S.S.R., 3-272
Typhoons: Formosa, 4-364; Indonesia, 4-371; Japan, 4-371; Oceania, 6-494; Philippines, 4-371
Tyrrhenian Sea, 3-239°

Ubangi-Uélé Rivers, Africa, 5-*437*°: length, 5-480
Uganda, Africa, 5-*418*°, 5-*437*°: area and population, 5-480; description, 5-*451;* rainforest, 5-*391;* village scene, 5-*452*
Ukrainian Union Republic, U.S.S.R.: capital, 3-275; collective farm, 3-*279;* industry, 3-280; people, 3-268; state farm, 3-*278;* village street, 3-*264;* wheatfield, 3-*276*
Ulawan, Mt., New Britain: height, 6-544
Uncia, Bolivia, 2-185
Ungava, Can., 1-32
Union of South Africa, 5-*418*°, 5-*456*°: apartheid policy, 5-454; area, 6-480; capital, 5-*464;* game reserves, 5-465; Indian population, 5-*405,* 5-461; land and people, 5-458; mineral resources, 5-466; native reserves, 5-471; population, 5-480; provinces, 5-459
Union of Soviet Socialist Republics (U.S.S.R.), 3-*260*°, 4-*294*°: agriculture, 3-276; aid to China, 4-363; airlines, 3-*273*°; alphabet, 3-204; Antarctic research, 6-542; apartment house, 3-287; Arctic peoples, 3-270; area, 3-262, 3-288; borders, 3-262; challenge to U.S., 3-287; cities, 3-274; climate, 3-267; coal reserves, 3-284; coastline, 3-262; coldest town, 3-267; forests, 3-285; future, 3-286; history, 3-265; hydroelectric power, 3-282; industry, 3-280; influence on Eastern Europe, 3-250; landforms, 3-263; languages, 3-269; latitudes, 3-267; mineral resources, 3-282; peoples, 3-268°; physical education parade, 3-*269;* population, 3-262, 3-288; railroads, 3-*272*°; rainfall, 3-*267;* religion, 3-269, 3-270; rivers, 3-263; roads, 3-*273*°; science laboratory, 3-*286;* State Planning Board, 3-283; steel mill, 3-*281;* subtropical areas, 3-279; sunflower field, 3-*276;* temperature averages, 3-*266*°; textile mill, 3-*283;* transportation, 3-272; Union Republics, 3-268; vegetation, 3-*264*°; Young Pioneers, 3-287
United Arab Republic: formation, 5-433; see also Egypt; Syria
United Nations: Antarctic administration, 6-543; Asia, aid to, 4-379, 4-381; India, aid to, 4-336
United States, 1-38°: Antarctic research, 6-542; area, 1-96; Canal Zone, 1-86; cities, population, 1-96; climate, 1-8°; manufacturing belt, 1-18; Midwest, see Midwestern U. S.; Northeast, see Northeastern U. S.; Pacific Northwest, 1-68 ; population, 1-96; settlement, 1-40; South, see Southern U. S.; territorial expansion, 1-12; transportation, 1-15°; West, see Western U. S.
Ural Mountains, U.S.S.R., 3-*260*°: description, 3-263; mining and industry, 3-284
Ural River, U.S.S.R., 3-*260*°: length, 3-288
Uranium: Arctic Regions, 6-543; Australia, 6-511; Belgian Congo, 5-446; Canada, 1-*30*°; Czechoslovakia, 3-198; worldwide sources, 6-551°
Uranium City, Canada, 1-32
Urmia, Lake, Iran, 4-314°: area, 4-384
Uruguay, 2-*99*°, 2-*156*°: agriculture, 2-117; area, 2-192; capital, 2-124; cattle industry, 2-165; land and people, 2-164; Paraguayan war, 2-182; population, 2-192; railroads, 2-121
Uruguay River, South America, 2-*156*°, 2-*167*°: Argentina, 2-159; length, 2-192
Ushuaia, Argentina, 2-*154,* 2-160
U.S.S.R., see Union of Soviet Socialist Republics
Utah, 1-38°, 1-64°
Uzbek Union Republic, U.S.S.R.: capital, 3-283; people, 3-269, 3-*271*

Valdivia, Chile, 2-153
Valencia, Venezuela, 2-132
Valle de Gŭadalupe, Mexico, 1-76
Valparaíso, Chile, 2-*153*
Van, Lake, Turkey: area, 4-384
Vanadium: worldwide sources, 6-564°
Vancouver, Mt., Canada, 1-96
Vancouver Island, Br. Col., Can., 1-24°, 1-35
Vaner, Lake, Sweden, 3-*214*°: area, 3-288
Vatican City, Rome, 3-*211,* 3-239°
Vegetation: worldwide, 6-*552*°

Veld, South African, 5-388, 5-462, 5-*470*
Venezuela, 2-*99*°, 2-*128*°: agriculture, 2-136; area, 2-192; capital, 2-126; coastal area, 2-127; highlands, 2-132; industry, 2-132; mineral resources, 2-118; oil production, 2-134; oil refinery, 2-*132;* population, 2-192; population distribution, 2-132; railroads, 2-120; transportation, 2-139
Venice, Italy: canal, 3-*238;* handicraftsmen, 3-247
Verde, Cape, Africa, 5-*436*°
Vereeniging, U. of S. Africa, 5-464
Verkhoyansk, U.S.S.R., 3-267: temperature, 4-300
Vermont, 1-39°, 1-43°, 1-48: mountain village, 1-*4*
Victoria, British Columbia, 1-28
Victoria, Lake, Africa, 5-*437*°, 5-452: area, 5-480
Victoria, Mt., New Guinea: height, 6-544
Victoria, state, Australia, 6-501°: apple production, 6-505; gold, 6-510; industry, 6-513
Victoria Falls, Africa, 5-*393:* African name, 5-392; discovery, 5-412
Victoria Land, Antarctica, 6-*533*°
Viedma, Lake, Argentina, 2-*156*°: area, 2-192
Vienna, Austria: development, 3-208; population, 3-288; St. Stephen's Cathedral, 3-*212*
Vietnam, North, 4-293°, 4-308°, 4-341°: area and population, 4-384; see also Indochina
Vietnam, South, 4-293°, 4-308°, 4-341°: area and population, 4-384; capital, 4-312°; see also Indochina
Vikings, 3-215
Virgin Islands, (U. S.) Caribbean Sea, 1-87°, 1-88
Virginia, 1-39°, 1-*58*°
Vistula River, Poland, 3-249, 3-*251*°
Viti Levu, Fiji Islands, 6-499
Vladivostok, U.S.S.R., 3-275
Vltava (Moldau) River, Czechoslovakia, 3-*212*
Volcanic island, landform, Oceania, 6-487
Volga River, U.S.S.R., 3-*260*°: barge, 3-*265;* course, 3-263; length, 3-288; navigable distance, 3-272; Stalingrad dam, 3-*280*
Volkswagen factory, Germany, 3-*236*
Volta Redonda, Brazil, 2-*176*
Voltaic Republic, Africa, 5-*418*°, 5-*436*°
Voronezh, U.S.S.R., 3-282
Vosges, mts., France, 3-*223*°, 3-224

Wabash River, Ind., 1-50°
Wachagga, African people, 5-*404*
Wakatipu, Lake, New Zealand: area, 6-544
Wake Island, Polynesia, 6-521°
Wales, 3-*223*°: landforms, 3-224; people, 3-202; shepherds, 3-*229;* see also Great Britain
Walker Lake, Nev., 1-*54*
Wanaka, Lake, New Zealand, 6-*516*
Wankie, Southern Rhodesia, 5-468
Warsaw, Poland: climate, 3-*200*°; development, 3-208; population, 3-288
Washington, California, 1-68
Washington, D. C.: capitol, 1-*17;* population, 1-96
Washington, Mt., New Hampshire, 1-43°
Washington, state, 1-38°, 1-64°: farmland, 1-65
Water power: worldwide, 6-551°
Watusi, African people, 5-*403*
Weddell Sea, Antarctica, 6-*533*°
Weisshorn, Mt., Switzerland, 3-288
Wellington, New Zealand: description, 6-498; population, 6-544
West Germany, see Germany, West
West Indies, 1-87°, 1-88
West Virginia, 1-39°, 1-*58*°
Western Australia, state, Australia, 6-501°: apple production, 6-505;
gold, 6-510; plateau, 6-501
Western Hemisphere, 6-547°
Western U. S., 1-63, 1-64°: agriculture and industry, 1-67
Westminster Bridge, London, 3-*208*
Whaling: International Commission, 3-216
Wheat: world production, 6-560°
Wheelus Field, U. S. air base, Libya, 5-425
White Sea, U.S.S.R., 3-*260*°
White Mts., New Hampshire, 1-43°
Whiteface Mt., N.Y., 1-43°
Whitney, Mt., Calif., 1-64°: height, 1-96
Whyalla, Australia, 6-511
Wichita, Kansas, 1-55
Wilhelm, Mt., New Guinea: height, 6-544
Wilhelmina, Mt., New Guinea: height, 6-544
Willamette Valley, Oregon, 1-66
Windsor, Ontario, 1-37
Windward Islands, Caribbean Sea, 1-87°
Winnipeg, Lake, Can., 1-*24*°: area, 1-96
Winnipegosis, Lake, Can., 1-*24*°: area, 1-96
Winnipesaukee, Lake, New Hampshire, 1-43°
Wisconsin, 1-39°, 1-50°, 1-55: dairy farm, 1-*53*
Wisconsin River, Wis., 1-50°
Witwatersrand, U. of S. Africa, 5-466
Wood, Mt., Can., 1-96
Wool: Australia, 6-513; New Zealand, 6-519; world production, 6-562°
World maps: economic, 6-558°; physical, 6-548°; political, 6-554°; population density, 6-556°; transportation routes, 6-566°
Wuhan, China: population, 4-384
Wyoming, 1-38°, 1-64°: mountain scene, 1-40

Xingú River, Brazil, 2-167°: length, 2-192

Yakut Union Republic, U.S.S.R.: gold production, 3-285; people, 3-268
Yalu River, Asia, 4-366
Yampi Sound, Australia: iron ore deposits, 6-511
Yangtze River, Asia, 4-351°: houseboats, 4-*361;* length, 4-384; source, 4-299
Yaroslavl, U.S.S.R., 3-282
Yawata, Japan: steel mill, 4-*377.*
Yellow River, see Hwang Ho River
Yellow Sea, 4-293°, 4-351°
Yellowknife Mine, Can., 1-30
Yellowstone River, Mont., 1-64°
Yemen, Arabian Peninsula, 4-314°
Yenisei River, U.S.S.R., 3-*261*°: course, 3-263; length, 3-288; source, 4-297
Yerupaja, Mt., Peru, 2-192
Yokohama, Japan: population, 4-384
Yucatan Peninsula, Mexico, 1-79
Yugoslavia, 3-*206*°, 3-*251*°: alphabet, 3-204; area, 3-288; farmer, 3-*252;* language, 3-249; mining and industry, 3-257; population, 3-288; steel workers, 3-*256*
Yukon River, Alaska- Can., 1-38°, 1-70; length, 1-96
Yukon Territory, Can., 1-24°
Yungas, Bolivian, 2-184

Zambezi River, Africa, 5-*456*°: course, 5-392; Kariba Dam, 5-*469;* length, 5-480
Zanzibar (Br.), isl., Africa, 5-*437*°, 5-394, 5-453
Zaporozhe, U.S.S.R., 3-282
Zinc: Australia, 6-510; worldwide sources, 6-565°
Zlatoust, U.S.S.R., 3-284
Zugspite, Mt., Germany, 3-*196*
Zuider Zee, Netherlands, 3-*223*°: reclamation, 3-222
Zulus, people, Africa, 5-*404*